Living
the
American
Dream

Pentair, Inc.
The First
Twenty-Five
Years

Living the American Dream

Pentair, Inc.
The First
Twenty-Five
Years

by
Murray J.
Harpole

St. Thomas Technology Press
St. Paul, Minnesota

St. Thomas Technology Press
University of St. Thomas
2115 Summit Avenue
St. Paul, Minnesota 55105

ISBN 0-9624229-5-9

Printed in the United States by
Arcata Graphics Book Group, Kingsport, Tennessee

Printed on acid-free 60 lb. Troy Book Satin
(50 percent recycled, 10 percent post consumer)
manufactured by Cross Pointe Paper, St. Paul, Minnesota
a subsidiary of Pentair, Inc.

Dedicated to all the women and men who made the Pentair story possible.

CONTENTS

Chapter One
   Beginnings 1965–1966 1

Chapter Two
   Survival 1967–1968 17

Chapter Three
   Success 1968–1972 31

Chapter Four
   Momentum 1972–1974 67

Chapter Five
   Transition 1975–1976 83

Chapter Six
   Maturation 1977–1979 99

Chapter Seven
   Diversification 1980–1981 115

Chapter Eight
   Expansion 1982–1984 141

Chapter Nine
   Satisfaction 1985–1986 157

Chapter Ten
   Carrying On 1987–1991 173

Chapter Eleven
   Lessons and Observations 1966–1991 199

Appendix

Pentair Code of Business Conduct...................... 225

Corporate Officers 227

Corporate Directors 229

Acquisitions 231

Divestitures 232

Subsidiary Profiles 233

Growth Record 234

Performance Record 235

Share Value...................................... 236

Net Earnings..................................... 237

Net Sales.. 237

Market Value of Shares........................... 238

Book Value of Shares 238

Capital Investments 239

Significant Events in Pentair History 241

FOREWORD

Living the American Dream is, first and foremost, a compelling history of the first 25 years of Pentair, Inc., how it was born in the heartland of America and how it grew.

Perhaps more importantly, it is the story of Murray James Harpole, whose courage, intelligence, and determination built this company and whose keen sense of values helped forge a code of business conduct that guides Pentair to this day.

I will always remember the circumstances surrounding my first meeting with this remarkable man. It was in 1975; Murray had phoned me saying he was looking for someone to help him manage Pentair. I told him that I was looking for a company to help build. We clearly had something in common and agreed to meet for breakfast the next day.

Since we didn't know each other, descriptions were in order. I told Murray I was six feet five inches. He said that he was five feet six. Needless to say, we easily located each other and the ensuing breakfast was for me the start of a challenging and satisfying relationship with a man who has since become my closest business associate and valued friend.

That meeting also prompted Murray to observe frequently in the future: "If you want to get the long and short on Pentair, talk to Gene and me."

Now, many years later, Murray Harpole has translated the "long and short" of Pentair into this fascinating book. *Living the American Dream* describes the start-up and development of a company that by traditional standards was highly unlikely to survive. Fortunately, for more than 14,000 stakeholders, Pentair not only survived, it became a billion-dollar industrial leader.

This book is also a report card on Murray's career from the time he and four others founded the company to its 25th anniversary. It is the story of how people – the founders, stockholders, employees, associates and Murray's family and friends – nurtured and shaped Pentair into the successful corporation it is today.

Living the American Dream has many aspects that make it a different kind of corporate history. How often do you find such a book that is actually written by the person who served as the company's chief executive officer for the first 15 years of its existence?

Over the years, Murray carefully recorded the significant events. The result was 25 volumes of diaries and notes which became the source material for this fascinating document. Since I have shared many experiences with him over the past 16 years, I can assure you that *Living the American Dream* presents a truly accurate picture of Pentair, past and present.

My relationship with Murray has provided tremendous excitement and the pride of knowing and working with a business leader of high ethics and great stature. This Iowa farm boy, who grew up in the Great Depression, is the most direct, honest, self-effacing business executive I have ever known. As I reflect on our relationship, the real Murray Harpole and the importance of this book come into perspective. *Living the American Dream*, written by the man who lived the events he describes, answers questions that are frequently asked of today's Pentair leaders.

- How does a business that was started with just a few thousand dollars to make research balloons grow in just 25 years into a billion-dollar industrial corporation with 10 subsidiaries in four countries?

- How does a company with a policy of independence survive three pernicious, unfriendly takeover attempts and create significantly greater shareholder value in the process?

- What is it about business leadership that creates a unique value system and culture that enables underperforming acquired businesses to produce long-term results that rank the performance of Pentair in the top 10 percent of U.S. corporations?

Our employees will find within these pages a sense of tradition that has shaped our corporate culture while reinforcing the values that are inherent in our code of business conduct.

Our shareholders will discover insights into the evolution and growth of a dynamic organization of which they share ownership.

Our customers, suppliers and other corporate executives will find meaning in the in-depth perspective this book sheds on the personal characteristics and organizational values so important to business success.

Murray titled this book carefully. He believes fervently that he and those who have worked with him have indeed been fortunate to live the American dream.

All of us—employees, shareholders, business associates, many friends, his wife of 43 years and his children—appreciate that Murray Harpole made the effort to document the history of Pentair and consolidate countless facts and observations into an enjoyable and insightful reading experience.

His effort, which Pentair is proud to have published at the end of its 25th anniversary year, has captured the essence of our company—both the long and the short of it.

D. Eugene Nugent
Chairman and Chief Executive Officer
Pentair, Inc.

PREFACE

Between 1966 and 1991 I lived the particularly compelling American dream of starting a business of one's own and then helping lead its development into a major industrial corporation, a life many people only dream about.

My dream and my business career are certainly not unique, but they have provided me with experience and insight I could not have fully imagined without them. For me entrepreneurs and corporations were transformed from imposing wonders to be revered, feared, or cursed into living, breathing phenomena capable of great strength and woeful vulnerability, in some cases at the same time. I discovered that a corporation's capacity to grow, overcome obstacles, and do either good or evil is not determined by some mysterious, otherworldly power, but by the will and leadership of a handful of individuals with normal human strengths and weaknesses. The story that follows is intended to bring to life the human side of both entrepreneurs and corporations as seen by one such entrepreneur who was privileged to help found and develop one such corporation.

Pentair, Inc., the subject of this story, began as an idea. I am one of five founders who were naive and inexperienced enough to start a company on the basis of that idea. As the company's senior promoter, I was, for the ensuing 25 years, an active participant in that company's growth. I was a product of rural America and America's private enterprise system. Growing up on a farm in southern Iowa, the oldest of 10 children, I identified with the consummate entreprener—the American farmer. My education in a one-room elementary school and slightly larger high school was grounded in the fundamentals. My early life was a rich mixture of hard work, good fun, few luxuries, and seemingly limitless opportunities. My hometown was a community of equals where everyone knew that Cyrus McCormick, Thomas Edison, and Henry Ford had all come out of similar beginnings. And look what they accomplished!

A career in farming ended for me one year after high school and the beginning of World War II. Color blindness ruled out the possibility of officer training in the military, but not the filling of a wartime need as an engineer. With a degree in electrical engineering from Iowa State College (now Iowa State University), I took a job on the Manhattan District Project for nuclear-weapon development. Over the course of the next two decades, I worked for four different companies in engineering, research, and development. At the age of 45, I became one of the five founders of Pentair.

In telling the Pentair story, I have several objectives in mind. First of all, I wish to provide further proof (if further proof is needed) that the American private enterprise system does work. I also wish to show that individuals with limited experience and financial resources can develop a respected, significant, and long-lived business by dint of commitment, hard work, and integrity, and with the willing support of others. I would be pleased if this book provides both an example and meaningful encouragement to others thinking about starting a business of their own, and if it inspires current and future Pentair employees and associates to draw on the best of Pentair's past for the good of Pentair's future.

Finally, I would hope that this account will encourage readers to fight to preserve our system of independent, publicly held corporations, focused on long-term benefits for all of their stakeholders and for society at large.

ACKNOWLEDGEMENTS

The writing of this book had much in common with the development of Pentair, Inc. What was envisioned as the personal commitment of a few soon depended on the work of many. Neither venture would have succeeded without a great deal of help and encouragement. Regrettably, not all of the persons who contributed to both could be included in this account. The unselfish support of all, however, is deeply appreciated. If, besides the inevitable omissions, there are errors of fact or misinterpretation of opinion, I am solely responsible. If the account wounds or offends in any way, I sincerely apologize.

I the writer and you the reader have benefitted greatly from the work of William Swanson. His suggestions, assistance, and skillful editing transformed my collage of information and prose into the finished account you hold in your hands. Equally important has been the excellent work of Maureen Olsen, who converted my dictation and handwriting into impeccably typed pages of organized and readable text. I will be forever grateful to both Bill and Maureen for their professional assistance, patience, and understanding.

My work on this book was made much easier by the responsive and courteous staff of Pentair. They greatly aided and accommodated my efforts to collect and verify information. I'm particularly grateful for the assistance of Gene Nugent. The encouragement and commentary of Henry Conor and Quentin Hietpas provided impetus and direction to both the starting and the finishing of the text.

The lion's share of the credit must go to my wife Ruth and my family for their understanding and assistance in this effort. After 24 years of living with Pentair, they could hardly be expected to live a like number of months with the writing of Pentair's story — but they did. Their support and comfort was, as always, invaluable. Thank you all.

INTRODUCTION

How does one tell the story of the first 25 years of a corporation? Its development was not logical, nor did it follow any grand plan or scheme. The countless surprises, changes in direction, diverse personalities, shifting fortunes, and ever-present threat of defeat are like the ups and downs of a long, drawn-out battle. Eventually a sense of order develops and a measure of control and direction becomes apparent; eventually there is stability and success. Pentair's first quarter-century was like that, and it is a challenge to describe.

This book endeavors to relate the development of Pentair, Inc., through a chronological account that begins with its founding in 1966 and concludes at the end of its 25th year. The story is told from my point of view from the beginning of my tenure to my retirement. This is not simply a story about a company, but a story about people, about human moods and emotions, as I look back on the evolution of a particular American dream.

While the observations, evaluations, and opinions reflect my personal biases, the order of events and activities is as objectively correct as I can make it. Thankfully, I had more to rely on than memory. I had the benefit of a daily diary that I began the day the company was founded. Corporate minute books, shareholder reports, and correspondence files provided supplemental documentation, all of which was drawn upon for this book. (Additional material, including a list of significant events, a roster of company directors, and graphs tracking Pentair's achievements are provided in the Appendix.)

The idea for such a company was conceived in 1965. Pentair Industries, Incorporated (as it was originally called), was brought to life on July 6, 1966, by five partners who planned to engineer and manufacture high-altitude research balloons, inflatable devices, and associated instrumentation. Neither the company's $26,000 capitalization nor the market for such products proved sufficient for survival, however. Pentair thus became a public corporation, with the sale of 200,000 shares at one dollar per share in early 1967. From that point forward, the company grew by acquiring, developing, and expanding existing (and usually underperforming) businesses, which included mostly paper mills and industrial-product manufacturers.

Pentair became profitable within two years of its founding and has remained profitable since. Following about six years in a start-up and survival mode, the company achieved a measure of stability and the maturity to develop long-range plans. Then the pace and scope of development increased as the company evolved into a diversified industrial manufacturing business. Eighteen years after its founding, Pentair became one of America's 500 largest industrial companies, with annual sales of $545 million, net earnings of $21 million, and some 4,800 employees. Today, at 25 years of age, Pentair's annual sales are $1.2 billion, and the company employs about 9,000 persons at operations in eight states and five foreign countries.

Pentair's management has been characterized by a small corporate staff operating through largely autonomous subsidiaries in accord with a published Code of Business Conduct. Management has conducted the company's business with a long-range objective, investing aggressively in facilities, products, and organization, and striving to be a highly respected, top-performing, and independent public company.

Pentair's accomplishments reflect the dedication, skill, and hard work of many people at all levels of the organization. Those people, supported by public investors, have once again proved that individuals possessing little in the way of either money or experience can build a mighty corporation from the seed of an idea. They have shown that success can be achieved and maintained despite the concerted efforts of outside interests to take control of the business for the short-term profit of a few.

Books, like careers, eventually must come to an end. This book presents the observations and experiences of one person who was privileged to take part in the American dream of taking an idea and helping it grow into a major corporation. In this book the corporation is called Pentair, and the good news is, its story has just begun.

Chapter One

Beginnings 1965-1966

One day in early 1965, two employees of the Litton Industries, Inc., Applied Science Division in Minneapolis took a long, hard look at the future. The outlook for the business was not bright, they concluded. As far as Litton was concerned, balloons and related inflatable products were going nowhere. But, with high-altitude balloons for near-space research, aerodynamic-shaped balloons for elevating air samplers, tethered balloons for carrying weapons-testing instruments, and inflated roughened spheres for radar tracking at satellite launches, there seemed to be enough current and potential applications to keep the business airborne for some time.

The men, neither brash youngsters nor cynical graybeards, had participated in various parts of the inflatables business over the past 15 years, first at General Mills, Inc., where much of the design and development of the high-altitude, free-floating devices had taken place since the end of World War II, and then at Litton, which had acquired the business from General Mills in 1962. At the time of the discussion, Vernon Stone was a 34-year-old engineering program manager with 10 years of experience in balloon development. I was the other man, a 44-year-old electrical engineer who had spent the past 21 years in a wide range of engineering research and development work, including some instrumentation and measurement equipment for research balloons and other inflatables.

Together we discerned a decline in emphasis on the products since Litton's acquisition. Moreover, we watched as some of the people who had worked on the products at General Mills and Litton left to establish competitive businesses. The balloon and inflatables business was a minor part of Litton's overall operations, with only a limited potential for growth.

We decided that if the business was going to go anywhere at all, it would have to be as part of a brand new company—one that we would have to start ourselves.

Billion-dollar companies, like the mighty oak, often begin modestly, with the acorn of an idea lying all but invisible on the forest floor. In Pentair's case, the acorn was the idea that the balloon and inflatable-systems business of Litton Industries could grow and prosper on its own, out of the shadows of Litton's larger products, as a new and independent organism. Vern Stone and I were the two original tenders of that "acorn."

After those initial conversations, we began to take the first tentative steps toward what would eventually be a new company that would design, manufacture, and sell balloons and inflatable systems. Vern concentrated on new business opportunities and on how we could service customers currently using Litton products or those of the competition. I worked on pro forma cash-flow projections and estimates of the capital needed to start and to maintain the business for one to three years. By the end of 1965, Vern and I were working nights and weekends at the kitchen table. We began to convince ourselves that the idea of going out on our own might just succeed.

Up until that time, we kept our plans close to the vest. But in early 1966, Vern and I began feeling out other individuals with specific skills and interests who might be interested in joining us. However, we found mostly skepticism about our prospects. While we generated some interest and enthusiasm among our colleagues, the size of the risk and commitment involved was enough to dissuade most of those we approached. "A new company sounds great, but I can't afford to take the risk right now, and I really don't think you'll ever get that particular 'balloon' off the ground," was the common response.

Nevertheless, by May 1966, three men were willing to take the leap. Vincent Follmer was a manufacturing supervisor with more than 10 years of experience in the manufacture of balloons and inflatables. Leroy Nelson was a senior mechanical design engineer experienced in the design of balloons and inflatable systems and in the machine design of specialized manufacturing equipment. Gary

Ostrand was a junior engineer not long out of college with limited experience in both design and technical sales. They joined us virtually every weekend in the planning of the new company.

We spent a great deal of time refining our sales projections, cash requirements, and cash-flow situation. Corporate organization and finance were new to me, and my first tentative calls on bankers and venture capitalists had not resulted in any financial support for our business plan. Clearly, we were going to have to pool our resources and set up the business as a partnership.

At the same time, we were defining specific projects that we could start on in early July. July is the beginning of the federal government's fiscal year, and the government was historically the major customer of the balloon and inflatable-systems business. New funding would be available, and small jobs such as retrofit, repair, and modification of existing inflatable systems could begin quickly, too. We believed we could be very competitive with these smaller projects, which required only limited facilities and personnel.

Defining such work helped us to focus our planning for the special fabrication and sealing equipment we would have to design and build before we could begin work, the materials we would have to buy, the size of the manufacturing space we would need to lease, the number of people we would need on our staff, and so on. Our very limited capital—that is, our collective life savings of $26,000—required that the projects we took on generate the cash flow necessary to support operations while we developed the size and strength to handle larger, more complicated, and potentially more profitable projects.

We were prepared to perform most of the fabrication and assembly work ourselves, while designing our own specialized fabrication equipment, and handling procurement, sales, purchasing, and all the other responsibilities involved in starting and running a business. The budget was very tight, but we believed that if everything fell into place, we could be successful. Our plan called for immediate sales and prompt payment for completed work to generate the necessary cash flow. We could break even on first-year sales of about $225,000, according to our projections.

In early May, we had proceeded far enough with our plans and projections to commit ourselves to the new venture. We decided not to mention our intentions to our supervisors in order to avoid discussion and possible delay. We would give Litton Industries two weeks' notice in June and begin our own operations on or about July 6. We agreed to keep our plans strictly confidential for as long as possible before giving notice. We also agreed to be extremely careful not to take any drawings, documents, or other data from the company. When we walked out of Litton's door for the final time, we would carry nothing except the knowledge in our heads. This had been gained under government contract and seemed to us to be in the public domain.

Understandably, those last two months proved to be an anxious and fearful time. We were committing ourselves and our resources to an unknown and questionable future, despite our best projections. We were about to walk away from secure jobs, paid vacations, corporate pension plans, and company-sponsored health insurance. We were placing at risk our children's education, our retirement plans, and many of the things we considered to be well-earned rewards for years of honest labor. Our frequent after-hours meetings—usually running late into the night around the kitchen table at Vern's house or mine—became occasions on which we would reinforce each other's resolve. As the senior promoter of the venture, I sometimes felt hard-pressed to maintain my *own* enthusiasm, let alone to buck up my partners'.

But on the other side of the coin was the tremendous sense of adventure and euphoria we felt on the threshold of starting a new company. We were embarking on an important journey that many people dreamed about, but few were ever able to make. In hindsight, we were too naive to recognize the dangers and pitfalls that lay ahead, but that naivete might have been our salvation. If we had seen all the twists and turns our path would take, we might never have started out in the first place.

Several important decisions remained. Although we never drew up a formal partnership agreement, the others insisted that I become president if the new company were to go ahead. We also agreed that Vern would become vice president and Vince, treasurer. Aldo Pieri, the general-practice attorney we met through Leroy, would be secretary. Our board of directors would comprise the five founders, Aldo, and Wallace Wells. Wally, a friend and a former Litton associate, was keenly interested in our venture. We welcomed him as an investor and advisor.

Also, we had to decide what to name the new enterprise and we developed a long list of possibilities. Among the names suggested were the 4M Company (one better than 3M); the Har-Stone Company (for Harpole and Stone); Multech Industries; Inflatable Products Company; and Air-Tech Industries. None of these names became a consensus favorite. Finally, Aldo insisted that we had to agree on something. After one of our late evening meetings we stopped at a downtown coffee shop and came up with the name Pentair Industries, Incorporated. The Greek root penta- referred to the five founders, -air to the air-inflatable products we planned to produce. We unanimously agreed that Pentair would be our corporate identity.

By this time we were only a month shy of our launch date, and there were additional concerns that demanded our attention. We needed a building, office furniture and supplies, an accountant, and a secretary. We also needed to draw up specific proposals and formal bids for the business we planned to secure.

As it happened, a major source of that business was becoming unexpectedly problematical. President Lyndon Johnson had declared that, beginning with the government's fiscal year starting July 1, much of the money budgeted for government research and development would be redirected to support the nation's growing military involvement in Vietnam. At first, the full significance of the president's declaration did not register; we were too busy with the business at hand. The net effect, of course, rendered our $26,000 in pledged capital inadequate. Nevertheless, on June 21 we gave Litton our two-week notice. Beginning July 6, we would be on our own.

Of course, my wife Ruth and I had discussed the risk to our own livelihood and well-being. We discussed the possible ramifications with our four children, then aged 15, 13, 11, and six. We accepted the possibility of failure as well as of success. We all understood that our education and retirement funds were gone, our liquid assets had been committed to the new venture, and both our house and car were heavily mortgaged. Through it all, Ruth was thoroughly supportive, and together we agreed that we would commit the next five years to making Pentair succeed. No matter how tough things got, we would stay the course, stopping only if we ran out of money or became too sick to carry on with the work. From that point on, I heard neither my wife nor any of my children seriously second-guess our decision.

At the company level, we engaged the services of Breitman, Orenstein, and Schweitzer, a local accounting firm, whom we had been referred to by Aldo. None of us had any real accounting or financial experience, so we were heartened by their practical and sympathetic approach to our fledgling, low-budget enterprise. I remember Harvey Orenstein and Stanley Schweitzer telling us to keep the company's records just like we tend our checkbooks at home. "Place all of your invoices and other financial data in a box," they advised. They would come in once a month to keep the records straight. "Don't worry about the financial reporting," they said. "Concentrate instead on developing the business." Because of such down-to-earth advice, I never worried about our recordkeeping again.

The business was already having a significant impact on my personal life. I was no longer able to leave business matters at the office. On June 26, I drove my family to Buffalo, New York, to celebrate Ruth's parents' 40th wedding anniversary. Though Ruth had spent considerable effort planning the party, I was preoccupied with thoughts about the new company, its many challenges and opportunities, and the seemingly countless tasks awaiting my attention. That was the first of many family events that found me present in body but not in spirit. The concerns of the new business were all consuming.

My partners and I sat down for our exit interviews at Litton on July 5. As we cleaned out our desks and bundled up our personal belongings, we realized we had crossed a bridge in our lives and careers, and there was no turning back. We felt a tremendous exhilaration at the thought of stepping forth to create a new enterprise. At the same time, we could not help but feel butterflies in our stomachs, having severed our ties with the world of stable employment.

———

If our brand-new company had an official "birthday," it was July 6, 1966. On that day, we opened an account at Fidelity Bank and Trust in Minneapolis in the name of Pentair Industries, Incorporated and deposited $26,000 pledged by the founders.

On that day, Vince, Gary, and I talked with a Fidelity banker about our plans for the company and asked him about the possibility of borrowing money in the future. (The founders' capital would probably not cover us, we told him, until the business got firmly established.) The three of us were naive enough to think that because we now had a company, it would be a relatively simple matter to borrow funds in the company's name. We learned right then and there it would not be as easy as we thought. The banker informed us that if we would give him our personal net worth statements and guarantee the loan, he would determine how much the bank would be willing to lend us. By now our personal net worth, aside from the funds we had committed to Pentair, was essentially zero. Whatever additional funding the company needed would have to come from other sources.

That night we arranged a meeting at our lawyer's office with about two dozen friends and acquaintances earlier identified as potential investors. Vern and I told the gathering about our plans to design, develop, and manufacture balloons, inflatable systems, and associated instrumentation. We explained that we did not have any firm contracts in hand, but that we had a number of prospects. We showed them our cost projections and the amount of money already committed to the operation, and we told them we needed additional funds to tide us over until the business was up and running. When we were through, a few guests signed the subscription forms we had passed out. A few more took the forms with them when they left, assuring us that they would give our request some thought.

After the meeting, our accountants expressed surprise and concern that we were soliciting subscription agreements without first preparing a prospectus and filing the pertinent data with the federal Securities and Exchange Commission (SEC) and the state of Minnesota. They thought a solicitation without such filings might be of questionable legality. As it happened, Aldo was out of town, and neither the young lawyer who was filling in for him nor the Pentair founders had the slightest idea that they might have been breaking the rules!

On the brighter side, one acquaintance at the subscription meeting suggested we contact a certain commercial property developer he knew. Perhaps the developer would lease us space for a year in exchange for company stock.

The property in question comprised 5,000 square feet in a new development in a St. Paul suburb which was conveniently located about five miles from my home and even closer to Vern's. The empty building included some office space and a long manufacturing area suitable for fabricating balloons, with a high ceiling and large doors opening onto a loading dock. We promptly signed a lease for the building and agreed to pay the first year's rent of $5,000 with Pentair stock valued at a dollar a share. If our planned stock issue flopped, we agreed to pay the $5,000 in cash. That proved to be a good deal, even though the landlord, after selling his shares for a profit, would later sue us, claiming that he should also have received the founders' stock at fifty cents a share.

Although lacking contracts, Pentair had its first official address: 3756 North Dunlap Street, Arden Hills, Minnesota. We immediately began equipping the office with used desks, file cabinets, drafting tables, and wastebaskets purchased from Litton. (In some instances, the items we bought as surplus had been the ones we had used ourselves while working for our erstwhile employer.) We also bought a pair of air conditioners for the office, because the building had a furnace for wintertime heating but no windows that could be opened in the summer. Soon we outfitted the factory space with electric power, long layout tables, tools, and the special equipment needed to fabricate and assemble balloons and other inflatable products. We had all been working at home, developing lists of equipment and supplies to be purchased and installed before we could really get down to business.

I was also developing a brochure to mail to prospective customers. No small amount of time was spent agonizing over a corporate logo and typeface for our printed materials. With the help of a printer who had attended our subscription meeting, we decided on an Irish script for our name, to be printed in gold ink on letterhead and business cards. The logo was tougher to agree on. After much discussion, we selected a pentagon with the Greek letter *pi* in the center. Of course, the letters P and I stood for Pentair Industries. Looking back, I cannot help but be amused by the number of discussions and the amount of mental energy we invested in that relatively simple symbol.

There were certainly more pressing concerns. We agreed that each of us would be paid at the same rate we were paid at Litton. Though our salaries hardly added up to a staggering amount, writing out the company's first payroll on July 15, our first payday, was a sobering experience. It was abundantly clear that the $26,000 with which we capitalized the company was not going to take us very far. The new business we had counted on during our planning was not yet there. Until we had that new business, we were simply eating our own lunch.

Vern was spending most of his time contacting would-be customers that we had been counting on for the early going. What he was learning we had already surmised from the newspapers but had not taken seriously enough in our planning: The government funding essential to so many of our possible projects had been placed in grave doubt by the president's decision to beef up our military presence in Vietnam. Without much of any real business to attend to, four of the five founders decided to take little unpaid vacations; none of the four had taken any vacation time during our last year at Litton. I had already taken a few days for my in-laws' wedding anniversary and did not feel I could take any more time away from the problems at hand. I doubt if I would have enjoyed myself anyway.

It did not take long to realize the seriousness of our financial condition. The euphoria we felt setting out on our own under the bright new Pentair banner was quickly wearing thin. Replacing it was the certain knowledge that the fledgling company was not going to survive without a significant influx of equity capital.

Writing all the company's checks, I was painfully aware of our rapidly dwindling resources with each and every expenditure, be it for manufacturing equipment or postage stamps. To make our resources stretch as far as possible, we adopted a set of informal rules that made up an austerity program. One of the rules was: *No travel if a long-distance telephone call will suffice.* Another was: *No long-distance telephone call if a letter can do the job.* However, our largest single expenditure was the payroll. We decided to cut it in half. I reduced my $19,500 annual salary to $700 a month, and my partners followed suit. None of us had any other sources of income at the time, yet we felt we had no choice but to make the cuts.

On July 20, we met with Aldo, our attorney, to discuss our financial situation and outlook. We agreed that selling shares of stock to the public was the only way to keep the company afloat. None of us had ever been involved in a public financing arrangement, but we all knew the next step would be to incorporate and register a stock sale with the SEC.

It became my responsibility to develop the public financing program while my partners continued preparing our factory and developing customers for our products and services. I redrew our internal financing plans based on downwardly revised estimates of government spending. Using books and documents borrowed from the library and other sources, I took a crash course on offering circulars, prospectuses, and articles of incorporation. To my dismay, I found that the market for new stock offerings was in a decided slump, despite vivid memories of the "go-go" years earlier in the decade and the great success of the locally based Control Data Corporation's dollar stock.

Drafts of the various documents were passed among the partners and our attorney. We generally agreed on the content except for the portion covering stock options; that language was revised and adjusted until we finally concurred. Without guidelines dealing with the number of shares we should issue, the price of each share, and the number of appropriate options, we were, at best, only feeling our way along.

Stan Schweitzer, one of our accountants, had some public offering experience and gave us much needed direction and advice. Stan also introduced us to P.R. Peterson of the P.R. Peterson Company, a two-man stockbrokerage that specialized in the initial public offerings of fledgling companies. It proved to be a fortunate meeting. Peterson may well have been the only broker in town willing to take a chance on us. We talked with other brokers in the Twin Cities, but no one besides Peterson expressed much interest. We were a tough sell because we were not in a particularly glamorous industry, government procurement policies were unfavorable, and we had no business yet in hand. Outsiders could be forgiven for not finding our prospects very bright.

I pooled the information we had gathered from Schweitzer, Peterson, our legal counsel, and other sources, and presented that information to my partners. Time was important; we needed the new financing as quickly as we could get it. According to the information, a stockbroker could probably sell 125,000 shares of Pentair stock at $1.15 a share. The founders could convert their equity to stock at the rate of 60 cents per share. We could also sell the stock to those potential investors who attended our early subscription meeting at a price of 80 cents per share and include them in the prospectus as incorporators. We could issue stock at a dollar per share to our landlord for the first year's rent.

In the meantime, Aldo recommended we retain an attorney with experience in corporate law and SEC matters. His choice was Stanley Efron, who from that point on would work with us on all aspects of the public offering. Our meeting with Efron proved fortuitous. Stan was then an energetic young attorney specializing in corporate law. Though we were taken aback by his no-nonsense appraisal of the time and money required to get SEC clearance for a stock offering, we liked his take-charge attitude and intelligence. Stan eventually became our general corporate counsel and played a central role in the company's development for more than 25 years.

While we fretted over our financial plans, we also tried our best to drum up some business. Our short-term prospects being virtually nonexistent, we decided to sow seeds for the future. We mailed scores of new-company announcements, resumes, and business plans to every prospective customer we could think of, and we filed the necessary forms to be placed on the bid lists of dozens of governmental agencies. Vern called or visited the most promising prospects. Leroy worked hard to complete the design of our manufacturing equipment. Meanwhile, Vince and Gary concentrated on equipping the office and getting the shop ready to go.

The financing challenge hung over us like a heavy, black cloud. Our orders for the special machines and equipment we would need to operate the business were committing our limited resources at a frightening rate, and the five of us were feeling increasingly desperate.

Stan, our new securities counsel, did not ease our concern when he told us that we would need three times the $100,000 we believed would be sufficient. Not only that, we could expect to wait up to six months to get SEC comments for a Regulation A offering of up to $300,000. Struggling to find something hopeful to tell us, Stan said we might be able to borrow some money from the people who had expressed interest in the company at that subscriber meeting in July. Maybe we could borrow enough money from them to tide us over until the offering could be completed.

After I discussed our plans with several local banks, brokerages, and venture capital companies, it was apparent that if anybody was going to find a way to help us with a public offering it was P.R. Peterson. Peterson had expressed a tentative interest in taking Pentair public, which was more than any other local professional had done. He and another local broker, John R. Stephens, visited our plant and talked with us in mid-August. Peterson decided he would work with us on a best-effort basis, developing an offering to be sold within the state of Minnesota. He believed that an exclusive Minnesota registration would be the only way we could get money soon enough to stay alive.

We filed our articles of incorporation with the state of Minnesota on August 26, 1966, transforming Pentair from a partnership into a full-fledged corporation. We listed our board of directors as comprising the five founders, plus Wally Wells and Aldo Pieri. The articles of incorporation provided stock at a par value of 50 cents a share. According to company bylaws drawn up a few days later, officers of the new corporation were Murray Harpole, president; Vern Stone, vice president; Vince Follmer, treasurer; and Aldo Pieri, secretary.

While I worked on the language of our offering circular, Stan Schweitzer finished the financial part, using a closing date of August 31. His figures were decidedly grim: of the $26,000 contributed, only $16,000 remained. Less than $13,000 remained when we subtracted our equipment and machinery commitments. Another $5,000 would be eaten up in the securities filing process, thus reducing our working capital to a paltry $8,000. If that was not bad enough, the report would show that the company's five principals had lost more than six percent of their investment, thus reducing their anticipated equity to be transferred from the partnership to the corporation.

Another hitch: Stan Efron, when reviewing our completed materials, vehemently disagreed with the idea of state registration only and said he would work with us only if we filed with the SEC under a Regulation A offering. He argued that a federal SEC registration, as opposed to a Minnesota-only approach, would eliminate any legal risk from inadvertent out-of-state sales and would pave the way for national distribution of our stock. He was right, of course. We made plans to engage Fidelity Bank as our registrar and transfer agent.

Thankfully, after a couple of months in business, we were beginning to receive responses from our mailings, calls, and visits. The responses did not translate into any immediate paying business, but they did reassure us that potential customers were becoming aware of Pentair. We promptly began preparing specific proposals and letters of quotation, while fabricating samples of some of the smaller balloons and inflatables we were planning to produce.

Just in the nick of time, we felt temporary relief from our financial bind. Wally Wells paid in $7,000 as one of the incorporators of the company. Some individuals lent us $16,500, following the solicitation of the people who had signed subscription agreements at the July meeting. We received an additional $2,000 from those subscribers by early December, for a grand total of $18,500.

All in all, we were heartened and surprised by the response to our call. Surprised because the individuals who lent us the money were not the wealthy individuals we expected to invest in such a speculative project. They were machinists, mechanics, engineers, secretaries, and clergymen, among other folk, who were willing to lend us $500 to $2,000 each. We gave them notes providing that if our stock offering was successful, they would be repaid with stock at $1 a share; if the stock did not sell, the founders would repay the notes in cash. We did not have the slightest idea of where that cash would come from, but that was something we could worry about later, if we had to. In the meantime, we were cheered that someone out there believed Pentair had a future!

Autumn of our first year in business found us laboring, day by day, over the fine points of an underwriting agreement, offering circular, and other SEC-required documents, while doing what we could to bring in business.

Eventually, the founders and our advisers agreed on the document language. For the SEC, we described our business as engineering and manufacturing inflatable systems, including tethered balloons, inflatable antenna masts, marker buoys, inflatable shelters, free-floating balloons, super-pressure balloons, and related valves, controls, inflation means, gas generators, containers, and accessories. We said that we had neither any sales nor any manu-factured product, and that our business was heavily dependent on government contract work. We added, perhaps needlessly, that it was a highly speculative business in which we were operating.

The final offering arrangement stipulated that what money remained of the founders' investment would be converted to stock at 50 cents a share. The 200,000 shares that would be offered to the public would be valued at $1 a share, proceeds to the company. Wally would get 7,000 shares for his investment, and the landlord would get 5,000 shares for the first year's rent. A total of 18,500 shares would go to the individual investors who had come to our aid during the past couple of months. Upon the offering's completion, the founders would own about 17.6 percent of the company.

The terms were difficult for us to swallow. After all, we had set out to establish a company that we would own, run, and profit from all by ourselves. Our plans, worries, and labors had been dedicated to that end. Now, after only half a year of operation, we were about to give up roughly 80 percent of our ownership. We were convinced by that time that we had no real choice. Did we want 20 percent of something, or 100 percent of nothing?

I recalled a conversation with a venture capitalist that summer, when I had been beating the bushes for funds. Alan Ruvelson, president of First Midwest Capital Corporation in Minneapolis, had seen many start-up operations come and go, and I listened care-fully to what he had to say.

Ruvelson said it took a great deal of commitment to launch a new company such as ours, and even that commitment did not guarantee the venture's success. Entrepreneurs risked not only their financial investment, but their physical and mental health and the well-being of their families. "Try as you might," he said, "you won't be able to anticipate all of the problems you're going to encounter, much less the severity of those problems and the amount of time and effort it will take to overcome them."

Ruvelson advised me that if we were not prepared to accept the risks and their manifold stresses, we would be doing ourselves a favor by bowing out as quickly as possible, before we harmed ourselves and others, strangers and loved ones alike. On the other hand, if we were prepared to accept the risks and to make the commitment, there was no telling how far we could go. He wished us luck and said he would be following us, if we proceeded, with great interest. He chose not to provide any financing.

I had much occasion to think about Ruvelson's remarks during the first years of Pentair's existence, but never did they seem more to the point than during those first few months in business.

Displays of canoes and inflatable products were the star attractions at Pentair's first annual meeting, October 30, 1967. About 20 shareholders showed up at the 1161 Grey Fox Road, Arden Hills, Minnesota location.

Pentair's first stock certificate, Number 101, was part of a 200,000 share offering sold to the public for one dollar per share. The stock was sold in January 1967.

Chapter Two

Survival 1967-1968

During the fall of our first year in business, our hopes were boosted by the possibility of a large contract from the Unidynamics Corporation. (Our bid proposal to Unidynamics had been a follow-up to contacts first made while we were working for Litton.) The contract, worth the considerable sum of $125,000, involved the construction of a torpedo-recovery system that would be used by the U.S. Navy. The system centered on an ammonia-inflated octa-hedron containing a radar corner reflector. The device would be released by a test torpedo at the end of its run and rise to the ocean's surface. There it would signal the torpedo's presence to a recovery ship. We were told we had probably submitted the winning bid, but the final decision would not be announced for several months. In other words, the prospect did nothing to relieve our immediate problems.

Morale was predictably low. Occasionally, we were irritable and short with each other. The great expectations and brave ambitions of only four months ago had been dramatically diminished by a harsh dose of business reality. Our working capital drained away like water out of a bathtub. For instance, almost $10,000 was necessary to cover accounting and legal fees and other costs connected with the SEC filing. Meanwhile, bills continued to mount for the special manufacturing equipment we had ordered.

Even the little things seemed to be working against us. The office area of our building faced north, and when our typically frigid Minnesota winter set in, the space was much too cold for comfort. Every time the front door opened, our secretary was buffeted by a blast of chill air. To make the situation tolerable, we needed to add an anteroom, which meant another expense we could ill afford. About the same time, a potential investor sent our way by P.R. Peterson showed up unannounced one day during a mid-afternoon break—just in time to see us tossing around a football in the plant. The investor, drawing his own conclusions about our hard-working staff, reported back to Peterson, who called to tell us that we were not exactly helping to sell Pentair stock.

Then, in early November, our landlord gave us a lead on something new. A small operation, the Thunder Aircraft and Marine Company, located in an adjacent building, was on the verge of bankruptcy and possibly for sale. I discovered that the firm had transferred its assets into a new company called American Thermo-Vac Tooling headed by Harvey Anderson and his two sons, Terry and Bob.

I quickly discovered the Andersons were smooth-talking entrepreneurs with unusual technical and business experience and quick, creative minds. They came up with the idea of thermo-forming large plastic parts for diverse products such as canoes, aircraft shipping containers, and golf carts. Their plan was to buy large sheets of acrylonitrile butadiene styrene (ABS) plastic, heat the plastic until it was pliable, place it over a mold, and draw a vacuum that would cause the plastic to conform to the shape of the mold and harden. Their plant was equipped with a vacuum system and a gas-fired oven, but both were inadequate to the task. Nonetheless, they had convinced a number of investors and suppliers that their prospects were good. In late 1966, the Andersons were on the cutting edge of that technology.

Bob Anderson was the spokesman for the group. He was a tall, presentable man with a confident yet self-effacing manner and an easy way with words that made him both engaging and believable. He told me he was interested in exploring the sale of the company. He said he had patents, supply agreements, and large orders in hand; all he needed was a little more capital and some technical assistance. However, the Andersons had no patents and what they owned by way of technical information they had only in their heads. Their accounting procedures were in shambles, and creditors were constantly hounding them.

Still, American Thermo-Vac was an intriguing possibility. The idea behind the company seemed sound. Furthermore, in light of Pentair's immediate prospects in the balloon and inflatables business, the idea of a new and potentially faster-moving activity was difficult to ignore. P.R. Peterson was intrigued as well. Peterson not only harbored grave doubts about the salability of Pentair's stock, he was involved in a toboggan-slide program that possibly could use vacuum-formed plastic sections for assembling seasonal toboggan runs. He suggested that if we acquired American Thermo-Vac, he could sell the 200,000 shares of Pentair stock during its forthcoming offering.

At an impromptu meeting of the Pentair board, I argued that the acquisition of the Andersons' business would help us raise desperately needed capital through the sale of our shares and give us the business we needed to stay on our feet. My colleagues were skeptical. They agreed the prospects were inviting, but the thought of diverting energy and attention to an unfamiliar business made them uneasy. I received their approval to go ahead with the acquisition, although it was less than enthusiastic.

Our accounting and legal counsel were not much more enthusiastic than the board. However, the next hitch proved to be the sellers themselves. Over the next six months, we were continually frustrated by the Andersons' actions. Meetings were either postponed or canceled; those few that did come off as scheduled were confusing, to say the least. Key accounting information was unavailable, promised product orders never materialized, and the roster of potential customers seemed to change daily. When we proposed a particular set of terms for acquisition, the Andersons asked for another set. One Anderson did not always speak for another, and it was unclear just who would be making the decision. Their company's creditors and suppliers were as confused by their modus operandi as we were. A few of their creditors were coming to us seeking payment of debts in anticipation of a Pentair acquisition of American Thermo-Vac.

On December 6, we received the go-ahead for our stock offering from the SEC though Peterson and broker John Stephens were reluctant to proceed without the new business. After reviewing the options with our directors and advisors, I told the brokers that we were going to develop the vacuum-forming business with or without the Andersons. The brokers immediately began promoting the Pentair stock and were soon receiving queries from other small brokers and local investors.

Six months after embarking into the balloon and inflatable systems business, we were committed to a vacuum-forming operation that we did not yet own. While we prepared new brochures and supporting information and struggled to land orders for balloons and inflatables, I was desperately trying to reach agreement with the Andersons, hoping to acquire some or all of their operation in order to reduce the time and cost of getting established on our own. The effort proved to be as difficult and as frustrating as anything I have ever experienced in my life. Meetings were set up, then canceled. One Anderson would agree to terms only to be overruled by another. Nights and weekends were consumed trying to hammer out a binding accord.

I might have given up the whole thing if it was not for a couple of the Andersons' broker friends promising significant interest from large customers around the country. Montgomery Ward and other large marine distributors expressed interest in buying quantities of up to 2,000 vacuum-formed canoes. The potential for vacuum-formed products seemed real. If only we could move swiftly enough to take advantage of it.

———

By mid-January 1967, P.R. Peterson had subscription agreements for the 200,000 shares of stock and was ready to close. We moved as quickly as possible on the design of an oven for vacuum-forming large parts. The new gas-fired, insulated oven measured about 6' x 7' x 20' in size and cost about $10,000. To accommodate the vacuum-forming operation, we rented larger space next door to our original facility, ordered a large vacuum pump and accumulator tanks, and moved in on January 26.

By this time, the Andersons had all but run out of operating capital, and they were aware that we were preparing to go ahead without them. In late January they finally agreed to sell us American Thermo-Vac's tooling, molds, shop equipment, and technical know-how for $50,000. According to the agreement, the Andersons would receive $25,000 down, then the second $25,000 at the end of 12 months. They would help operate the business for six weeks, then turn the operation over to Pentair. They would not compete, they agreed, for three years within 200 miles of our plant. On January 26 Bob Anderson showed up unexpectedly at our office eager to sign the agreement and receive $12,500 as a portion of the down payment. Four days later I received the fully executed agreement along with a visit from Harvey Anderson, who asked for an additional $2,000 payment for a critical COD delivery. I paid him the money with a sigh of relief, not knowing that we were far from done with the Andersons.

During the first part of 1967, we began to see some fruits of our earlier labors on behalf of balloons and inflatable systems. One contract called for the production of a quarter-scale inflatable submarine for Navy rescue experiments; another for radar reflecting spheres with unique surfaces for the National Aeronautics and Space Administration (NASA). The orders, and the prospect of a new business, went a long way toward restoring morale which had been sinking like a rock the previous autumn.

However, uncertainty remained. The balloon and inflatables business was more competitive than ever, due to the limited amount of government funding, and the projects we did land were likely to be only marginally profitable. The vacuum-forming business was highly promising, but we still did not have any firm orders. We had to design and procure our own vacuum-forming system, and we did not yet have a knowledgeable work force. Our advisors fretted about plunging into vacuum-forming activity when our offering circular described only the balloon and inflatables business. Money remained tight. Then matters took a turn for the worse.

The Andersons began talking about scrapping our agreement. American Thermo-Vac creditors became increasingly demanding. We discovered that liens existed against most of the operation's equipment and assets.

Moreover, by the middle of February, we had received only about half of the money coming from our stock offering. It took a letter from our attorney to the underwriters to shake loose the balance. We were now able to repay those persons who had lent us money back in September, using shares of stock valued at $1 a share. Because this did not include the interest payments due those early investors, the company's founders were obligated to pay the interest out of their own pockets.

I had assumed that the pressures of the business would let up with the influx of public financing. Instead, the pressures increased. Our shareholders were mostly small, unsophisticated clients of small, local brokerage firms. They seemed to understand the risks involved, but I had the uneasy feeling that they expected Pentair's dollar stock to perform on the order of Control Data's dollar stock, which had risen to dizzying heights a few years earlier. Those investors included friends and relatives who had lent us money that had since been repaid with our stock. They had invested a significant portion of their life's savings in Pentair and were betting their future that we would succeed. Little did we know then that their wildest expectations would be exceeded!

It was a very uncomfortable position for me. There I was, expected to talk up the company's products and prospects to the investors our brokers would bring around to the shop, while, privately, the uncertain realities of the business made it difficult for me to say too much to friends and family members. While I was committed to assuring a bright future for Pentair, there was almost nothing we could promise them beyond 100 percent of our efforts.

Our uneasy relationship with the Andersons continued, as they struggled to keep American Thermo-Vac alive. After considerable research and exploration, it became apparent that our best bet for early sales lay in the manufacture of a 17-foot canoe. Bob Anderson had what appeared to be an excellent mold, which was one of the items we were presumably buying as part of our deal.

We still lacked many tools and pieces of equipment the Andersons had agreed to sell us, however, and no amount of asking and cajoling was able to shake the stuff loose. Frustrated, we finally asked our lawyer to start legal proceedings, in an attempt to get either the tools and equipment or the $14,500 down payment. We were not the only ones seeking relief. By the end of May 1967, the Andersons' landlord, the phone company, and the IRS had all begun legal action. The sheriff placed a seal on the Andersons' factory door with a court order attaching all of their assets.

By mid-1967, Pentair had grown to about 15 persons, including the five principals, our inflatable-systems assemblers, and four of the Andersons' vacuum-forming workers we had added to our staff. The growing number of employees meant the company was landing more business, which was good news, but it also meant more work on our part. For the first time, we were managing a work force, which meant keeping additional records, preparing a payroll, withholding tax monies, arranging for medical benefits, and performing other essential tasks. The nature of our manufacturing activity was such that we had to wrestle with concerns about solvents, toxic materials, and plant-floor safety. Keeping expenses in line with our marginally profitable contract work was essential.

A year after the company's founding, I was totally consumed by the work of managing Pentair. Even when I was not at the plant, my mind was preoccupied with finding solutions to our problems. My two sons sometimes helped out in the evenings or on weekends, mowing the plant's lawn, shoveling snow, and straightening things up inside, but other than that, I did not try to involve my family in the business. As a matter of fact, I found it almost impossible to even describe to them what I was doing at work, much less promise them the situation would soon improve. I managed a week's vacation in July 1967, taking my family to a lakeside cabin in northern Wisconsin; but even then I found it impossible to keep my mind off the business.

In addition, we suffered some personal shocks. Our attorney and advisor, Aldo Pieri, died suddenly of a heart attack in June. Then, in late July, Vern went to the doctor with an apparent sprained ankle. Incredibly, Vern was diagnosed as having a malignant growth between his heart and a lung. Surgery, followed by chemotherapy, took him out of circulation for three weeks. Vern's indomitable spirit was obvious in his desire to continue working from his sick bed and in his insistence that he would "lick this thing," carry his fair share of the load, and maintain a leadership role with the company. Nevertheless, his absence on top of the other pressures we faced ate into morale and led us to wonder if we had made any progress at all that first tough year on our own.

In the meantime, the Anderson saga became more bizarre. Late one night that summer of 1967, the canoe mold together with some hand tools, woodworking machinery, and furniture from the American Thermo-Vac plant disappeared. Within the next few days we got a court order allowing us to claim what little remained at the facility. We retrieved an 11-foot boat mold, a 15-foot boat plug, mold-handling equipment, and a partially finished plastic canoe. Bob Anderson himself showed up at our office a few days after that, angrily demanding payment on the balance of our agreement but offering no information on the missing materials. He seemed truly desperate, alternately threatening legal action and pleading for understanding in an effort to avoid criminal prosecution and salvage something from the family's collapsing business.

About two weeks later our attorney received a phone call advising us that Bob had delivered the missing canoe mold to a nearby warehouse. Accompanied by the sheriff, we went to the warehouse, found the mold partially filled with rainwater but otherwise in reasonably good shape, and took it back to our own plant.

Through much of the summer we received a series of calls and correspondence from American Thermo-Vac creditors (including the IRS), all seeking to recover costs from us, but those contacts eventually ceased. Bob Anderson harassed us for a while, but he eventually went away, too.

———————————

Our payroll now included four skilled craftsmen from American Thermo-Vac. We tried to keep them gainfully employed by selling pattern and mold work for other companies in addition to doing custom vacuum-forming work until we could start making canoes. By summer's end, efforts to sell either tooling or vacuumed formed products had resulted in very limited business: some hulls for self-propelled surfboards, a few air-conditioner enclosures, and sample hulls for 14-foot runabout boats. With Vern ill, we could not go after additional work as aggressively as we should have, and once more we faced a severe shortage of immediate business. Thankfully, we did have the torpedo-recovery system job for the Navy and the small NASA reflector project, both of which were proceeding as planned. Under the circumstances we had little choice but to go ahead with the 17-foot vacuum-formed canoes and to continue earlier work on the development of the hull structure for motorized surfboards.

Our fiscal year ended on August 31, and we were planning our first annual meeting. Using other public companies' materials as models, I worked hard to develop our first annual report, an employee stock-option plan, and an annual meeting notice.

I approached that first annual meeting with considerable apprehension. Pentair had lost $106,000 during its initial year in business, and its outlook was unclear. To make matters worse, Vern, a key member of management, was in failing health. Expenses were a problem, so we decided to hold the annual meeting at the plant and serve coffee from our office coffee pot. On October 30, we spent the evening tidying up the place, setting out folding chairs, and arranging displays in the canoe assembly area.

The next day, 21 persons were shown the full panoply of Pentair's products including a vacuum-formed canoe, surfboard, air-conditioner cover, inflatable torpedo-recovery system, reflector spheres, and assorted balloons arranged as artistically as possible in a corner of our plant. The guests were also invited to inspect our tooling, oven, vacuum system, balloon-fabrication equipment, and other tangible assets. What we could not show them in a display we described in as upbeat a fashion as we could manage.

Sales for Pentair's first full year in business totaled about $30,000. Our net loss was more than $100,000. Only $130,000 of operating capital remained. Still, the stockholders appeared satisfied, if not particularly heartened, by what they saw and heard. Our employee-option plan, which we believed would encourage further growth, was overwhelmingly approved.

We principals indulged in a rare celebration by having lunch at a local restaurant, the lunch paid for by money from our factory's coffee fund. Vince Follmer made coffee every day in a big, 100-cup coffeemaker. Management and employees paid a nickel a cup for the daily brew. While the coffee was of dubious quality, it seemed to be the most profitable enterprise we had going at the time.

———

As we moved into our second year, the demands on management grew more onerous.

Despite his illness, Vern came to work every day, courageously doing his best to stay on top of the job; however, it was becoming too much for him in his worsening condition. With Aldo gone, we depended on one of his young partners, who, although hard-working and diligent, lacked Pieri's legal knowledge and experience. Other friends and advisors helped the best they could, but the burden on the company's day-to-day leadership only grew heavier. Clearly, we needed help.

One day in September 1967, our accountant Stan Schweitzer told me about another client, Ben Westby, who Stan said had a great deal of business experience and just might be interested in working with a small public company such as ours. I told Stan I would be glad to talk with him, not realizing how significant that contact would turn out to be.

My first meeting with Ben was not particularly auspicious. His office, which was adjacent to a small shop area in the warehouse district of downtown Minneapolis, was cluttered and unimpressive. Westby was dressed in a sweater, slacks, and tennis shoes. I found his flamboyant style of speech intriguing, though, and there was no denying the breadth of his experience. He had been a union organizer and newspaper editor in the meat-packing industry, and he later developed and sold a string of small manufacturing businesses. There was no denying the man's energy and inventiveness, and it was apparent that he was accustomed to, maybe even comfortable with, surviving by his wits. In spite of obvious differences in our personalities, I took a quick liking to him.

Ben offered much-needed management dash to Pentair, and Pentair had attractive features for Ben, too. Primarily, Pentair offered him a chance to work with a publicly held company with the potential to make some real money. The gamble involved in such an operation appealed to him as well. One of Ben's favorite sayings was, "Business is a game, and you keep score with dollars."

Over the next several months Ben visited our plant and met with me over breakfast or lunch at irregular intervals. He was not particularly excited about the stability and growth potential of our business, but then, our commitments notwithstanding, neither was I. Ben continued to impress me with his business acumen, new-product ideas, and wide-ranging contacts in the region. Between our meetings, I checked out as many outside references as I could. Ben was the kind of man you either liked a lot or did not like at all. He had many enthusiastic supporters and a few detractors. During that period, Ben and I exchanged offers and counteroffers. For the time being, his demands were too great for us. We still had a strong desire to go it alone.

While we talked to Ben, we began to see a glimmer of hope for our canoe-manufacturing business. The large order, quantities of between 1,000 and 3,000 units, promised by a sales representative never materialized, but there was little question that interest in the product did exist.

It was probably fortunate that we did not have all those orders because the only canoe in our inventory was the eye-catching red-and-white, 17-foot handmade unit we had displayed at our shareholders' meeting. Vince, my two sons, and I had tested the craft on nearby Turtle Lake one weekend and found it both sturdy and stable. It would look even better when we received the trim pieces we had designed and were having manufactured for us. But that single unit was the only one we had.

As quickly as we could, we began building more, using the mold we had finally obtained, the tooling we had developed, and the new oven and vacuum system. We were beginners, and the process was slow-going at first, but the product came out of the process sturdier and better looking than any of us had expected. By the end of December 1967, we had turned out several units as part of our line of snappy, red-and-white "Penta Craft" canoes.

At the same time, we formed hulls for motorized surfboards as part of a project managed by a promoter in northern Minnesota. The project would shortly come to naught when the promoter's financiers, a group of Red River Valley potato farmers, ran out of money and a public stock offering failed to raise the necessary cash. Symbolically, one of the surfboards literally blew to pieces when an accumulation of hydrogen in the battery compartment exploded during a test run in the spring of 1968. Thankfully, no one was hurt in the blast.

We continued to manufacture metalized spheres and torpedo-recovery systems as well as to receive occasional small orders for aerodynamic-shaped balloons. Also, now that our vacuum-forming system was up and running, we were getting more visits from representatives of boat and recreation-equipment manufacturers interested in the possibility of doing some business. Indeed, our little operation appeared attractive enough to get a few inquiries into our willingness to sell out. (Those early overtures, though tempting, were never seriously pursued. Unfortunately, large-size plastic products were being promoted beyond the real capability of the materials and producers like us.) But Vern's condition and absences made it difficult for the company to remain on top of the inflatables business the way we planned and maintain operations on a day-to-day basis.

Vern was giving everything he could to help deal with the demands at the office, but his health was deteriorating. The strain among us was very telling during that difficult period. After one especially trying day in February 1968, Leroy Nelson resigned as both officer and director. While regrettable, Leroy's resignation was not hard to understand. Pentair was operating in businesses far different from those spelled out in our original plan, and the work

environment was much more stressful than any of us had anticipated.

Big problems, small problems. For Pentair during those first
couple of years, even the small ones seemed large, sometimes
overwhelming. For instance, shipping 100 canoes from St. Paul to
Detroit does not sound too difficult, does it? Yet, during the winter
of 1967-1968, it proved to be a major challenge.

First, we could not find any common carriers equipped to
transport large numbers of canoes. The canoes could not be stuffed
into conventional semi-trailer trucks without damaging the craft.
Specially equipped vehicles would be prohibitively expensive.
The only practical solution was to lease a modified trailer of the
kind used by automobile manufacturers to haul cars. That is exactly
what we did, and we thought our problem was solved.

When the trailer arrived for loading, our dock and alley were
buried beneath three feet of fresh, drifting snow. Then, in sub-zero
temperatures, we had to arrange the vehicle's heavy adjustable
supports so they could safely accommodate as many of our 75-
pound canoes as possible. After considerable effort, we hitched 32
canoes onto the rig and then spent the next few days getting the
shipping instructions in order.

The driver, a small, no-nonsense man, knew the pounding
punishment a lightly loaded trailer could give a load. He took one
look at the rig and said the canoes would never survive the
journey. He kindly helped us rearrange the load, and, miracu-
lously, the canoes made it to Detroit intact. But at what cost in
terms of employee hours and effort? I still shudder at the thought.

In fact, we were getting more and more orders for our canoes.
The major problem with that was the timing, since canoes were
manufactured in the winter, shipped in late winter and spring, and
paid for in the summer. It was costing us too much to make each
unit, but the greater hitch was the capital tied up in receivables and
inventory. By the spring of 1968, we were almost out of cash.

Our bank was unwilling to lend us any more money. About the
same time, David Hyduke, an officer of the First National Bank of
St. Paul, called on us out of the blue. Hyduke was carrying out a
long-range policy of bank president Clarence Frame to develop
new business with small, start-up companies. He arranged an
unsecured loan of $50,000 at 7½ percent interest. A month later I
was able to borrow another $30,000 from the same source. It was

the beginning of a banking relationship that would prove essential to us on more than one occasion.

As ever, for every step forward we seemed to take two steps back, or at least sideways. Leroy's resignation and Vern's absences made it impossible for us to keep abreast of our current business, much less to add more.

Ben Westby and I had kept in touch over the winter, and in March 1968 I asked him to help us appraise the prospects for our collection of businesses. Together we visited several boat and marine dealers to assess the market potential for canoes and other products. We also spent hours examining the possibilities of our balloon and inflatables operation and other activities. We finally concluded that Pentair could not expect to survive if it followed its current course with its current businesses. Realistically, our choices narrowed down to three: sell the company, merge it with another company, or acquire something new.

Ben was interested in taking part in an acquisition or joining Pentair if an acquisition could be found. He had been told by a banker in Ladysmith, Wisconsin, that the Peavey Paper Mill in that community was in trouble and its owners were eager to sell. Ben was not interested in acquiring the mill himself, but he thought that Pentair might be a potential buyer. It was a possibility, and one day in March my wife and I stopped by the plant en route home after delivering a repaired canoe in northern Wisconsin. The plant's managers were not on the premises at the time so a tour was not possible. I was awestruck by the idea that Pentair could acquire something so big as that plant, even if the plant did appear old and somewhat run-down from the outside. On the drive home I could not stop talking about the unbelievable possibility of parlaying our little canoe-and-balloon business into a big paper-making operation.

Over the next several weeks, my attempts to find a buyer or a merger partner for Pentair were unsuccessful, and our bankers suggested that liquidation might be the best solution to our on-going problems.

On May 9, 1968, our board of directors decided to shut down Pentair's canoe-manufacturing operation. We also decided to lay off our skilled tool-and-pattern-makers and take a 30 percent cut in pay ourselves, effective immediately. Most difficult of all, we would have to take Vern off the payroll. By taking those steps, collecting our receivables, finishing our balloon contracts, and selling what remained of our inventory, we determined that we would be able to stay in business until at least September and pay off the bank and other obligations to our creditors. The plan called for harsh measures, but it reflected the reality of our situation. In addition, the plan provided us with the opportunity to seek a new direction for the company.

At that May 9 meeting, the board took two steps that would have far-reaching significance. One of those steps authorized me to negotiate a formal corporate relationship with Ben. The other step was to talk with the people at the Peavey mill in Ladysmith about getting into the paper business.

Chapter Three

Success 1968-1972

On May 13, 1968, Ben and I drove to Ladysmith to take a good look at the Peavey Paper Mill. Inside, we saw a busy but cramped and cluttered facility with three old paper machines, the smallest of which was on the fritz. The mill produced about 50 tons of single-ply toilet tissue and napkins a day, using wastepaper as raw material. Ben and I were hardly experts; neither one of us had ever been in an operating mill. But it did not take an expert to see that the machinery was old and in dubious repair, and that the plant was in need of organization and maintenance. Even the offices were across the Flambeau River from the factory.

Surprisingly, the plant's operators were three hard-working men all under 30. The production manager was a part-time farmer. The business manager was a part-time preacher. The man in charge of engineering and maintenance was a recent technical-school graduate. Of special interest to us was that the sales manager was moving about $3.5-million worth of product a year, selling under both private and proprietary labels mostly to large grocery chains. Surely, a company could find a way to make some profit with annual sales of $3.5 million.

The mill was privately owned by members of the Peavey family of Ladysmith, and from time to time it had been quite profitable. Then a bitter struggle seven years earlier resulted in management ousting the union. This severely damaged the operation. The Patrician Paper Company of New York had been recruited to make an investment and help turn things around, but its efforts had been for naught. The mill was on the verge of bankruptcy. Both Peavey and Patrician wanted out and were willing to negotiate an attractive deal. Because the mill was Ladysmith's

31

major employer, local bankers and other community leaders were eager to see it sold to someone who would keep it in business.

Ben and I agreed that the Peavey mill offered an opportunity. But first Ben and Pentair had to work out an employment agreement that included an equity participation. This would not prove as easy as I thought.

We had to move fast. The Peavey deal had to be settled quickly because Peavey was for all intents and purposes bankrupt. This meant we had to get Ben's situation settled. We also needed to sign a pact with Peavey's sales manager, Fred Whiting, who was critical to whatever success we might make of the mill and who was most likely, if left unprotected, to be hired by someone else. For the next several days I virtually lived with John Abdo, our new legal counsel, and together forged agreements with both Westby and Whiting. We also worked out the wrinkles of the acquisition deal as negotiated with Patrician and Peavey.

On Saturday, June 1, the Pentair board accepted the agreements. Peavey would become a wholly owned subsidiary of Pentair with a separate board of directors and with Ben and me as its principal officers.

There was a snag: The agreement called for a $10,000 down payment at the closing, and the closing was scheduled for the following Monday. Pentair had neither the cash nor the available credit with its banks. Thus, come Monday, Ben and I stopped en route to the closing at his bank, the Third Northwestern in Minneapolis, and opened an account in Pentair's name. We then borrowed $10,000 guaranteed by both Ben and Pentair, and proceeded to the closing.

The closing took place at the Howard Johnson hotel in Bloomington. Members of the Peavey family, officers from Patrician, and the Pentair delegation comprised of Ben, John Abdo, and I were present. With little discussion, we reviewed and signed the documents and handed over the check for $10,000. Allen Schultz of Patrician and Pete Peavey had only one overriding concern: that we knowingly assume all obligations of the business and hold them free and clear. The complete terms of the agreement provided for another $20,000 to be paid at the end of one year, plus 20 percent of the mill's after-tax profits for the next five years. There had been no due diligence, no review of liabilities, assets, contracts, or obligations. We simply bought the mill and stepped into the shoes of the previous owners. We did know that Peavey had about $1.4 million in debts with more than $900,000 of it unsecured.

Just like that, almost two years after Pentair went into business as a manufacturer of balloons and inflatables, the company was the owner of a paper mill. Peavey became our first wholly owned subsidiary.

If I thought my life as a papermaker would somehow be less complicated than the life I had become used to, I was once again mistaken. Pentair was not yet exclusively a papermaker, for one thing; we had a balloon and inflatables business as well as a vacuum-forming operation awaiting disposition. Furthermore, we had no cash to work with, and the paper mill itself was teetering on the brink of bankruptcy.

On a personal level, the reconstituted Pentair bore little resemblance to the original five-man partnership that had opened for business just two years earlier. On June 7, 1968, Gary Ostrand resigned as a company officer (he remained a director); the next day, Vern, I, and our wives attended Gary's wedding. Five days after the wedding, Vern passed away, succumbing to his year-long struggle with cancer.

Vern's death was an immeasurable loss. Indeed, I sometimes wonder how the company might be different today if Vern had remained healthy. He was a creative and committed engineer and manager whose enthusiasm for and expertise in inflatable systems and plastic fabrication were critical to our business. We had just begun to develop momentum in those parts of the business when he got sick. His illness and resulting absence had added to the tensions among the original management, which was already spread dreadfully thin. If Vern had stayed healthy, I suspect the company would not only have developed more extensively along its original direction, it would have done so with the original leadership team intact for a long period of time.

However, despite Vern's death, the company's fundamental objective remained the same during the summer of 1968. Our goal was still to build a successful public company that would be respected for its conduct of business and would provide a meaningful return to its investors.

With the addition of the Peavey mill as a wholly owned subsidiary, I was heartened by the company's prospects. Rather than struggling for a few thousand dollars in sales every month, we suddenly had a business selling $3.5 million a year. We now owned a physical plant filled with huge (albeit antiquated) machines producing goods that left the dock by rail-carload. That the plant was old and the business was losing money could not be any worse than our experience of the previous two years.

In any case, we were determined to make things work. I was willing to do anything ethically acceptable to achieve success. My pride was at stake, true. But an even greater factor was the obligation I felt to all those persons who had staked their limited savings on Pentair and were banking on me to make their investments worthwhile.

The prospect of working with Ben Westby, meanwhile, was both exciting and a little unsettling. Ben's experience and savvy were adding a great deal to my education as a business manager, and his pragmatic approach to management and finance was compatible with mine. On the other hand, his overall approach to the business was much shorter-term than mine was. His approach was: "Get in, do the job, get paid, and get out." Ben had been educated in the School of Hard Knocks, both as a union official and a business manager. He could be suave, diplomatic, and persuasive or, depending on the situation, a rough-and-tumble sort of fellow who could cut a corner or two. Personally so inexperienced, and coming out of a comparatively sheltered background, I was anxious about Ben's way of doing things.

Under the terms of our agreements, Ben received 30,000 unregistered shares of Pentair stock and Fred Whiting, the Peavey salesman, 10,000, both amounts to be supplemented later with options. Ben's 30,000 shares gave him, in fact, greater equity in the company than I ever had. The agreements also called for Pentair's registering Ben's and Fred's shares for sale at their request. Presumably, both men were thinking that we could fairly quickly turn the Peavey mill's operations around and thus enhance the value of Pentair stock, upon which they could liquidate their holdings for a handsome profit. However, unbeknownst to any of us at the time we signed the agreements, SEC regulations would prevent any early or unrestricted sale of shares. We soon learned that because Peavey had no audited financial statements, we would not be able to register their shares for three years. In addition, if and when we were able to register, the shares would have to be sold as soon as that registration was effective, thus eliminating flexibility in liquidation.

The situation generated some ill feelings and distrust. Ben had many business scars, and he was very wary that I might take unfair advantage of any success the company might achieve because my shares had been previously registered. He was concerned that once we achieved success, I would sell my shares at a profit, pack my bags, and leave him to run the company by himself, which was an intolerable prospect to him.

As a good-faith gesture, I transferred half of my shares as a loan to Ben, with the condition that he could sell them and replace them with shares of his own if he chose to do so before the sale of his shares would be legal. That smoothed things over for a while; unfortunately, concern about the stock would be a source of conflict for the next several years, regularly disrupting our relationship.

As the "new" Pentair moved forward during the summer and fall of 1968, I tried to sell our inventory of canoes and collect our receivables, looked for a buyer for both our canoe and inflatables businesses, and helped to get the paper mill running profitably. While my attention was drawn to the mill, Vince managed the day-to-day fabricating and shipping operation, met our contractual obligations to NASA and other inflatables customers, and moved out our gradually diminishing inventory of canoes.

As far as the Peavey mill was concerned, our first job was to head off bankruptcy. The $900,000 in unsecured debt was largely trade accounts payable. I wrote letters to all of the mill's customers and suppliers, advising them of its sale to Pentair and expressing our determination to make the business successful. Immediate cash needs for payroll and COD deliveries were met by factoring receivables. A factoring agreement between Peavey and Commercial Trading Company of New York City was in place when we acquired the business. We continued the relationship, which not only aided our cash flow but provided hard-nosed discipline in cash management. Commercial Trading lent us 85 percent on our receivables at 17 percent interest when the product was shipped. We asked creditors for patience and support during the turn-around. In the meantime, Ben tried to establish a creditors' committee and negotiate some sort of settlement before the mill could be thrown into involuntary bankruptcy.

I was heartened and amazed by the response of both suppliers and creditors. Though we were new and unknown to most of them, they continued to do business with Peavey and most continued shipping under an open line of credit. They accepted us as honest and sincerely committed to making the business a success, and we did not fail to meet a single obligation. I give a great deal of credit to Ben, whose nerve, intelligence, and experience were invaluable in managing a very delicate situation.

In acquiring Peavey we also acquired the services of their New York-based insurance broker, James Partington. Peavey's casualty insurance underwriter was in the process of terminating the mill's insurance for failing to maintain equipment and safety practices. Jim, a tall, distinguished gentleman with a distinctive British accent, was totally committed to helping us get the insurance promptly and soundly reinstated. He quickly became a valued member of our team, handling insurance matters in subsequent business acquisitions and playing a key role in our insurance program for the next 20 years.

On July 29, 1968, we sold the assets (not including finished goods and receivables) of our thermo-forming business to a newly created local company, Technical Products, Inc., for $25,000 in cash. As part of the agreement, Vince would continue to supervise both the canoe-manufacturing operation and the inflatables work, thus remaining on the Pentair payroll but receiving part of his salary from the new thermo-forming owners.

Two months later, Technical Products also bought the fixed assets of our inflatables business for $5,000, and Vince became one of that company's employees. Technical Products agreed to fabricate and deliver the remaining products due NASA under terms of the space administration's contract with Pentair. Pentair was thus entirely out of its original businesses. We were able to liquidate our inventory, collect our receivables, and pay off our obligations in full — leaving us with some cash in hand and the freedom to concentrate on our paper mill.

We moved corporate headquarters to a new location at the Apache Office Park in St. Anthony, a northern Minneapolis suburb. The corporate staff consisted of Ben, me, and a part-time office manager and secretary. Vince continued to serve as a Pentair director but was now working full time for Technical Products. Vince's commitment to Pentair's interests in overseeing the successful completion of the company's inflatables and vacuum forming contracts is typical of the commitment and integrity needed to build a successful and respected business.

As we were making those changes, we were also making some progress with the mill in Ladysmith. In August we reached a tentative agreement with the operation's creditors. We received the needed approval of a majority of the creditors in both number and dollar amount. Our proposal provided that all unsecured debts and bills for less than $500 would be paid in full, while debts exceeding $500 would be paid off at 50 cents on the dollar over a three-year period. The $500,000 in secured debt would be paid in full per the agreements. I was again surprised by the willingness of creditors and suppliers to accept such a plan despite our new and inexperienced management. I told myself that if the tables were ever turned, I would be obliged to demonstrate the same level of support.

Indeed, my initial experience at the Peavey mill under Ben's tutoring provided wide-ranging experience in sales, corporate finance, and employee relations amounting to a graduate education in business. It laid the groundwork for many of the principles and policies that would guide Pentair.

We immediately went to work trying to make our employees, long estranged by labor strife and union-busting discord, a positive and cohesive part of the operation. The task was made easier by the fact that the sale removed their former adversary. Following Ben's example, we acquainted ourselves with every worker at the mill, visiting each one on the job during all three shifts. The workers responded favorably, pleased that we were interested in what they had to say about running the business. They wanted to do a good job and were eager to be part of a successful enterprise. We assured them that we would give them every opportunity to do both.

The young plant managers were similarly eager and amenable to improvements. We were fortunate that these managers were relatively inexperienced and thus not set in their ways. Ben and I had only so much time we could actually spend in Ladysmith and this gave them the opportunity to implement the new policies without our constant looking over their shoulders, thus strengthening trust and confidence on all sides. We were laying the foundation for an operating philosophy that would serve Pentair well for decades to come.

Improvements showed immediately. The work force and management became more enthusiastic and productive, and they contributed much to problem solving. For instance, the mill had been trying to fix its profit problem by reducing the cost of raw material through the use of lower-grade wastepaper. When asked about problem areas, the workers described the problems of runability, clean-up, and low-quality product caused by cheap raw material. We switched to buying higher-priced, higher-quality raw material, and productivity, product quality, and worker satisfaction increased markedly. Customers were willing to pay more for a better product.

The Peavey mill showed its first profit in six years in August, following its acquisition by Pentair. It was only $15,000, but it demonstrated that changes in management and operations could push the business in a successful direction.

But we refused to kid ourselves. It was going to be a long, uphill struggle. Relative to the paper industry as a whole, Peavey was a small mill that could produce only single-ply toilet tissue and a limited quantity of napkins. Moreover, those products could be sold on price only at the low end of the market. The plant was old, and breakdowns were frequent. I sometimes thought the only way we were able to keep the operation going was through the stalwart efforts of our engineering and maintenance chief, Leland Peterson. Lee, a soft-spoken young man, was respected by everyone, totally dedicated to the mill, and able to take care of almost any machinery or operating problem with a minimum of time and money. I doubt we could have been successful without him, his energy and his ingenuity.

Not long after our entry into the paper business, another opportunity came to our attention by the Patrician Paper Company, one of the Peavey mill's former owners. Some enterprising people had recently helped build a small tissue-paper mill on the Caribbean island of Trinidad; the mill, which had not yet opened, had somehow been promoted along with the construction of a telephone system on the island. The promoters were no longer interested in the project and would sell their interest for a small part of future profits. The Trinidad government was willing to negotiate tax breaks and other concessions in order to get the plant up and running and reduce paper imports to the island. We decided we would look into the possibility, which seemed to offer profit opportunity as the only domestic manufacturer of toilet tissue in a country needing to reduce imports.

The Trinidad workload and our desire to change accounting periods to a calendar year forced us to change our 1968 annual shareholder's meeting from October to December. When we finally did get together on December 6, shareholders approved increasing the authorized shares from 500,000 to 2.5 million. This would makes shares available for future acquisitions and for incentive options and bonuses to employees. Shareholders also ratified a new set of directors, replacing Gary Ostrand, who had resigned, and adding Fred Whiting and Daniel Miller, the Peavey mill's general manager. Ben did not wish to stand for election at that time.

The shareholders also approved the board's broadening of Pentair's charter. Our original corporate charter was quite specific in defining the general nature of the business: "To conceive, design, make, manufacture, purchase, and sell: a) devices which are inflatable with air and/or other gas or substance; and b) electronic and mechanical devices." We were currently in violation of the charter, with growing concerns for possible legal exposure if our new business failed. The approved amendment broadly stated, "The corporation has general business purposes." The new wording gave us the freedom to pursue virtually any kind of business.

I thought the shareholders' votes reflected the unaccustomed upbeat mood that carried throughout that 1968 annual meeting. Nearly 50 shareholders came to the meeting, which backed up the increased attention Pentair had been getting from the financial community. Analysts and investors were impressed by the company's new dynamism, represented by its ownership of a paper mill, as well as by its annual sales rate of $4 million and the modest profit deriving from those sales.

By the end of calendar 1968, we had reached a settlement with Peavey's creditors. Also, out of concern for the high-risk decisions we were making, we amended our corporate bylaws to provide for indemnification of officers and directors. We also had moved our fiscal year-end from August 31 to December 31, beefed up our banking relationship with Third Northwestern, and changed our corporate counsel, appointing William Lapp to the position. Vince resigned his directorship so he could devote all his attention to Technical Products, and he was replaced by Ben.

———

While the turnaround at Peavey was a continuing struggle, we were beginning to see something hitherto unknown to Pentair in its first two years: momentum.

We bought into the Trinidad tissue-paper mill in March 1969, paying no cash but agreeing to pay a percentage of future profits. The plant was located on a new site on a very small river near the center of the island. It was isolated on a plot of land surrounded by a bend in the river and tropical forests. The buildings were new and constructed in an open, tropical fashion. Access was by way of a concrete ford across the river, which flooded after every heavy rain. The paper-making machinery was really a collection of antiques designed to produce 10 tons of toilet tissue a day, but it was never successfully operated. It was intended to use bagasse (sugarcane waste) as a fiber source, but we set it up to use wastepaper as a raw material. We took a few Peavey personnel to the site to bring the machinery up to operating condition and prepare to make paper. While this added to our costs and diverted attention away from the Peavey plant, it did not seem an undue burden and did offer the possibility of a decent return. Ben and I made several trips to Trinidad to manage the machinery refurbishment and to negotiate with the government on taxes, imports, and licenses.

More importantly, Peavey's industrious Fred Whiting learned in November 1968 that consumer-goods giant Procter & Gamble (P&G) was eagerly seeking new sources of highly absorbent wadding for its popular Pampers-brand disposable diaper. Most manufacturers were unwilling to divert production from their proprietary products, especially in light of the fact that P&G expected to need the wadding supply for only three years. We told P&G officials that we would activate our third machine and, with their technical assistance, demonstrate that we could make product for them. Within two months we were able to make promising production runs. We then proposed converting our entire mill to the production of absorbent wadding. P&G accepted our offer, lent us $80,000 to refurbish and adapt our machinery, and provided continuing technical help to get the process on line. By spring 1969, we were in production under a 36-month contract, with, at P&G's discretion, a three-year extension. The wadding production went smoothly, and the mill was suddenly earning more than $50,000 a month.

Not only was this a profitable business, it was easy, too. No changes in grades and colors, no converting, no sales promotion— just continuous operation on one product for one customer. Furthermore, the high-quality raw materials were very clean, thus eliminating the environmental problems confronting us with wastepaper use.

The P&G contract gave us breathing room, but in three years we would have to return to the manufacture of single-ply toilet tissue, which was a very difficult and marginal business for a small, one-product mill. We had to use the three years to look hard at acquiring other businesses to strengthen the company. The Trinidad paper mill was the initial result of this effort. Over the next year we seriously considered almost a dozen different companies, including a die-castings and hand-tool manufacturer, a bakery, another tissue-paper mill, and a company that made automobile heaters. None of them seemed right for us.

Our P&G contract together with the acquisition of the Trinidad mill (officially, Caribbean Paper Industries, Ltd.) had a startling effect on Pentair's image. We were no longer perceived as a struggling, obscure company. Our P&G contract and new international operation drew nationwide attention. (We aided the publicity process by placing a paid notice in *The Wall Street Journal* and holding a meeting for local stockbrokers to talk about our expanding business.) The price of our stock went from $2 per share to $25. In April 1969 we split the shares three for one and gained new shareholders all over the United States. Our enhanced stature in the investment community proved valuable in the company's future financing.

In August 1969 we got the Trinidad mill operating and made our first reels of paper. However, soon afterward as we prepared for production, social and political unrest on the island led to an insurrection. There were shootings, a sundown-to-sunrise curfew, and definite hostility to outsiders. We closed the plant, arranged for a security guard at the facility, and came home. We returned some time later to complete arrangements with the Trinidad and Tobago government, but we were never able to resume operations.

Unfortunately, my working relationship with Ben was not progressing very smoothly during this period. Ben was continually concerned about liquidity and how he could cash out his interest at Pentair. He would talk about selling the company, I would say we were not going to do that, and he would threaten to sue both me and Pentair.

The discord and threats eventually began to distract folks both inside and outside the company. The situation finally reached the point where I visited the lawyer Ben had repeatedly threatened to engage in a lawsuit against me and Pentair. I asked the man if he was representing Ben in any such litigation, and he replied he was not and, furthermore, would not. I then asked him if he would represent me if push came to shove. He said that he would. I told Ben I had talked to the lawyer, and that ended Ben's threat to sue. Unhappy over the developments, Ben then resigned as both an employee and director of Pentair. It was, however, only one of a series of such resignations, and Ben was back at work within six weeks.

At about the same time, late 1969, Fred resigned, amicably. Since Peavey was now selling solely on contract to Procter & Gamble, Fred's services were no longer urgent, and he had plans to go into business for himself as a paper broker. A few years later he handled some of Peavey's products.

In January 1970, Pentair added two new directors to the board, joining Wally Wells, Dan Miller, and me. One was William Thayer, a local stockbroker and business analyst whom I had come to know through the sale of our inflatables and vacuum-forming businesses in 1968. The other was Henry Conor, an entrepreneur and investor who had visited the company during our formative months and had stayed in contact ever since. Henry had a long and stabilizing influence on Pentair, serving 21 years as a director. He provided critical assistance to management as a consultant, corporate representative, and treasurer when business demand became overwhelming.

Another fortuitous event was the hiring of Irene Roettger in April 1970. Irene played a key role for the next nine years. Starting as a part-time employee, she was soon managing our office and serving as corporate secretary. Rapid developments were taking Ben and me out of the office frequently; fortunately, Irene was on hand to take care of the many needs and demands that required corporate attention. In fact, Irene became the glue that held affairs together over the next few years as Ben and I scrambled to develop the company.

Moving ahead, we continued to explore various acquisition possibilities. One of these, in early 1970, was a husband-and-wife moccasin-manufacturing operation in Spooner, Wisconsin. Financed by a local bank and private lender, Namekagon Leather, Inc. was producing high-quality moccasins in a range of styles and sizes. Local Chippewa Indians fashioned the decorative beading. However, the company was losing money and facing financial collapse.

Intrigued as we were, we did not want to make Namekagon Leather a part of Pentair and thus accept its financial exposure. Instead, we decided to acquire the controlling position in a shell corporation called Plastineers, Inc., at a price based on the shell's asset value, which was cash in the bank. Plastineers would then acquire Namekagon.

With Ben back on the job and devoting his tremendous energy to our acquisition activity, we completed the Plastineers/Namekagon deal in March 1970. At the same time, we were overcommitting our time and effort by looking into a Rockville, Maryland-based company called Universal Systems, Inc. (USI).

Founded by some Minnesotans and bolstered by more than $1 million raised in a public stock offering, USI was developing software programs and associated data banks to service motor freight carriers with an automated rating and billing system. But by the time we came along, the company had spent most of its funds and needed both new funding and management help to complete demonstrations of its computerized systems and capitalize on the response. We did not want to buy USI outright but negotiated a one-year investment and management agreement with an option to buy the promising start-up company. Our concerns were heightened by the company's inordinately plush offices, which we recognized as a sure sign of misplaced priorities in a faltering business.

On February 27, 1970, we agreed to lend USI working capital and manage the company during the term of the agreement. We could terminate the agreement, however, any time after four months, with an obligation to manage the company and to lend USI not less than $85,000 during the four months. In exchange, we would receive 44,000 restricted shares of USI common stock and a two-year option to buy 51 percent of the company at 50 cents a share. If successful, the high-risk venture had potential for enormous profits.

However, we soon discovered that we had made a big mistake. Our only consolation was that it could have been much bigger. The much-touted USI software system did not work the way it was supposed to work. Tests showed it to be a complete failure. Of course, we would have liked to pull out of the deal, but we knew that some of USI's large shareholders, not to mention the New York brokerage firm that had sold its shares, would probably sue us if we did. We were stuck. USI was on the verge of bankruptcy, creditors were clamoring at the door, and we were obliged, with no less than $85,000 and who knew how much more of our own money, to keep the company alive for at least four months.

Biting the bullet, we hired a bright and energetic businessman, Donald Hawes, to run the Maryland operation. Don was a shrewd executive, accustomed to living by his wits and currently between business deals. Despite considerable pressure, he performed flawlessly and managed to keep the business alive over the next several months, contain our financial exposure, and even push some of the developmental work forward. He also helped us work out an agreement with another Maryland company, The Resource Management Corporation of Bethesda, to take over USI. USI shareholders agreed to the plan, provided that the company's creditors accept delayed payment of their debt. But two of those creditors refused, killing the deal, and after much discussion and our decision to withdraw entirely from the mess, the two creditors sued Pentair.

On July 1, the day after our four-month commitment ended, I returned to the Twin Cities from Maryland to find my phones ringing constantly both at home and at the office. The calls were from USI shareholders and creditors, either pleading for help or threatening to sue. Finally, I took the phones off the hook. I was bushed. Pentair had done the best it possibly could under the circumstances and had lived up to its part of the agreement. It cost us more than $200,000, but I felt fortunate that we had not lost our shirts.

The two lawsuits, which amounted to more than $100,000 in claims, required significant amounts of our time and money to fight over the next 13 months before we emerged with a favorable out-of-court settlement. The plaintiffs ended up paying us enough to cover our legal fees, and we learned the importance of taking quick and aggressive action against persons suing us on questionable grounds. But it was a slow and painful lesson.

The annual meeting of shareholders in the spring of 1970 proved to be the worst I would ever experience. The problems of the Trinidad and USI operations made for a real contrast to the euphoria of the preceding year. I was the only Pentair officer to address the meeting and was appropriately criticized.

To this day I remember an elderly shareholder loudly stating that we should get out of Trinidad. He had been there on vacation and had observed that there was no market for toilet paper. Everyone on the island used old newspapers instead.

———

In calmer waters closer to home, Pentair, thanks to its acquisition of Plastineers and, through Plastineers, Namekagon Leathers, was in the clothing business.

Besides making moccasins worth more than $100,000 in sales a year, we set up a small factory for Namekagon to produce samples of fringed leather vests and skirts that a Minneapolis clothing distributor agreed to help promote and sell. We called the operation Federated Industries, Inc.

Federated comprised two operating divisions, Namekagon Leather, which concentrated on its moccasins, and What's New, which made the leather goods sold through the Minneapolis distributor. The husband-and-wife team that had founded Namekagon were kept in charge of the moccasin manufacturing, while Dan Miller (from the Peavey mill) and Wally Wells, Pentair's long-time investor and board member, were put in overall charge of the new business. Vince, one of Pentair's founders, came back from Technical Products and was named manager of What's New.

For a while everything went well. By late spring 1970 our tiny plants in Spooner were turning out fringed leather jackets, skirts, and purses in a variety of colors and styles. The market was eager for leather clothing, and sales through our Minneapolis distributor were brisk. Interest in the moccasins was rising, too. Then, late in the year, the little boom turned to bust as leather suddenly lost its fashion appeal, and we could not give the product away. Though our moccasin sales were steady, sales of all our other leather goods plummeted, and we had to scramble to shut down production and move out the remaining inventory.

The business limped along until February 1971, at which time Pentair sold a significant portion of its equity in Federated Industries to Dan and the original owners of the moccasin business. Plagued by a lagging market and other problems, Federated closed its doors for good in February 1972. By that time Dan had converted the What's New division over to contract sewing of winter garments; the moccasin inventory and production equipment were taken over by the operation's creditors.

Throughout its brief existence, Federated Industries required financing help from Pentair. During its final year in business, Pentair was guaranteeing the loans of smaller lenders, and in some cases I had to provide a personal guarantee. Even though Pentair had a reasonable balance sheet, lenders required the added comfort of a personal guarantee on marginal programs. It was effective in assuring personal attention to loan repayment.

When all was said and done, all the loans were repaid, and there were no debts outstanding when the business shut down for good.

In 1971 our efforts to make Pentair a stable operating company were entering their fifth year. If not as stable as we would have wished, Pentair was operating profitably, thanks largely to the Peavey mill's contract with P&G. On the negative side were the ongoing lawsuits stemming from the USI debacle, the decline and failure of the Federated business, and a confusingly bleak scenario in Trinidad, where Caribbean Paper Industries was requiring nominal monthly payments to secure the facility. (The guard we hired had moved into the plant with his family. On one visit I discovered the family's clothes hanging out to dry on a clothesline strung between the paper machine and one of the plant's walls.)

Early in the year Ben returned, after another temporary departure, as executive vice president of Pentair. Ben soon rejoined the board as well. A short while later Wally resigned from both the company's management and board. Five years after the company's founding, I was now the only one of the founding group left.

By that time, I was approaching my job with considerable confidence. The past four and a half years had both educated and toughened me. Convinced that things could not get any worse than during the dark days of the recent past, I believed I was reasonably well-equipped to handle whatever opportunities and problems might arise.

This much was apparent: Pentair was destined to be a marginal company with our existing businesses. If we were to prosper and become a stable and respected company, we would have to acquire other companies or add to the business in some other way. We seemed to be confronted with a bad-news, good-news situation. The bad news was that because of our own less-than-robust financial condition, the best we could expect to acquire at the time was another distressed company with a bargain-basement price tag. The good news was that our experience at the Peavey mill made it clear that we had the ability to turn around such a company. Never mind that at that stage of development our corporate management consisted of only Ben, Irene, and me.

Meanwhile, the Peavey operation was becoming more and more complex. Pressing environmental concerns were being raised by tough new state of Wisconsin regulations governing water and air emissions. Litigation was brought by an equipment supplier centering on machinery purchased prior to Pentair's ownership of the plant. The P&G arrangement was scheduled to lapse come the end of 1971. We were preparing to return to the production of toilet tissue from waste paper with all the attendant operating and pollution problems.

The environmental concerns were new to us. We retained the services of a New Richmond, Wisconsin, law firm with experience in environmental issues and began a long series of discussions with the state's Department of Natural Resources, trying to develop a mutual understanding and respect. A paper mill's effluent when processing waste paper is considerable. At Peavey, it would pose a significant threat to the Flambeau River. The city of Ladysmith, eager to assist its largest private employer, agreed to treat our effluent in the municipal wastewater facility. That worked well for a while, but the discharge eventually overwhelmed the city's treating capacity. Our next step was to build a lagoon system at the plant site. That system, which allowed us to treat the waste before it entered the river, proved effective for the next few years. During the same period we also added and updated equipment inside the plant that would remove a greater amount of fiber pollutants from the discharge waters and return those waters to the production process.

As for the P&G deal, we negotiated a contract extension that would carry the wadding-production business through the first half of 1972, albeit at about half the original volume. At the same time we converted one of our paper machines, unneeded for the wadding process, to a toilet-tissue maker. We also refurbished our toilet-tissue converting and packaging equipment for a return to that market.

When we acquired Peavey in 1968, one of the plant's most successful products was a four-roll pack of toilet tissue labeled Sail. The product included a dish-cloth premium that was contained in every package and sold extremely well, primarily in the southeastern United States. We were impressed with the power of a small premium to help boost both the selling price and the demand for the product. We thought perhaps a larger premium in a package of higher-quality tissue would do even better. We badly needed both a selling advantage and a product we could produce from high-priced raw material that would minimize water-pollution problems.

In early 1971, we began to manufacture a higher-quality tissue with unique premiums in the package. The tissue itself used wood pulp, not waste paper (with its negative environmental ramifications), as its raw material, and the premiums included hair trimmers, lint brushes, inflatable pillows, and similar personal-care items. The product was called Plus. We bought large quantities of the premiums and began promoting and shipping four-roll packs of Plus.

Plus was launched in late spring 1971, but we soon discovered that our positive experience with Sail could not be replicated with a new item. We could not achieve the volume and price to support production of this higher-cost product. Entering 1972, after making a valiant effort with Plus, we understood that wadding and other absorbent-tissue production would have to supplement our toilet-tissue line if the mill was to stay profitable.

Throughout 1971 we continued to explore acquisition possibilities. Early in the year, we looked at the Clary Corporation of California, an old-line producer of adding machines, before deciding that the diversified manufacturer posed too great a risk for Pentair. Its financial condition was shaky, and its operations seemed unstable. We learned from USI that running troubled operations in distant locations with limited corporate staff could be hazardous to a company's health.

Then, in August, we were alerted by Stan Efron, our securities counsel when we registered our stock back in 1966, that a rendering plant for sale in Arden Hills, a St. Paul suburb, might be an interesting acquisition. Though the plant's business was somewhat cyclical, it had been profitable for a long time. Its roughly $1.5 million in annual sales derived from two related operations. Minneapolis Hide and Tallow collected meat and bone scraps from stores and restaurants and offal from meat-packing plants, from which it rendered nonedible oils and tallow and cracklings. Kem Milling, Inc., ground the cracklings into high-protein food supplements for livestock and poultry.

The rendering business was entirely foreign to Pentair, but its acquisition was financially attractive. Its owners wanted $700,000 for the business, with $125,000 down. There was $250,000 in cash in the business, so we used half for the down payment. We believed the business had considerable potential for growth. Besides, the paper business had been foreign to Pentair before we acquired the Peavey plant; our experience there had shown that we could "learn" a new business. As was the case at Peavey, the rendering business' managers were interested in staying on to run the plant, thus providing us with management continuity and operational expertise.

We bought the business in the fall of 1971 and merged it into a new Pentair subsidiary named Conserve Industries, Inc. Immediately following the acquisition, we retained Stan Efron's services as Pentair's corporate legal counsel, a relationship that we have maintained to this day. Conserve would be a sound operation for the next 10 years. The acquisition received favorable local publicity, although the business would later be questioned as an unrelated orphan operation of Pentair.

Of even greater long-term importance to the company, however, was an acquisition whose story began in October 1971, when Dan Miller, then heading Federated Industries, sent us a copy of *Wisconsin Investor* magazine. Dan thought we might be interested in an article headlined "A Town for Sale." We were interested, all right. The article stopped us in our tracks.

The "town for sale" was the small Wisconsin community of Niagara, where the local paper mill, which employed more than a third of its 2,000 residents, had been put on the sales block by the Kimberly-Clark Corporation. The point of the article was that whoever bought the plant would in effect be buying the town.

On the plus side, the plant was a major producer of coated groundwood paper used in magazines and catalogues; it had been recently upgraded and was currently churning out product at the rate of about 350 tons a day. Its customers included *The New Yorker* and *Southern Living* magazines, Conde Nast Publications, and Sears Roebuck. On the negative side, demand for the coated paper had grown soft and probably would grow softer; the recent demise of *Life* and *Look* magazines was believed to be the harbinger of bad times for the industry. The plant had been losing money for the past several months, and there were severe labor and environmental problems a new owner would have to confront. Small wonder, given the preponderance of negatives, that Kimberly-Clark was having trouble finding a buyer.

Ben and I talked about the article and concluded that the Niagara plant would be an unlikely acquisition candidate. Nonetheless, we contacted Kimberly-Clark. After investigating our background, Kimberly-Clark officials arranged for us to visit the facility on October 27.

We were very impressed, to say the least. Niagara, on that bright fall day, was very scenic beneath the bluffs along the Menominee River. The plant was huge, well equipped, and well maintained.

Logs came in one end of the mill and were ground into pulp; then the pulp was mixed with purchased fiber and run over paper machines nearly 20 feet wide. The multi-storied building housed not only the pulping and paper-making equipment, but facilities for preparing the coating material, winding and roll-wrapping equipment for the finished product, and hydroelectric generators for converting a large waterfall into power.

I do not know how well Ben and I hid our excitement during the first tour. We could scarcely believe that our little company might be able to buy such a plant. We were so distracted by the prospect of the plant's acquisition that we made a wrong turn leaving Niagara and drove 30 miles out of our way before we realized the mistake! Like kids in a candy store, we planned our due-diligence investigations and the pro forma financials for this acquisition, knowing full well that our few pennies might not be enough to swing the deal.

Our eagerness was tempered by the need to gain some understanding of the business, negotiate a purchase agreement, arrange financing, and settle labor and environmental matters. We discovered that vice president Bob Ernest and other Kimberly-Clark officials were honest and forthright, candidly providing us whatever data we requested about the plant. We learned that the mill's annual sales totaled about $30 million and that it was currently losing about a quarter-of-a-million dollars a month. The previous year there had been a seven-month strike, and there was no love lost between management and union employees. Fixed assets of the mill had a net book value of $22 million. Despite the difficulties, we decided to try to acquire the mill.

Discussions and negotiations with Kimberly-Clark resulted in a preliminary purchase agreement in early January 1972. On January 27, we signed a conditional purchase agreement and paid $100,000 in earnest money. The purchase price was $7.5 million for fixed assets plus the actual value of mill inventories estimated at $2.5 million. We were to pay $1.5 million at the time of closing with the balance in notes to Kimberly-Clark. The sale was conditional on, among other things, Pentair reaching a satisfactory agreement with the plant's labor unions, postponement until 1974 of Wisconsin water-pollution abatement orders, and a reduction in property taxes based on our purchase price being lower than previous valuations. Niagara was one of four paper mills Kimberly-Clark was selling. The company had made a strategic decision to concentrate its resources on consumer products.

We spent four months putting the details of the deal together and preparing to take over the operation. On top of all that, we were still assimilating Conserve Industries and converting part of Peavey's operations to the production and marketing of toilet tissue. Our earnings were depressed to less than $10,000 a month as we made these transitions.

Financing the Niagara acquisition proved to be a formidable task. Our meetings with investment bankers in New York were initially encouraging, but we soon met great resistance in the financing of any coated-paper operation. Government-supported economic development financing seemed possible, but the time-consuming red tape and lack of independence in a government program were unacceptable. Having less than $1.5 million in net worth and depressed performance, and the requirement for $1.5 million in new working capital made the $10-million acquisition of a new business a tough sell.

Negotiations with local banks and venture capital firms seemed our only hope, but a high level of skepticism kept the talks operating on an on-again, off-again basis. Finally, on March 24, 1972, we reached agreement on a financing package involving First National Bank of St. Paul and the venture capital firms of Community Investment and Northwest Growth Fund to lend us $1.4 million, which, in addition to our $100,000 down payment, would allow us to purchase the Niagara mill. All closing documentation was reviewed and approved on March 25, and the closing was set for 11 a.m., Monday, April 3.

While the financial negotiations were going on, the other conditions in the agreement had to be satisfied. We reached agreement with the Wisconsin Department of Natural Resources to extend the completion date for the water-pollution abatement system to August 1974. That extension would give us sufficient time to engineer and to construct the system, assuming we found financing. A reduction in property taxes was a tough proposition; it meant a $265,000 per year impact on the Niagara village and school district budgets. However, a new property valuation based on our purchase price for the mill was eventually accepted for tax purposes. The major stumbling block remained an acceptable labor contract.

Our pro forma estimates showed that significant cost savings in operations were required to turn Niagara from a quarter-million-dollar monthly loss to break-even. The major source of the cost reductions would be in payroll. Necessary savings could be accomplished by eliminating the employee pension plan, reducing vacations, cutting out sick-leave pay, and certain other items for all employees. We decided that wages and salaries could be frozen at existing levels. As far as vacations were concerned, we would treat everyone as a new employee, with one week of vacation the first year and increases in later years depending on company performance. Admittedly, these were drastic cuts. In return, the most we could promise was to do our best to assure the survival of the business, initiate a profit-sharing plan, and restore some of the benefits as the business became profitable.

Needless to say, negotiations were difficult. The first union vote, on March 17, decisively rejected our plan. As a result, we formally notified Kimberly-Clark that we could not proceed with the agreement. Kimberly-Clark then posted a notice at the mill that the sale agreement was suspended, that there were no other potential buyers, and that the mill would cease operations on May 15. The fat was in the fire. Either we reached a compromise with the union or the deal was dead. The union agreed to informal discussions over the next few days, and those discussions led to a resumption of negotiations. We made minor adjustments to our original offer, but the decision rested on our verbal assurances that we would initiate a profit-sharing program and begin restoring benefits as soon as sound profitability was achieved. The union reluctantly accepted our proposal and the new contract was accepted by the union membership on March 30. The vote was 396 in favor to 73 against.

During those difficult labor negotiations I became acquainted with the president of the local union, Martin V. Ponzio, known to everyone as "Pope." Pope was a sturdy, burly man whose tough-guy exterior did not hide a compassionate heart. Pope had been union president for 24 of the previous 25 years and would continue to serve in that role, except for one term, until his retirement 12 years later. Pope was an intelligent and natural leader, a tough negotiator, and a staunch union man who not only fought for what he believed to be in the best interests of his people but understood the demands of the business. I respected Pope and learned a great deal from him. While he made life difficult for us at times, he was predictable, trustworthy, and sincere within the best context of strenuous negotiations. He would sometimes threaten, "If we can't get this resolved, I'll tear the plant down brick by brick." But he was also fond of saying, "We're all in the same canoe."

Then, on Friday afternoon, March 31, the roof fell in. Don Soukup of Community Investment called and told me the venture capital firms were withdrawing their support, having become nervous about the merits of the deal. I hung up the phone, speechless. When I recovered, I called the venture capital firms, but my calls went unanswered. After all our work, I could not believe what had happened. Unable to get hold of anyone who could explain what had gone wrong, I went home that evening and did not sleep a wink.

The next two days, Easter weekend, were a nightmare. Ben was vacationing in Phoenix; Stan, who had prepared or coordinated all the closing documents, was in Phoenix on business, and most of the parties to our deal were enjoying the holiday. Telephone calls and meetings with the venture capital people led nowhere. On Easter Sunday, Stan (who had returned home late Saturday evening) and I were able to reach officials at both First National Bank of St. Paul and Kimberly-Clark. Over the phone we put together an amended agreement in which both parties would assume portions of the venture capital firm's funding. Pentair would provide additional warrants to sweeten the deal. Surprisingly, the warrants were under more favorable terms than those initially specified by the venture capitalists.

The agreement was still subject to approval by Kimberly-Clark's Executive Committee meeting in an emergency session on Monday morning. Ben returned from Arizona late Sunday, and he, Stan, and I met at the bank on Monday morning with our fingers crossed, hoping Kimberly-Clark would get the needed approval and come to the closing. As it turned out, we received the approvals and were able to close the deal and pay over the funds as scheduled on April 3, albeit leaving several loose ends still to be tied up.

Pentair became the owner of another paper business, to be known as the Niagara of Wisconsin Paper Corporation, on April 3, 1972. We had bought the factory, if not quite a town. Ben and I were overjoyed by what we had done and by what we had yet to do. Our confidence was buoyed by the attitude of Niagara's work force. Almost to a person the plant's employees were dedicated to avenging what they saw as a slap in the face from Kimberly-Clark. They would make Niagara a very successful paper mill. As it turned out, Niagara became the most successful of the four mills sold by Kimberly-Clark.

Ben and I met immediately with both the work force and Niagara's civic leaders. As we did during our early days at Peavey, we made it a point of getting to know the people and visiting them on the job. Our first task was convincing folks that Pentair was committed to the plant's success and the well-being of the town, and, as at Peavey, the folks responded with enthusiasm and good will. The friction between management and labor vanished with the change of ownership. It was a new beginning for everyone.

Strains between Pentair and the plant's on-site managers persisted for a while. In large part, this was due to our insistence that the managers listen to every employee suggestion and either implement changes or provide a specific reason why the change would not improve operations. In one telling incident, management asked a machine operator about a streak on the paper. The operator acknowledged the defect and explained how its cause could easily be eliminated. Why hadn't he corrected the problem until then? "Nobody seemed to give a damn," he replied. Some local managers grumbled that we were selling out to the union. The transformation of the mill was astonishing despite the strains, however. Its productivity, in terms of both quality and quantity, increased dramatically almost overnight.

To keep abreast of the Niagara operations, we hired one of our directors, Henry Conor, to represent Pentair at the mill for the next three months on a resident basis. Meanwhile, Ben and I spent a great deal of time cleaning up purchase-agreement details, developing a pollution-control program, setting up sales and market development activity with Kimberly-Clark salespeople, and meeting with the mill's suppliers and customers. Fortunately, the market was showing signs of improvement by mid-1972. By August we had sufficient business to crank up to a full seven-day-a-week production schedule. The mill was even beginning to make a little profit.

Six years had passed since Pentair's founding. My five-year commitment passed without notice as the enterprise now engendered perseverance.

Difficult as it was to believe, the company was becoming a major corporation. In the summer of 1972, we could boast of 850 employees, projected annual sales of $45 million, and a debt-to-equity ratio greater than seven to one. The future was still uncertain, but I believed we had the ingredients to build a stable operation. Our primary objective was no longer merely to survive but to succeed.

However, my personal convictions about the company's future were tempered by exhaustion. I was drained both physically and emotionally by the pressures and problems of the past six years, and I wanted a break.

At our regular board meeting on June 26, I asked the directors to replace me as president so I could get a rest and recharge my batteries. The directors said they would not replace me and encouraged me to stay the course. They said the company had grown large enough to increase the management staff and that a larger staff would give me the organizational support I needed.

Reluctantly but with renewed enthusiasm, I accepted the board's decision. Tired as I was, I had a hunch the best was yet to come.

The founders of Pentair were (top left) Murray J. Harpole; (top right) Vincent Follmer; (botton left) Vernon Stone; and (botton right) Leroy Nelson and Gary Ostrand. Three years after Pentair's founding in 1966, only Murray Harpole remained in the business.

Pentair Industries, Incorporated's first home, 3756 North Dunlap Street, Arden Hills, Minnesota included 5,000 square feet of manufacturing area with a high ceiling suitable for balloon and inflatables fabrication, a loading dock, and office space with a northern exposure. Later an anteroom was added to spare office employees a blast of the state's frigid weather.

Pentair Industries employees during a lunch break in the Arden Hills, Minnesota plant.

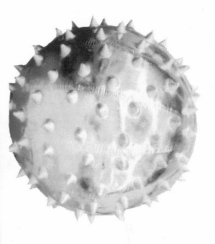

Tools of Pentair's trade—specialized machine for balloon and inflatables manufacturing...

two-meter spiny-like roughened sphere used for radar tracking of upper air winds...

tethered balloon known as the Penta Kite.

A pyramid of Penta Craft canoes were among Pentair's first vacuum-formed products.

The sporty, red-and-white canoes were made from acrylonitrile butadiene styrene (ABS) plastic and could withstand the Joe Sparma batting practice demo. Sparma, Detroit Tigers pitcher, takes a swing during the greater Michigan boat show. Note the Pentair logo on the tip of the canoe: a pentagon containing the Greek letter pi.

Benjamin Westby (left) joined Murray Harpole in the Pentair venture in 1968. One of Westby's favorite sayings: "Business is a game and you keep score with dollars."

Corporate secretary and office manager Irene Roettger worked for Pentair from 1970-1979. She held the works together during some very turbulent times at Pentair.

Welcome to PEAVEY PAPER MILLS

The Peavey Paper Mill of Ladysmith, Wisconsin became Pentair's first wholly owned subsidiary in 1968. It produced 50 tons of single-ply toilet tissue and napkins a day.

Lee Peterson, engineering and maintenance chief, and later mill manager, was known for prompt, cost effective resolution of problems. The energetic Lee was totally dedicated to the mill.

Absorbent tissue wadding for Procter & Gamble's Pampers-brand disposable diapers is manufactured at the Peavey mill.

Notice to Shareholders
of
PENTAIR INDUSTRIES, Incorporated

Your management has announced recent developments that are expected to have favorable impact on the future of Pentair Industries. This announcement covers:

(1) A Long Term Contract
(2) An Acquisition in the Caribbean
(3) Projections of Operations

You are encouraged to request a copy of this announcement if you have not received one. Send request and self-addressed return envelope to **Pentair Industries, Incorporated, 2500 39th Ave. N.E., Minneapolis, Minn. 55421.**

The Wall Street Journal notice (top) regarding Pentair's acquisition of Caribbean Paper Industries, Ltd., (bottom) drew nationwide attention in 1969. Stock prices went from $2 to $25 per share. Less than a year later, political instability forced the plant's closing.

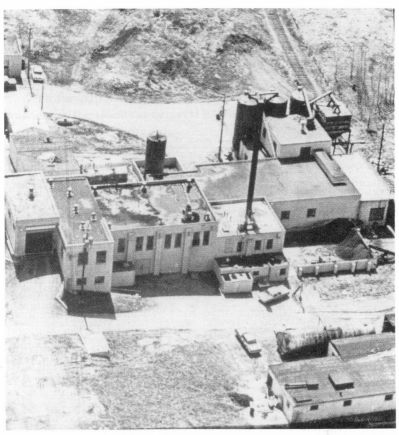

In 1971 Pentair entered a new business as it acquired Conserve Industries, Inc.,
a renderer of meat by-products. Pentair owned Conserve for twelve years.

Enterpreneur and investor Henry Conor became a member of the board of directors in January 1970 and served 21 years. During his long-standing relationship with Pentair he acted as consultant, corporate representative, and treasurer.

Managers Ernest (left) and Don Roberg stayed on after the Conserve Industries, Inc. acquisition and provided managerial continuity and operational expertise.

Chapter Four

Momentum 1972-1974

Our first six years now seemed like a dream, or maybe a nightmare. Pentair was like a runaway horse; the best I could do was guide it toward smooth and stable terrain, avoiding swamps and ravines, and hope to stay in the wagon.

We had reached a higher plateau by mid-1972. We were on the right road and heading in the right direction. Now the task was a matter of staying on track.

On a business level, we had acquired troubled, underperforming companies and turned them around with a small but energetic corporate staff that operated through wholly owned, yet autonomous subsidiaries. We handled and resolved knotty union and morale problems through common sense and respect for other human beings. Through determination and hard work, we could make more good things happen than bad.

I had learned how important it was to build a team, to earn the good will and to make the most of the support of others, and to recognize the importance of individual commitment and integrity to a successful business. I also learned to trust and expect the best of others, as well as to keep an eye out for occasional bad apples who conduct their affairs with little regard for honesty and ethics.

But survival and education were not enough. Pentair was still facing many uncertainties and problems. Moreover, our problems could not be solved overnight. It would take time and a great deal more determination and hard work to keep the horse on the course, moving toward its objectives.

Our corporate staff remained thin, ensuring workdays that routinely extended into the evening and workweeks that regularly swallowed up Saturdays and Sundays. Ben and I spent as much time as possible at our mills and plants in Minnesota and Wisconsin, while Irene Roettger, our corporate secretary, and Bill Zolchonock, our new accountant, held down the fort at the home office. Periodically, Ben would grow disenchanted with the operation and take one of his "leaves," although his contributions were invaluable.

My personal concerns were lessened by my ability to sell enough stock to replenish my children's education fund. By that time, two of my children were already in college.

At the Peavey mill, the P&G contract was fast approaching an end. Converting that operation to the manufacture of other products for other customers was proving difficult. For one thing, corporate energy and attention were distracted by the demands of our new acquisitions at Conserve Industries and Niagara Paper Corporation. For another, environmental concerns and restrictions required spending significant effort and money on pollution control facilities at Peavey before returning to the use of wastepaper as a raw material.

At Peavey, our attempts to make a high-grade, single-ply tissue with a premium in every package had not been successful. During the year-long trial, we sold as many as 25,000 cases a month, but we were not able to generate meaningful profits. Thus, in April 1972, we ceased production of toilet tissue and shut down the number 3 paper machine. To offset the loss of that business, we did our best to develop additional sales for wadding and other absorbent products, thus, maintaining at least nominally profitable operations for the rest of the year.

Meanwhile, Conserve Industries required hard work to bring us up to speed on the nature of the business and to make sure it was contributing to the overall corporate development. Don and Ernie Roberg were committed and capable managers, and the business was running smoothly and profitably enough so that Ben and I were not needed on a daily basis.

However, Conserve's future did not look especially bright. The meat-packing industry was changing, with less and less meat scraps and other raw material available to us. Somehow we had to find a way to deal with the changes and expand the business. Conserve's Kem Milling operation had grown to include the processing of material purchased from others for high-protein animal and poultry food supplements, but that growth was limited by the size of its equipment and declining supplies. Our investigation of other rendering plants, with an eye to further acquisition, yielded nothing. Actually, I had visited more than enough rendering plants to satisfy my interest. We were also facing increasing pressure to deal with air emissions and water-effluent discharge at the plant's suburban location. All in all, while Conserve was adding to our stability and cash flow, it did not offer Pentair the opportunity for significant future growth.

In the meantime, our paper mill at Niagara promised the most exciting possibilities and therefore took the lion's share of our time and corporate resources. Financially, we were barely breaking even at Niagara, but the demand for the product was growing by the day. Ben and I were working to meld the plant's management and work force into a highly efficient team, and we were exhilarated by the staff's enthusiasm and cooperation. Despite eliminating vacations and pensions, productivity was running high. Everybody was determined to show Kimberly-Clark and the world that the plant was a good one. The mill's workers expected to succeed and to see their benefits restored as we had promised. As a matter of fact, I do not recall a single employee leaving Niagara during that period to work for someone else.

Under the terms of our purchase agreement, Kimberly-Clark would continue to sell at commission the Niagara mill's products through 1973. This important provision maintained the mill's credibility in the marketplace while we developed our own sales force. During the transition, we were also given permission to hire Tom Thomsen, an outstanding salesman in Kimberly-Clark's New York office. A tall, mild-mannered man, Tom knew his customers' needs and fully understood the capabilities of the Niagara mill. Tom became sales manager at Niagara, where his customer relationships and market savvy maintained sales volume and product offerings that capitalized on the mill's economic and technical strengths over the next twelve years. Eventually, he was named Niagara's president.

We benefitted as well from an improvement in the coated publication-grade paper market that began shortly after we acquired the mill. By August 1972, the mill was running 24 hours a day, seven days a week. Although pricing remained soft, profits were beginning to build. By late fall, the market was becoming downright robust again, and price increases were warranted. Mill productivity continued to rise, enhancing our growing profits.

One of the most astounding and emotionally rewarding aspects of our Niagara acquisition was the way we were received into that small Wisconsin community. Despite the fact that we had negotiated reductions both in employee benefits at the mill and in our tax obligation to the town of Niagara, the local workers and the citizens were genuinely warm and enthusiastic about us, and that was never more apparent than on September 20, 1972.

The occasion was the community's official welcome of Pentair. As the company's representative, I expected a simple ceremony with perhaps a luncheon or a dinner followed by a few speeches. Driving into town that morning, however, I was surprised to see all the lampposts along the main street festooned with American flags. I wondered if I had overlooked a national holiday. At the approach to the mill there was a huge "Welcome Pentair" banner stretched above the street and the Niagara High School band playing rousing music on the lawn. The flags, the banner, the music – it was all for Pentair!

Additional surprises awaited me. Crepe paper and bunting hung from the walls and ceilings of the mill. An incredible variety of posters and banners that had been painstakingly crafted by Niagara schoolchildren were prominently displayed on tables and walls. The messages that sang out from the posters and banners were as moving to me as the long hours and hard work that went into them:

"Welcome To Niagara"
"Thank You For Saving Our Mill"
"Thank You For Providing A Job For My Father...
For Helping Build Our Community...
For Helping Keep Our Environment Clean"

During that unforgettable day there were greetings from Wisconsin's Governor Patrick Lucey, local civic leaders, and hundreds of citizens. In the evening, in front of an overflow crowd at Niagara's St. Anthony's Catholic church, the governor, civic leaders, and Miss Niagara, Karen Bartolac, welcomed Pentair with official speeches.

By the time some response was required of me, I was so overwhelmed by the community's welcome I was virtually speechless. I did say a few words of greeting and thanks, but for the life of me I cannot tell you exactly what I said. I know that I was impressed as never before by the importance of Pentair to the communities where it did business. I vowed that Pentair would do everything possible not only to make those businesses succeed, but to look out for the best interests of the individual locations, school systems, and citizens that depended on them. If I had ever doubted it in the past, the demonstration of friendship and good will in Niagara that day convinced me that the long-term interests of a business and its community were inextricably entwined.

Three months later, the good feelings were still apparent in the response we received from the Christmas cards Ben and I signed and sent every Pentair employee. Many Niagara workers returned our greetings, saying they had never before received a personalized card from the top officials of a company. Taking a sincere personal interest in the welfare of a work force was essential to developing a supportive, productive team.

By the end of 1972, Pentair comprised three operating subsidiaries, employed about 900 people, and was approaching $50 million in annual sales. The corporate staff was as lean as ever, with Ben, Irene, Bill, and I making up the home office in St. Paul. Of course, we were very ably supported by Stan Efron, our legal counsel; Stan Schweitzer, our CPA; and Jim Partington, our insurance advisor.

Operations at the Peavey mill remained problematical as we sought ways to replace the P&G business. Conserve was operating profitably in an industry with limited prospects for significant growth. Niagara (officially, the Niagara of Wisconsin Paper Corporation, or NOW) was doing well enough for us to begin restoring employee benefits. In all of our facilities, we were making sizable capital investments aimed at heightening productivity. In addition, there were increasingly stringent environmental requirements demanding expensive improvements. The Niagara plant was well along toward completing the engineering design of a $1.6 million water-effluent treatment facility and looking forward to an $2 million air-quality control investment. At the end of 1972, our long-term debt was more than $9 million, with equity of $2 million, and it was imperative that we find fresh sources of financing for the pollution-control equipment.

Our modest success was causing unexpected pressures as well. When we announced that our first-quarter 1973 earnings of $660,000 exceeded our earnings for the entire year of 1972, several of our newer shareholders, led by Robert Politte, insisted that we more aggressively promote the company and boost the price of the shares. At the end of 1972, our price/earnings ratio was about 12-to-one, with our stock price at $6.50 a share. To me, that seemed a reasonable level in light of the company's enormous debt and short track record. Besides, those shareholders who had been with us from the beginning had already benefitted from a three-for-one stock split and had a twentyfold increase in their original investment.

On December 1, we chartered a plane and took 21 stockbrokers and financial analysts on a tour of the Niagara mill. Five days later we convened a meeting in Minneapolis to provide information and to answer questions for those we could not accommodate on the plane trip. Our job was now to deliver on the rosy outlook we had presented during those information sessions.

However, I was not comfortable working with public relations firms, other than when putting together routine communications such as quarterly reports and setting up meetings with members of the financial community. To me outside PR practitioners tended to overpromote a business or product without first developing a realistic understanding of what they were promoting as well as a client's long-term goals. We believed the best course was to under-promise and overdeliver. I was gearing Pentair's operations to long-range growth based on continuing operational success rather than hit-and-run hype, and I believed that what we did, as opposed to what we merely said we were going to do, would secure for us a proper valuation in the market. To my mind, performance was worth a thousand words.

For all the progress we were making at Niagara, the Peavey mill continued to lose money during the first three quarters of 1973. Monthly losses reached as high as $80,000 in May 1973. For one thing, the mill's paper markets were soft; for another, new federal price and profit controls were causing large portions of U.S. and

Canadian pulp to be sold overseas, thus reducing the availability of raw material to domestic mills. Exacerbating these problems was our discovery of a kickback scheme involving a Peavey employee. We solved the problem by quietly terminating that employee; criminal prosecution was not considered appropriate.

In July 1973, we named Lee Peterson president and general manager of the Peavey subsidiary. Perhaps we should have recognized the breadth of Lee's talents earlier, because the plant's operations soon began to show marked improvement. The paper market showed renewed strength during the fourth quarter, and with better sources of raw material and increased productivity, the mill returned to profitability.

Meanwhile, at Conserve, sales and earnings slowed somewhat during the first half of 1973 but strengthened appreciably during the second half. New pollution-control equipment was installed at the suburban St. Paul facility during the year, and we carefully considered acquiring a rendering plant and cold-storage facility in St. Joseph, Missouri. We also negotiated for additional raw material from a small meat-packing company called Robel, Inc., in St. Cloud, Minnesota. In August these talks culminated in an agreement to begin servicing their plant immediately. Our facilities and equipment had to be modified to handle this new material, and the process caused some headaches before it operated smoothly. It also inadvertently contributed to one of our grislier moments when a hastily modified truck hauling the by-products between St. Cloud and the Twin Cities failed and spilled a load of bloody guts and other material on the highway. A construction gang working nearby dug a hole, shoved the mess into the hole, and covered it over with dirt. Talk about burying your mistakes!

The transportation and handling problems were resolved in a matter of months, and the Robel arrangement just about doubled the volume of work at Conserve. In fact, the Robel contract was important to maintaining high volume and acceptable profits at Conserve for as long as we owned the facility.

―――――――――

Throughout 1973, though, the Niagara mill played the dominant role in the Pentair story. The leadership of mill manager Bill Beerman greatly added to the organization's stability. Production manager Tharlie Olson became a strong supporter of the team approach and in later years became a key Pentair executive. A monthly cash production bonus for Niagara employees not only offset some of the employee benefits that had been reduced but provided a further incentive to boost productivity. We negotiated with the union a modest pension plan that helped further restore benefits and increase work force confidence and productivity. Because of both increased production and union-backed work-rule changes during the year, we were able to stabilize the Niagara work force with a total employment of 613 people.

Ever since Niagara tried to maximize employment during the Great Depression, the mill had worked four six-hour shifts per day. We were now operating 24 hours a day, seven days a week. This meant no days off during the week. The result was reduced productivity and increased accidents due to employee fatigue. Standard industry practice was to operate four crews on eight-hour shifts, with two or more days off per week. We finally negotiated a six-month trial of the standard schedule. Surprisingly, many Niagara employees opposed the change. Some of the senior workers actually asked, "What will I do with two days off every week?" Before long, though, no one wanted to go back to the old schedule.

Meanwhile, Kimberly-Clark proved to be a first-class corporation, honoring all of our agreements, assuring the mill of a constant supply of pulp in an exceedingly tight market, and providing crucial sales support in a very solid seller's market. In December, we hired Kenneth L. Wallace, a Kimberly-Clark marketing manager, as Niagara's executive vice president in charge of marketing. Ken had 31 years of experience with printing-grade papers, including printing and graphic arts, mill development of new printing grades, and sales and marketing. He and Tom Thomsen made a strong team, with Ken becoming president of the Niagara operation the following July. Niagara was now well along toward having its own sales and marketing staff.

While all of that was going on in Niagara, Wisconsin, Ben and I were spending a great deal of time looking at a paper mill in Niagara Falls, New York. The mill produced magazine-grade paper and a range of tissue products that could complement Peavey. The huge facility contained an extensive warehouse and distribution center. Formerly owned by Kimberly-Clark, it was now the property of Cellu-Products, Inc. Though the mill's operations were bogged down in contractual problems between Kimberly-Clark and its current owner, as well as between its union and its new management, we believed that we could run the plant successfully. However, union negotiations broke down, the plant was closed, and we walked away without a deal.

Nonetheless, Pentair ended 1973 on a strong note. All three subsidiaries were operating profitably, and Niagara was performing outstandingly. We had paid down a significant portion of debt and, through the sale of industrial revenue bonds, obtained financing for pollution-control improvements. In October, we declared a 10 percent stock dividend, giving each shareholder one new share for each 10 shares owned. Sales for the year totaled $44 million, a 74 percent increase over the previous year's amount. Net income was $3.4 million, a 429 percent leap up from 1972.

Our growing confidence in the company was bolstered by the continuing strength shown by all three subsidiaries in 1974. However, that confidence was not shared by the investment community, and the price-to-earnings ratio of Pentair stock responded poorly to our sales and earnings gains. The short track record of our earnings improvement, combined with our continuing debt (reduced but still high) and a small, relatively inexperienced management group, led many potential investors to perceive us as a flash in the pan. Financial analysts expressed interest, but most said, "We'll wait a few months and see how you do before recommending an investment." Our best response was to live with the frustration and to continue to develop the company.

Stock price notwithstanding, our asset value and earning power attracted the attention of both large investment houses and smaller speculators and promoters. At least once a month, we were contacted by financiers interested in helping us "take our company private." They would lend us money to make tender offers to repurchase the company's outstanding shares from our stockholders. They would give Ben and me large equity positions for facilitating the stock buy-back and for staying on and running the show.

For Ben, taking Pentair private had the appeal of producing liquidity for equity. What he did not like was the necessity of remaining part of management. For me, the whole idea ran counter to my long-term objectives. Furthermore, the continuing overtures and our willingness to speak with the various "suitors," caused serious problems. Some of our customers, suppliers, and employees were starting to question our commitment to the business.

In the fall of 1974, a number of smaller promoters and speculators grew more aggressive. A softening paper market had caused our stock price to decline to between two and three times earnings. With the stock at about $5 a share, a certain promoter was pressuring us to make an $8-per-share tender offer to our shareholders. The promoter's plan was to acquire 51 percent of the outstanding stock and then depress the attractiveness of the stock in the marketplace. When the stock price dropped, we could then buy the remaining 49 percent on the cheap. According to the plan, Ben and I would be assured large salaries and a greater chunk of the equity; of course, we would be expected to sell the plan to the shareholders and continue to run the business as a private corporation. We were told that if we did not go along, the promoter would do the deal without us and install his own management. This package of blackmail, greed, and deception was designed to appeal to selfish interests.

The plan itself was bad enough; the threat was intolerable. Such activities might not have been illegal, but they surely were unethical and immoral and not in the best interests of the shareholders and the other groups that held a stake in the company.

The episode demonstrated to me just how aggressive and unscrupulous people can become when large amounts of money are at stake. It also showed me the folly of talking to such people. Over the next decade-and-a-half we curtly refused to entertain such plans with several different promoters and speculators. We had learned to be firm, even rude, when badgered by fast-buck artists. However, this knowledge did not prevent future attempts to gain control of the company.

Ben's association with Pentair became more and more difficult for him during this period. The responsibility and workload for top management grew while at the same time the payout as determined by the market value of Pentair's stock did not match either the amount of sweat or the company's performance.

On July 1, 1974, Ben resigned as an officer of Pentair, only to resume work on July 15. On November 1, he resigned as both an officer and a director, and this time it was for good. He continued to consult with us and was heavily involved in company activities during the first half of 1975. His affiliation with Pentair ended entirely in the fall of 1975.

Also in 1974, we were faced with the task of developing information for and complying with newly instituted government price- and profit-control requirements. Such a job was tough enough under ordinary circumstances; for a company consisting of a group of newly acquired businesses lacking meaningful prior history, it was especially burdensome. At one point, we were told by the IRS that we had violated the regulations and had to return $450,000 in "excess" profits. It took four months of unflattering publicity, testimony, and painstaking paperwork before the IRS rescinded its order and Pentair was absolved of wrongdoing.

The squeeze on management became even more acute. I as board chairman and president, Bill Zolchonock as vice president and treasurer, and Irene Roettger as secretary remained. Early in 1974 I retained Henry Conor, one of our directors, as a consultant to develop new organizational plans and evaluate staff needs. That spring and summer we interviewed several candidates for Ben's position of executive vice president but could not locate the right person. Then we decided to recruit someone for president and chief operating officer, while I would assume the new title of chief executive officer as well as that of chairman.

That led to interviews with Peter King, a vice president of American Hoist & Derrick Company of St. Paul. Peter was bright and very energetic with good recommendations and a background of responsible executive experience. After interviews and clearance by the board of directors, it was up to me to make the hiring decision.

On September 3, 1974, Peter was hired as Pentair's president and COO, and on September 23 he was elected a director. For the next four months, we worked hard to get our new COO up to speed while integrating a new acquisition into the business. Unfortunately, Peter's management style did not mesh with the Pentair culture, and he was having a problem being accepted as a company leader. By the end of December, we agreed that his employment was not working out to anyone's satisfaction. In January, Peter departed Pentair.

That brief experience (debacle may be a better word for it) was very painful and embarrassing for me. I made the hiring decision, disrupted an individual's life, and raised questions among the public, our shareholders, and employees about the way Pentair was run. It was not one of my shining moments at the helm.

On the positive side, I very quickly had developed a keen appreciation for the demands on the positions of president and chief operating officer. I vowed that Pentair would not name a president or any other top officer until that person had spent time with the company at a lower level. I believed this resolution would help assure the compatibility of personalities and interests as well as the management ability of whomever assumed the most critical positions.

Pentair was not for everyone. It was a stimulating and highly challenging place to work, but the demands on a manager's time, energy, and commitment were enormous. In order to succeed, a top manager had to have a wide range of interests and talents, had to be concerned about people on all strata of the organization, and had to be willing to put in long hours with minimal staff support.

Those conditions and requirements would be the norm for several years, and I had the opportunity on more than one occasion to see just how difficult it could be for executives, especially those coming from larger, long-established corporations, to be truly effective at Pentair.

―――――――

One day in March 1974, Tom Oliver, a Chicago paper merchant, alerted us to the fact that a paper mill in the southwestern Ohio city of West Carrollton was for sale. Owned by the Ethyl Corporation, the mill was a four-machine operation annually producing about 60,000 tons of uncoated book-grade paper and using about 50 percent secondary fiber, or wastepaper, as raw material. Tom provided contacts, introductions, and assistance in making the acquisition; for his efforts, he would appreciate the assurance of a source of paper in what was then a very tight market.

The Ethyl Corporation was divesting its paper-making facilities to concentrate on the chemical business and was willing to sell the Ohio plant at book value. The mill had been highly regarded in the industry as a producer of quality products. The paper market was exceptionally strong at that time and, as a pioneer in paper recycling, this mill did not rely solely on kraft pulp (which was in extremely short supply). Its acquisition added a complementary line to our Niagara products. Particularly attractive was the mill's unique capability to make book-grade papers from secondary fiber or wastepaper. Its long-established customers included Encyclopedia Britannica, Macmillan, and Doubleday.

As our investigation and due diligence progressed, we had reason to be concerned about a number of items, including a tightening market for pulp and the transfer of environmental permits. Nonetheless, convinced that the mill would be a sound addition to the Pentair family, our directors approved a $100,000 earnest-money payment and a purchase agreement for about $5.6 million. At that time, our board of directors was made up of John Baird, Henry Conor, Don Roberg, Ken Wallace, Ben, and me. Before the closing, I set off for a week's vacation, but the vacation was interrupted by an urgent call to return home. Ben had changed his mind about the merits of the deal and was agitating to break our agreement. I called a special board meeting to review the concerns. The concerns were genuine but not materially different from those previously considered, and we had entered into the agreement in good faith. The board voted to proceed over Ben's objections, and the agreement was finalized on July 29. The acquisition became our Miami Paper Corporation subsidiary.

In hindsight, while the acquisition was sound, our timing was awful. Within a month of the closing, the market for the mill's book-grade paper deteriorated rapidly. Moreover, we soon discovered that we had underestimated (or failed to recognize) some of the mill's pervasive problems and many of the changes taking place in the industry. In any event, the Miami mill was from the beginning and for the next 10 years a troubled operation with labor problems, erratic quality, and marginal profitability. Only after a decade of hard work and significant investment would the mill finally realize its potential.

Those first several months of Pentair ownership revealed the extent of the problems. The mill was badly in need of upgraded facilities and organizational development. New environmental-protection equipment was required. The unionized work force, while initially cooperative and helpful, lacked direction and enthusiasm. In a strong market, the mill had been able to overcome its deficiencies and coast on its positive reputation. When the market faded, the mill could not respond with the quality and efficiency necessary to maintain profits and assure full production.

The problems at Miami also highlighted the chronic overextension of Pentair's corporate management. Because of the increased size and complexity of the corporation, we were simply unable to spend the time at the new mill that we had spent at Peavey and Niagara. The problems at Miami were more complicated and time-consuming than those we had encountered at our earlier acquisitions, and the mill's integration into the larger organization was consequently slower and less effective. We lost nearly a half-million dollars on Miami operations during those first five months of our ownership, and some losses continued through most of the following year.

Thankfully, the Niagara operation ran very strong throughout 1974. Despite concerns about the availability of pulp, we were able to maintain a steady supply and make the most of a strong market for the plant's end product. We also maintained our product offerings rather than taking advantage of the market and upgrading customers to higher-priced grades of paper. While foregoing some profits, we established strong new relationships with customers that would stand us in good stead when the paper market slid into a serious recession the following year, customers who would continue to support us for many years. A profit-sharing program we instituted at Niagara provided a distribution of $600,000, amounting to about $1,000 per employee, at the end of the year. (Early in 1975 we restored the mill's employee vacation program.) Operations at our Peavey mill steadily improved during 1974 and generated respectable profits. Having discontinued its original tissue production the previous year, the mill had cultivated a roster of new customers for specialty-tissue products and, as a result, enjoyed healthy sales in an increasingly tight market. By the end of the year, Peavey had installed new pollution-control equipment and had begun building an effluent-treatment plant. The plant resumed its single-ply toilet tissue production, too. Peavey was awarded a Certificate of Excellence from Parke-Davis, Inc., a major customer, in recognition of its quality improvements.

Conserve operated at full capacity during 1974, sustained in large part by our agreement with Robel. I was satisfied that Conserve represented a relatively stable and profitable business for the foreseeable future. It did not have a great deal of growth potential either on its own or through acquisition of other such facilities. Still, we could expect it to contribute meaningful profits to the corporation for several years without requiring excessive management time or capital investment.

In August 1974, we moved our corporate offices to the Roseville, Minnesota location, our home to this day. We were the second tenant in a new office building whose owner declared bankruptcy not long after our arrival. For most of the first year, we were occasionally without heating, cooling, and elevator service— sometimes for as long as a month. We got through that rough going, however, and the location has since served us well.

———————

In all, 1974 was another record year for Pentair, with sales of $70 million and earnings of $3.6 million. The corporation boasted those numbers even after absorbing both the operational losses at Miami and the cost of the Ohio plant's acquisition. In addition, we were free of bank debt and able to establish a new, $7.5-million credit line with First National Bank of St. Paul (which provided us with the funds to acquire the Miami mill). We made a series of far-reaching capital improvements resulting in increased productivity, higher quality, and a broader line of products at each of our operational facilities. At that year's annual meeting, our shareholders authorized 500,000 preferred shares of Pentair stock, which together with our strengthened ability to obtain debt financing, enhanced our flexibility for future acquisitions and capital improvements.

We still faced considerable problems (foremost among them a deteriorating paper market), but at the end of 1974 our operational strengths gave us the confidence to believe we were truly going to build a significant corporation in the years ahead.

Chapter Five

Transition 1975-1976

The year 1975 found Pentair in transition from an entrepreneurial start-up company to a corporation with increasing stability and a more professional management style.

By that time Ben Westby and I had managed the company for six years. Our relationship had been rocky, our styles contrasting dramatically, but together we had built a company with a great deal of promise. By 1975 Pentair had annual sales of $70 million, net profits of $3.5 million, and shareholder equity of nearly $10 million. Moreover, we had achieved those results without the sale of equity beyond the 200,000 shares the company sold at $1 per share in early 1967.

Ben had resigned as an officer and director, and he was working for us on a consulting basis. Ben's absence from the day-to-day operations paved the way for the recruitment of professional management that was essential to the company's long-term success. Additional corporate staff was critical in the short run also, since I was now the company's only operating officer. I must add, too, that Irene Roettger and Bill Zolchonock deserve much credit for helping hold our few but far-flung operations together during the early 1970s. Our outside advisors, Stan Efron and Stan Schweitzer, likewise merit strong commendation for their efforts.

Before the end of 1975, our total corporate staff would grow from five to 10 persons. We added a vice president for operations, controller, personnel officer, and labor-relations specialist. All four would become important long-term employees of Pentair, greatly adding to the company's strength and stability for several years.

That year proved almost as demanding of our time, energy, and attention as any in our history. A major complicating factor was a short but very severe recession in the paper industry—the worst, old-timers told us, since the Great Depression. The industry as a whole operated at an average of 75 percent of capacity for the entire year. Pentair's sales and earnings plummeted, and I requested a 10-percent salary reduction for myself in keeping with the expense controls we initiated.

At our Niagara paper mill, we took over sales responsibility on July 1, as Kimberly-Clark formally ended its ties with the plant, and we opened our own sales offices in New York and Chicago. At our Miami plant, we recruited a sales manager early in the year and began building a sales organization behind him. Unfortunately, both Niagara and Miami were faced with severe recessionary pressures which resulted in significant down-time at both locations. In March we shut down the smaller paper machine, number 1, at Niagara and did not start it up again until September. We even gave serious consideration to shutting down the entire Miami facility for a month during the worst of the trouble, but, thankfully, that drastic measure was averted. In any case, the long stretches of limited activity, the expense of weekly shut-downs and start-ups, and the generally depressed prices caused by the recession greatly reduced the profitability of both operations.

Ironically enough, the Peavey Mill enjoyed a very strong market all year. Peavey's products were diverse, including single-ply toilet tissue for both proprietary and private labels, carrier sheet and absorbent wadding for several smaller producers of disposable diapers and sanitary pads, and an absorbent pad for meat packaging. Prices remained firm, and our newly completed water-treatment system allowed us unprecedented flexibility in the use of wastepaper and thus in the range of paper grades the plant could produce. As a result, Peavey's sales and earnings reached record levels and helped us offset some of the problems at the other two mills.

Meanwhile, at Conserve the general economic slowdown reduced the subsidiary's earnings somewhat, but both sales and volume remained strong.

Our most serious problems that year were at Miami, where production and sales had declined until the mill was operating at less than 50 percent of capacity in March. In an attempt to capture new markets, we hurriedly developed new grades of paper and installed new process machinery but met with little success.

In fact, Miami operations ran at a loss until year-end, forcing layoffs among both salaried and hourly workers. A salary freeze was instituted at mid-year, but an attempt to negotiate a similar freeze for hourly employees, who were due for a wage increase in September, was blocked by the union. A batch of inherited sales agreements with unfavorable terms and a plant full of machinery in need of refurbishing added to the mill's woes.

Our difficulties at that Ohio facility were exacerbated by the lack of a sales and marketing organization. Sales and marketing personnel were retained at the corporate level by the mill's previous owners, and we discovered that our plans for covering Miami's market with the sales team from Niagara were impractical. Experience, technical knowledge, and contacts were not interchangeable between book-paper and magazine-paper markets. To remedy the situation, we hired Jim Grove, a career book-paper salesperson, as vice president for sales in February. We could not have found a better person for the job. Jim was a personable young man with much experience in book-paper sales, most recently working for Ethyl in selling Miami mill products, and he was highly regarded in the book-publishing industry. He began at once to sell Miami paper and to build a sales organization.

Results did not come overnight because of the recession. But by the end of the year Jim's small sales group was in place, and the mill was out of the red, although still a long way from becoming a truly successful and consistently profitable part of the growing Pentair corporation.

This was also a pivotal year for Pentair's on-again, off-again relationship with Ben. Consulting work did not suit Ben's style. He found neither satisfaction nor adequate remuneration, and the corporation's reduced earnings and depressed stock price caused by the recession did not help his mood. Frustrated by the situation, he was receptive to promoters and speculators who expressed interest in acquiring Pentair or taking the company private. This resulted in our having to take the time to discourage them. Going private was totally against our objective of remaining an independent public company, and it could only be accomplished by providing a large, short-term benefit for a few people at the long-term expense of shareholders and employees. As the year progressed, shareholders began to agitate for management either making a deal or squelching the persistent rumors that Pentair was on the block.

Ben finally hired a lawyer and demanded more compensation and a greater voice in the company's management. He filed suit against us in early 1976, but technically he remained on consulting status until the suit came to trial in the fall of 1977. After a week of testimony, a negotiated settlement finally and officially severed our working relationship.

Beginning in early 1975, we began to develop a pension plan that would cover all Pentair employees not covered by union plans. Lack of such a plan for our corporate staff, and senior management at Niagara and Peavey was interfering with our attempts to recruit qualified people for our most critical positions.

By December 1975, we decided on a pension plan that I believed to be in everybody's best interest. This was a money-purchase program that provided for flexible corporate contributions appropriate to our earnings in any given year; it also allowed employee contributions for those who wished to save for greater pension benefits. The plan met with instant disapproval. Everybody wanted a guaranteed pension payout at retirement age and was unwilling to accept the risks and uncertainty believed to be inherent in a money-purchase plan. Because of its unpopularity, the plan was scrapped after a little more than two years and replaced by a defined-benefit program. At least the original plan had the virtue of fixing initial pension costs in proportion to the depressed earnings of 1975 and set the stage for a new plan under more favorable economic conditions.

As we made Pentair a more attractive place to work, we began to build a corporate management staff that would carry on our transition from a start-up company to a thriving multimillion-dollar corporation.

Ken Seaman came on board as corporate personnel director early in 1975, transferring from the staff of the Miami mill. Ken's experience was needed to help with organizational development and labor relations at Miami and our other facilities. When Ken was transferred, we were employing more than 1,200 people whose daily concerns needed to be addressed; we were also putting together a pension plan that had to be administered. As our first personnel director, Ken developed and ran our initial personnel programs until March 1976.

Dick Jost was retained late in 1975 to recruit a new mill manager at Miami and to help fill other vacancies. We would employ Dick the following year as our first vice president for personnel and labor relations, and he would continue as a corporate vice president to this day.

Our accounting needs had outgrown Bill Zolchonock's control. He had expressed a desire to leave Pentair to become involved in the general management of a start-up company. Thus, during the first quarter of 1975, James Kaufenberg was brought on as our controller. Jim immediately proved helpful in setting up a corporate financial accounting and reporting system. Jim would work at Pentair corporate headquarters for the next seven years, before moving over to the operations side of the business and assuming management of the Miami mill.

Our greatest staff-development challenge was in filling the position of vice president for operations. Following the departure of Peter King, I was determined to leave the presidency open. I also resolved that I would be far more thorough in evaluating candidates for this second-in-command position. Finally, I decided that an engineering background would be required for the post. After all, we were dealing with subsidiaries we acquired because they had been underperforming for their previous owners and in most cases needed significant upgrading. Who better to wrestle with those challenges than someone with a technical as well as general business management background?

After months of interviewing applicants for the job, we ran an advertisement in *The Wall Street Journal*. The more than 150 replies that we received to the ad not only surprised us but overwhelmed our capacity to screen and to evaluate the candidates. I was getting nowhere with my limited time for recruiting and frankly wondered how we would ever find the right person.

Then in late March, I received a letter from the president of a local unit of the ITT Industrial Credit Company. The president described an executive vice president of operations within the ITT organization who was looking for a new post. The man was a mechanical engineer with about 25 years of industrial experience, including a variety of assignments with a major corporation as well as being president of a smaller company. Immediately intrigued by the man's qualifications, I responded to the letter and within a month was meeting with the candidate himself, D. Eugene Nugent.

I discovered Gene shared my interest in operations and said he was willing to spend the time and to make the effort to come up to speed in our businesses. We met several times over the next few months, during which we checked each other's backgrounds thoroughly. Finally, on August 1, 1975, Gene became our vice president for operations.

Over the next several weeks, I spent considerable time working Gene into our operations and familiarizing him with our plants, plans, and philosophies. We paid lengthy visits to each of the Pentair subsidiaries; Gene got to know not only how the subsidiaries worked, but the people who worked them. A quick study, he swiftly picked up on the activities I had neglected and gave those activities more time and attention than I could.

Our interests, objectives, and philosophies were compatible, even though our management styles were different. Gene was more the professional manager, with skills and interests in detailed planning, marketing, and external relations. This filled the longer-term need at Pentair and complemented my more entrepreneurial style of planning in broad terms, acting more on instinct, and concentrating on operations. During his first year, Gene was involved in dealing with our operating problems, establishing himself within the organization, and making the difficult transition from big-corporation to small-company culture. The results were good. Gene was made a corporate director in September 1975 and promoted to president and chief operating officer one year later. With Gene's addition to the staff, Pentair now had the core of a strong management organization that could carry the company into its second decade and beyond.

Our financial situation during 1975 was also going through major changes. Early in the year we had reason to be concerned. We had more than $11.5 million in secured debt with Kimberly-Clark and the bank, and we were committed to spending $2.5 million for a secondary water-treatment plant at Niagara. With our deteriorating earnings outlook, we would have to secure long-term financing soon. We decided to start the pollution-control system through internal funding and hoped to sell some long-term bonds in 1975.

However, the weak economy and our collapsed paper market made local financial institutions less than enthusiastic about handling our pollution-control bond financing. As a result, I flew to New York and after some discussion found the investment bankers at Drexel Burnham willing to listen. They assured me that there would be no problem in a private placement of $3 million for the financing of the pollution-control system. I was further led to believe that New York was the place for such assistance, New York institutions having far greater resources, not to mention imagination, than their humble counterparts in the Midwest.

Of course, I was pleased to have Drexel Burnham's support. Unfortunately, it was little more than talk. In August, four months after my visit in New York, I learned that the haughty New Yorkers were having trouble placing our bond. By November, after we spent considerable time and effort on the project, it was clear that Drexel was not going to come through for us.

Time had become critical. The pollution-control project at Niagara was moving steadily ahead, and we needed the money to support its cost. We also needed to sell our bonds before the project progressed beyond the point where it would qualify for tax-advantaged funding. I again approached local institutions, and by the end of November, the Twin Cities bond house of Miller & Schroeder agreed to sell $2.5 million in bonds for us. With no small amount of satisfaction, I terminated our relationship with Drexel Burnham and watched happily as Miller & Schroeder successfully completed the bond sale shortly after the first of the new year.

Looking back on 1975, I was satisfied with the overall progress the corporation had made in the teeth of a severe recession. Despite a sharp drop in earnings, we had significantly strengthened our management organization, invested $4.4 million in new production facilities and pollution controls, reduced long-term debt by 35 percent, and increased shareholder equity by 20 percent. (Our profits fell nearly 50 percent to $1.9 million for the year, the first time in the past four years that we had experienced a decrease in our earnings.) I was proud of what we accomplished and felt good about prospects for the year and years ahead. Furthermore, my pride and self-confidence were shared by others in the organization.

The year 1976 was the 10th anniversary of Pentair's founding. We marked the occasion modestly, with inscribed pen-and-pencil sets for the founders, customers, suppliers, friends, and other key people, and a dinner party honoring those of us involved in the founding. The dream had become a reality, as the company had grown in fits and starts from a struggling, highly leveraged little business to a maturing, financially substantial corporation. On one hand, we had earned the $90 million in sales and $4 million in earnings. On the other, it was a miracle that we had survived for as long as we had.

We were cautiously optimistic about 1976. We still faced pressing problems, but there were signs of good things ahead. The paper market, particularly as it affected our Niagara mill, was rapidly regaining its strength, and the economy seemed to be getting healthy again. It was time to consider a quarterly cash dividend to shareholders. We thought about such a dividend in 1975, but the board of directors was divided and we held back largely because of the recession. In 1976 the economy and, more particularly, our first-quarter results justified such a payout. Thus, on April 19, we declared our first quarterly cash dividend of 10 cents a share. We waited to start paying cash dividends until we were sure we could pay them without reduction or interruption; in fact, Pentair has paid a quarterly cash dividend ever since that first quarter in 1976, and the dividend has been increased every year.

Early in 1976, we were still concerned with the relatively short-term mortgage debt incurred in the purchases of the Niagara and Miami mills, so we selected Paine Webber for the private placement of $5 million in 10.4 percent five-year unsecured notes. We also negotiated a new, $7.5 million line of credit with First National Bank of St. Paul. Despite reservations among the Pentair board about this financing, I was heartened that the company was regarded enough to receive such consideration in the financial community. I also believe that the board's reservations made us all the more careful about how we put that new money to work.

On the down side, we continued to be distracted by both individuals and corporations threatening to take control of Pentair. Such threats were forthcoming at that time for two major reasons. First, while we were enjoying good profits and strong cash flow, the market was still undervaluing our stock, our shares trading at about four-and-a-half times earnings. In other words, our stock was a real steal. Second, Ben was still agitating for a takeover as a means for him to liquidate his equity position quickly and profitably.

Ben, Bob Politte, and others threatened a proxy fight to replace management. The challenge prompted us to take additional steps to thwart unwanted takeover attempts. For instance, we proposed changing our corporate charter to allow for staggered terms for our board of directors, with three classes of directors each serving three years, and to stipulate that any further change in the charter require a 60 percent vote in favor of a change, with not more than 20 percent opposed. We engaged Georgeson and Company, proxy solicitors, to help us secure the vote to approve management's proposals. Ben and his allies prepared a filing to the SEC covering their proxy solicitation, thus stepping up demands and threats to disrupt the annual meeting. But our swift and direct action discouraged them, while our shareholders overwhelmingly approved our proposed changes in the charter.

Even that did not end the takeover threats. We were repeatedly contacted and aggressively pursued by three different suitors in 1976. In each case, the suitor offered to pay management about 50 percent more than the marketplace for our Pentair shares and provide us with an attractive salary and equity position; of course, in return, we would be expected to support the suitor in acquiring the company and to run the operation under its new ownership. In each case, we refused to go along with the proposal.

In all of those proposals, the suitors were trying to take advantage of the shareholders and bribe management into giving them support for their personal gain. By the fall of 1976, we decided to take further preventive measures. The board of directors established a firm policy formalizing our intent to remain an independent public company.

Our formal antitakeover policy has since been refined to deal with subsequent contingencies, but action to formally establish that policy was essential to our maintaining independence over the years, as unfriendly takeover threats have remained a fact of Pentair life.

At that point in our development, the low market price of our shares was a continuing source of concern. One way we could improve the situation was to improve our financial public relations. For the past several years, the company had received mostly favorable press coverage, but that coverage alone had not increased knowledge of the company in the financial community or made much difference in the price-to-earnings ratio in our stock.

We now had both the staff and the resources to mount and to maintain the kind of public presence we needed to be recognized by the financial community, but we were inexperienced and needed some direction. While we had nine brokerage firms making a market in our stock, much of the trading was in the Twin Cities area. We needed more widespread familiarity with the company to assure better shareholder liquidity and improved access to future financing.

Help came in early 1976 when Bob Politte, one of our gadfly shareholders, suggested we think about Quentin Hietpas as a member of our board. Quent had built a successful career and achieved national recognition in both investor and public relations. He had effectively served several major Twin Cities corporations and organizations in one or both of those capacities. We were impressed by Quent's energy, knowledge, and enthusiasm, and promptly elected him to the Pentair board where he serves to this day. With Quent's help, we increased within three years the number of investment firms making a market in our stock to twenty-one and finally achieved the nationwide coverage we needed.

Later in 1976, we retained Georgeson and Company, who had handled our proxy solicitation, to help with investor communications. Georgeson set up our first formal meeting with financial analysts, portfolio managers, and other investors on April 12, 1977, in New York—an event we have repeated several times each year since in major cities throughout the United States. Ken Donenfeld, then a member of the Georgeson organization, has handled investor relations for us since 1976, though with different organization affiliations.

A milestone of another sort took place in 1976, when Pentair divested its Peavey paper mill. Peavey had been our entree into the paper business back in 1968 and, as such, was really our springboard to continuing success. Peavey was not only important to the growth of Pentair; it was also part of a group of employees and a community that had provided us with much warmth, encouragement, and support. For many reasons, the decision to sell the mill after our eight-year relationship was wrenching. At the same time, I had no doubt that its divestiture was in everybody's best interest.

We had made several unsuccessful attempts to acquire another tissue mill in order to strengthen our presence in that part of the market. We had tried to develop other related products for the mill but with only limited success and then only under strong market conditions. We had invested in facility, machinery, and pollution-control upgrades. But all of that tended to maintain our competitive position not improve it. We had done well at Peavey in 1975, and it entered 1976 as a profitable operation. However, looking ahead we could not be sure of a bright future for the mill, its employees, and its hometown. Moreover, we were expanding the corporation's paper business in the printing and writing grades instead of tissue.

Because Peavey was not a financial drain and because we truly believed it would do well under other ownership, we developed a divestiture philosophy. We would continue to make capital investments in the business and to manage it as though we were going to run it forever. While doing so, we would keep our eyes and ears open for a logical buyer who would both pay a fair price and assure continuity of operation. If we found such a buyer, fine. If not, we would continue to operate the plant the best way we knew how.

We did not have to wait long for a buyer. In January 1976, I got a call from Jim Alexy of the Brown Company of Eau Claire, Wisconsin. Jim wanted to know if either the Peavey plant or Pentair itself might be for sale. I assured him that while Pentair was definitely not for sale, we would consider selling Peavey under the proper conditions.

Over the next several weeks, Jim and I continued to talk; the more we talked, the better the idea sounded to us. Brown's Eau Claire facility included a modern recycled fiber plant that was producing more fiber than it could use. He said Brown could ship that excess fiber to Peavey. Furthermore, because Brown was turning out a wide range of tissue products, Peavey could concentrate on the single tissue line for which it was best suited. Our discussions led to negotiations during the next few months. Going into the talks, our asking price for the Peavey mill was $5 million.

We eventually settled on $3.2 million, which was higher than book value, and closed the deal on August 13.

All things considered, I could not have been more pleased with the outcome. Peavey had been an important part of Pentair's development; our original $10,000 investment in its purchase in 1968 had grown to more than $3 million in 1976. Now the mill would fit neatly into Brown's plans and operations, and it has continued to justify ongoing capital investment and expansion. Emotionally, it was very difficult to make the sale; yet, it was and continues to be very satisfying to see Peavey expand and develop while providing steady employment in the community. I still look forward to occasional visits to the mill and reminiscing with our former employees.

———————

While divesting the Peavey mill during 1976, we continued to look at additional acquisitions. One was another large printing-paper mill owned by Kimberly-Clark. The Kimberly mill in Kimberly, Wisconsin, was attractive to us for several reasons, one being that its production would nicely complement the production of our Niagara mill. Kimberly-Clark, with whom we already had a solid relationship, was very encouraging, but we just could not find the right combination to make the deal work. After much discussion, our board of directors decided that as attractive as the Kimberly mill might be, we already had too much going on to expend the time, attention, and dollars the additional plant would require.

In retrospect, I am satisfied that we made the correct decision, but it is interesting to think about what might have happened if we had gone ahead with the acquisition. Had we bought the Kimberly mill it is very likely that Pentair would have concentrated on the paper industry and would not have become an increasingly diversified corporation with significant operations in industrial products. The Kimberly mill would have forced us to develop or acquire a source of fiber to support our growing need, and to do that we would have had to focus so much of our resources in that particular area that further diversification would have been out of the question.

Meanwhile, Conserve made a strong recovery from the depressed market conditions of 1975. Its operating income increased by 190 percent on a 45-percent gain in revenues. By 1976, we were receiving more raw material in the form of meat by-products than we could efficiently process. To remedy that situation, we launched a $900,000 expansion program that would double our processing capacity and improve overall production activity and product quality.

The Miami mill showed a promising turnaround in its performance during 1976. Part of that turnaround was the result of the stronger market, but part of it was due to Jim Grove's sales organization. The forward momentum was given an additional push by Jim Winn, who was hired as Miami's executive vice president and general manager early in the year. Winn brought sorely needed paper-mill operating experience and technical expertise while strengthening its general management. Jim would be a long-term Pentair employee who would manage a number of our paper-manufacturing operations over the next several years.

The turnaround at Miami did not by any means remove all of our challenges. The plant still required a lot of hard work and investment in the development of new grades of paper, the upgrading of machinery, and improvements in its recycled-fiber system. We had to begin the arduous process of changing over to more specialty and commercial printing grades of paper in order to compete and realize acceptable profits. At the same time, we continued to serve the publishing sector of the industry that had historically been the mainstay of the mill's business. It became increasingly apparent that we would have to upgrade, and possibly rebuild, our waste-paper processing plant to achieve competitive productivity and consistently acceptable quality.

We were still trying to develop a good working relationship with the Miami mill's unionized employees. They were basically a good work force but seemed to distrust all management. Also, the union's leadership was simply not receptive to the idea of working with us to improve the plant's productivity. To me, the relationship was both frustrating and disappointing, particularly because we had been able to work so effectively with the unions and workers at both Peavey and Niagara.

We negotiated a new labor contract that called for an eight-percent wage increase. Ten-percent increases were the norm in similar negotiations at the time, but we believed the smaller amount was justified by the need for improved profitability as a means of affording badly needed capital improvements. However, our offer was rejected by the union's membership. After a 36-hour strike, we renegotiated the contract upward to the 10 percent the membership demanded. Relationships still did not improve, and grievances ran 10 times the industry experience. Nevertheless, Miami showed a very modest profit for 1976. Modest or not, the profit was a marked improvement over the sizable loss of the previous year.

The Niagara mill operated very well in 1976. Again, we were in a strong seller's market in the coated publication-grade papers, and the outlook called for continued strength for the next three to five years. Given that rosy forecast, we accelerated our efforts to speed up and improve the plant's production machinery and to continue the development of those paper grades in demand.

———————

At the beginning of our 10th year in business, we hoped to exceed $100 million in sales. However, with the sale of the Peavey mill at mid-year, our sales totaled slightly more than $90 million. Net income of more than $4 million was more than double the preceding year's figure, with a majority of those earnings deriving from our Niagara subsidiary.

In the meantime, our debt-to-equity ratio dropped below one-to-one, as our debt was reduced to only 75 percent of equity. That figure was especially meaningful to us, because of our struggle to lower the ratio from more than five-to-one over the previous four-and-a-half years. The greatly reduced debt ratio meant increased flexibility in acquisitions, capital investments, and other financial needs in the years ahead. Another reason to celebrate: The warrants that had been issued to Kimberly-Clark and the bank when we acquired the Niagara mill were redeemed in 1976. Thus, the Niagara facility had been acquired without our having to issue any new equity.

Despite the disappointing price/earnings ratio that continued to dog us, our increased earnings, stronger overall financial condition, and positive outlook slowly but surely pushed our stock price to $10.50 per share at the end of 1976, an increase 40 times the original offering price in early 1967, considering stock splits and dividends. The provision of our first quarterly cash dividend that spring was an especially bright sign.

The improved feelings of our shareholders were amusingly summed up by Pentair investor Paul Wilkins. During the question-and-answer period of our 1976 annual meeting, Wilkins, who had been critical of some of our past activities, identified himself as an 80-year-old retiree who had been holding Pentair stock since its initial offering. He said he had invested in a number of small companies and that while most earned him good money, most never paid a dividend. Dividend income was important to him in his retirement.

Addressing his remarks to me, Wilkins said, "Young man, you've taken my money, you've tried to make balloons, canoes, and leather moccasins, and operate a paper mill in Trinidad, and all of these things were failures. But you didn't give up. You bought a paper mill, then manufactured diapers, and have since bought more paper mills and reinvested the profits until now you have a successful company. This year you are returning some of that money to investors like me by paying a cash dividend."

Turning to the other shareholders, he concluded, "I recommend that this young man and his wife be given $40,000 and a year's leave-of-absence to take a trip around the world."

Wilkins' speech brought a hearty round of applause from the gathering, but, alas, no action was taken on the specifics of his proposal. Those comments were not the last we would hear from Wilkins. But from that point on I counted him as a good friend and steadfast supporter of management, and I always looked forward to hearing from him.

Chapter Six

Maturation 1977-1979

The year 1977 turned out to be a period of blessed relief from the internal crises and external pressures Pentair had struggled through for most of the previous decade. The relief did not come too soon. I needed the time to take a deep breath, recharge the batteries, and review our direction as much as the company did. Thankfully, 1977 provided for us both. The workload continued to be heavy, but the focus shifted from stabilizing operations to identifying and capitalizing on opportunities.

The national economy was strong, and our sales topped the $100-million mark for the first time, with earnings up 32 percent to $5.7 million. Our investor-relations program brought the first national report on the company by a financial analyst in the New York office of Shearson Hayden Stone. We sailed through the entire year without a major crisis. By year's end, our corporate staff numbered 14 persons, six of whom were operating executives. This larger team enabled us to handle all the home office functions while developing policies and procedures to effectively manage a group of wholly owned subsidiaries. It is interesting and important to note that the group of corporate officers assembled by 1977 would add greatly to the company's ongoing stability. In fact, five of the six are still with Pentair at this writing, almost 15 years later, and the sixth remained on board for more than six years.

This was not to say that all had become sweetness and light. While we had built a solid corporate staff, I was still occasionally frustrated, disappointed, and saddened by management difficulties, and I was continually challenged trying to recruit and integrate new people into important positions.

In years past we needed people who were willing and able to live with the risks and problems inherent in a free-wheeling, pressure-packed entrepreneurial environment. We learned from experience that specialists and professional managers usually could not or would not accept the risks, the uncertainties, or the workload of that environment. Moreover, the talent and experience of such applicants tended not to be broad enough to cover the diverse needs of a struggling, up-by-the-bootstraps type of operation. There are people who can start businesses and people who can run businesses, but there are very few who can do both.

It was always hard for me to see employees who had been important, in many cases, critically important, to the company's development leave Pentair. It was even harder for me to have to terminate one, which, fortunately, was seldom necessary. I was not worried about the individual's financial well-being, because most Pentair employees had the opportunity to profit through equity interests in the company. What bothered me was knowing the person had helped the business grow, then had to leave before he or she could fully enjoy its triumphs.

If there are truly indispensable people in a company's history, you will find them among the original entrepreneurs. Pentair owes its very existence to their invaluable contributions. However, in our middle years the challenge was to build and to maintain an increasingly professional management staff. The jack-of-all-trades mentality common to the entrepreneur was not common among the professionals Pentair was recruiting now. Unlike the entrepreneurs who were used to getting by on their wits in a free-form environment, the professionals we now needed to bring on board were familiar with the structure and specialization of large, long-established companies.

In many instances, those individuals were accustomed to having staff members do the detail work and bringing in outside consultants to deal with special problems. They worked regular hours, meaning eight to five or six, five days a week, and enjoyed the usual executive perks: club memberships, corporate cars, spouses on business trips. Of course, they traveled on company time, and their meals, accommodations, and services were first-class. All of those perks tended to be viewed as rights, not privileges. And many were expected from Pentair. Why not? Wasn't Pentair a profitable company with annual sales of $100 million?

I recall a small but telling incident from a Christmas season during the mid-1970s. One new executive presented handsome gifts to office staff members, impressing everyone with his generosity. However, the cost of those gifts later appeared on the executive's expense report. He and I had a short discussion on self-aggrandizement at company expense, and to my knowledge, such company-funded largesse did not happen again. But that was a case of the executive coming from a larger, freer-spending corporation and taking for granted his new company's willingness and ability to absorb incidental expenses, whether the expenses had anything to do with the business or not.

Coming to work at Pentair gave everyone a jolt of culture shock. It usually required six months to two years for new persons to adjust completely to our policies, procedures, and environment. Our corporate staff was always extremely lean in relation to the size and scope of our business, and our officers were given a great deal of responsibility and autonomy. Everyone was expected to keep a tight rein on ego and expense and to maintain open and honest communication – no covering behinds with memos! One of the toughest tasks required of a staff officer was to provide real support to an operating subsidiary while allowing that subsidiary the maximum amount of independence.

Newcomers to Pentair were not the only ones who had to make an adjustment. I, too, had to change my ways and my thinking, and I did not always make those changes willingly. Perhaps after spending so many years committing every available resource to the company's development, I found it difficult to accept the idea of personal perquisites. By that time, I had an unshakable belief that executives were stewards of the shareholders' money and that we were duty-bound to be wise and frugal in its use. That made it harder to accept perks for corporate executives whose salaries would seem to be sufficient to afford such extras themselves.

Maybe I paint too negative a picture. The truth is that we did find very fine, competent individuals who were committed, enthusiastic, and productive Pentair executives. Together we developed a culture and management team that has steered the company over the past decade and a half and positioned it solidly for the future. Whatever adjustments have been necessary along the line have paid off.

One key executive was our financial vice president, whose position we filled April 1, 1977. We had begun looking at candidates the previous autumn and interviewed more than a dozen applicants. The post was too important to be filled quickly, without confidence in having found the right person. That person was Jack Grunewald, a real find. Jack was a solid individual with the cost accounting, financial-management, and CPA training and experience we needed. After the usual adjustment period, he began making important contributions in finance, financial control, and investor relations. He filled perhaps the single most critical role on Pentair's management team.

With Jack on board, Jim Kaufenberg moved toward operations. He became director of operation services and was responsible for capital projects, long-range planning, and acquisitions. Gary Burwell was then hired as controller. Together, Jack, Jim, and Gary allowed us to cover all the primary financial and planning functions of the corporate office with competent and committed executives.

In 1977, we continued to refine a formal program of organizational development and training for our subsidiary operations. At our Niagara facility, promotions allowed us to replace two key retirees: the mill's manager Bill Beerman (August 1977) followed by president Ken Wallace (February 1978) turning control over to Tharlie Olson. Training programs were established to improve the management and communication skills of our supervisors at Niagara and Miami. Such programs were implemented throughout the company as it grew and contributed greatly to Pentair's success.

Meanwhile, our Miami organization began the year on a less than auspicious note. Extremely cold, snowy January weather put a severe crimp in the plant's operations that resulted in a nominal loss for the quarter. Then, in July, operations were adversely affected by an explosion in its primary boiler. On the positive side, we began work on a $2.2-million upgrade of our secondary- or recycled-fiber system to improve the quantity and quality of low-cost fiber. We also continued to develop new grades of paper and new markets for all its products, which helped assure profitability for the year albeit at a lower than acceptable level.

Conserve showed some small growth in both sales and earnings in 1977. Performance was hurt in 1976 by the effects of a drought that resulted in fewer cattle coming to market and consequently, a reduced amount of animal by-products available for processing. To make matters worse, prices for rendered animal fat and protein were depressed worldwide. Those problems were all the more troublesome because we were completing a $900,000 expansion that would double Conserve's capacity and upgrade its pollution-control facilities. The subsidiary dependably contributed to corporate earnings while requiring little of our time and attention. We did hear increasing concerns expressed by the investment community about Conserve. Why did Pentair persist in hanging on to it, given the modest size of its contributions, its limited potential, and the nature of its business, which seemed an odd fit with the rest of the corporation's activities? We had little trouble responding to those concerns, but they increased in number and intensity until the subsidiary was eventually sold.

Niagara, the dominant engine driving the corporation's growth, continued to be the primary source of Pentair's sales and earnings in 1977. The mill made the most of a seller's market and was shipping record numbers of tons of its paper products. The completion of its new secondary water-treatment plant maintained the mill in compliance with state and federal regulations for the next several years. We were also able to buy from Kimberly-Clark more than 300 acres of land adjacent to the plant for $200,000, providing an important buffer to outside developments and some elbow room for eventual expansion.

The fifth anniversary of our acquisition of Niagara was April 3, 1977. The event was marked by a festive community celebration featuring posters created by local schoolchildren, mill tours, a gala dinner, and several speeches. Later that year Niagara paid out a total of $850,000, or more than $1,200 per employee, as part of its profit-sharing plan, and that pay-out resulted in yet another civic celebration. Niagara's profit-sharing program continued to grow until its annual pay-outs reached between $5 million and $10 million in later years.

Ben formally ended his off-and-on relationship with Pentair in 1977. The lawsuit he initiated in 1976 dragged on through the deposition and interrogatory stages until it finally reached trial in late October of 1977. At that time, I took the stand and testified for five days. Then, when it was Ben's turn to testify, both parties decided to negotiate a settlement. That settlement effected a clean break in our relationship and eliminated any chance for lingering interference, frustration, and disappointment on either side.

I felt relief that our troubled relationship was over and sad, too, because I enjoyed Ben's company. He had contributed so much to my education and to our survival as a company. When all was said and done, Ben had played an important role in Pentair's success.

With the divestiture of our Peavey subsidiary the previous year, I believed that Pentair should acquire another paper mill. The new mill should manufacture printing- and writing-grade papers that would provide sufficient volume and diversification to more effectively compete in the market while giving greater clout in the purchase of raw materials for all of our facilities. My plan was not unanimously endorsed by Pentair's management group, some of whom believed we should be diversifying into nonpaper industrial products. At any rate, we set a year-end 1977 target date for another acquisition. Unfortunately, we were not able to hit it.

We did make a serious attempt to acquire the Blandin Paper Company in Grand Rapids, Minnesota. That company was a profitable and highly regarded producer of coated ground-wood papers owned by the Blandin Foundation, which was being forced to sell the operation in order to comply with tax regulations.

The cost of the paper mill, about $125 million, was too high for Pentair to tackle alone, so we solicited support from Canadian Pacific Investments of Montreal. In addition, we received commitments from several of our largest customers interested in an assured source of paper. Despite that support we were refused the opportunity to make a formal bid on the plant. The investment-banking firm engaged by the foundation's Minnesota trustees to handle the sale decided that Pentair was too small and had too short a track record to be an acceptable contender. I was greatly annoyed that a group of Minnesota trustees would not give a Minnesota corporation the chance to bid, although we were still a small operator in a giant industry.

That year we also had discussions (in one case, serious negotiations) with three other paper mills around the country. All three were profitable, well-established operations, but in each case it quickly became apparent that we would have trouble arranging the financing to meet the purchase price. Ego considerations were involved also. The owners of those businesses found it tough to accept the idea of a relatively small, upstart company like Pentair purchasing and managing a big, long-standing corporation. In any case, those talks came to naught, as did our objective to make a major acquisition in 1977.

Our investor-relations program kept us hopping, beginning with our initial presentation to security analysts in New York in April. By the end of the year, we had made twelve presentations in eight key corporate finance centers around the country, meeting with more than 200 analysts and brokers.

Our investor presentations were typically low key and candid. Most of the financial people we visited had little knowledge of Pentair and its businesses, so we were very direct and informal in both our talks and our printed communications. The information was very well received. As a matter of fact, as we spread the Pentair story there was increasing pressure for us to apply for listing on the New York Stock Exchange. We looked into a possible Big Board affiliation and we qualified. However, we decided that our interests were best served by remaining in the over-the-counter market, where we maintained up to 20 knowledgeable market-makers, including the largest investment-banking and brokerage firms in the nation. In the meantime, we were satisfied that we now had an effective investor-relations program under way.

Our increasing maturity and stability manifested in other ways. We leased additional office space in the Roseville building where we were headquartered. We developed a defined-benefit pension plan that replaced our original money-purchase program and covered all nonbargaining employees throughout the corporation and its subsidiaries. We retained a consultant to help us set up bonus and incentive programs; this resulted in our Management Incentive Plan covering annual bonuses and our Long-Term Executive Performance Plan providing long-term equity incentives to be used in conjunction with various options. Those plans have served the company well, with only minimal changes to this day.

Also in 1977 we replaced our public accountants with a Big Eight accounting firm. Discussions with investment bankers made it clear that as a matter of policy they would not consider future financings of the size we would need unless our financial statements were audited by a large accounting firm. Again we had the unpleasant task of ending a relationship with persons who had provided essential service and support during Pentair's development. The firm of Breitman, Orenstein, and Schweitzer was replaced by Haskins and Sells, who have since been annually reappointed as our independent auditors. As additional steps in our maturation, I developed a charter for an audit committee and for a personnel and compensation committee as well as a director's policy manual. All were adopted and implemented by our board of directors. These actions and activities added up to unprecedented status and stability for Pentair.

The following year, it was back to more challenge and change. Pentair Industries Incorporated (our formal name since 1966) became Pentair, Inc., in 1978. Along with the adoption of the simpler, more concise corporate designation came the switch from the Irish Script type we had used since our founding to a simpler, cleaner-looking block lettering for our name. We decided to cut back on the use of our original logo, the Greek letter *pi* enclosed in a pentagon, in the name of simplicity and directness. Those kinds of cosmetic changes signified a salutary transition toward a more professional image.

Revenues, earnings, and cash flow all increased rapidly during 1978. Earnings jumped 45 percent on a 37-percent gain in sales. Our growing cash position again encouraged Bob Politte to agitate for larger dividends, increased acquisitions, or the sale of the company. Our improving financial performance continued to draw inquiries about our willingness to sell out. Our greater size resulted in such inquiries coming from larger and more responsible potential suitors and were generally friendly in nature. It was a relief to have grown too large for the small-time promoters to hassle us and to find that strategic buyers, for the most part, were respectful and not yet caught up in the takeover frenzy to come. We were firmer than ever in our resolve to remain an independent public company, and we quickly rejected each overture. We made it clear to our shareholders that we would continue to oppose all takeover attempts.

Our strengthening financial condition enabled us to put our cash to work in significant ways. We increased our cash dividend by 40 percent for the year, declared a 50-percent stock dividend, purchased all remaining outstanding warrants for about $950,000, and initiated a series of capital improvements worth $35 million. We also acquired the Flambeau Paper Corporation for about $16 million.

Pentair's search for an additional paper operation continued from the previous year. During the winter of 1977-1978 and the following spring, we aggressively pursued three separate acquisition opportunities and, at one point, had three separate purchase offers outstanding.

One of the three was the St. Regis Paper Corporation mill in Rhinelander, Wisconsin. That facility included a sulphite pulp mill and a torula yeast plant (for processing the wood sugars from the pulp mill), and produced glassine, wax, packaging, and printing papers. We made some tentative proposals to St. Regis, but we were unable to justify its asking price.

The Port Huron Paper Company, the second possibility, was a publicly owned operation producing one-time carbonizing and lightweight printing papers at mills in Port Huron and Detroit, Michigan. Port Huron was an old-line, well-regarded company whose recent performance had been only marginal. While management and shareholders wanted to sell, the decision makers were determined to set aggressive terms. We satisfied all conditions, but we failed to meet their price. The talks broke down, and Port Huron did not become a Pentair subsidiary, at least not for another five years.

The third company we considered acquiring was the Flambeau mill located in Park Falls, Wisconsin. Owned by Capital Cities Communications as a property of its *Kansas City Star* newspaper, the mill had not been aggressively managed for several years and was currently in violation of pollution-control standards. The business comprised a sulphite pulp mill, paper-making machines producing business and commercial printing papers in a variety of colors, and a converting facility for cutting and packaging the papers. In 1977, when it was put up for sale, the plant was producing about 100,000 tons of paper a year for annual sales of about $50 million. Park Falls, like Niagara, was a scenic mill town in northern Wisconsin with a population of about 3,000. Its mill employed 550 people.

Clearly, Flambeau appealed to Pentair. It was a turnaround situation in an industry in which we had the experience and know-how, so we made a bid. However, negotiations were unusually difficult and complicated. Our difficulties centered on a competitive bidder who was one jump ahead of us. Some sleuthing by our insurance representative revealed that the officer with whom we were dealing in one of the seller's subsidiaries was also trying to buy the mill. He was functioning as a double agent who would use the information he received from our proposals to help craft ones of his own. Once we uncovered his role, we negotiated directly with Capital Cities and they finally accepted our $16 million cash offer in June 1978. We closed the deal on July 31.

As was standard practice, we corporate officers spent a great deal of time learning the specifics of the Flambeau operation firsthand, becoming acquainted with the plant and its people, and familiarizing the work force with our philosophy, policies, and procedures. To strengthen its on-site management, we moved Steve Semenchuk from the Niagara mill to Flambeau, where he became president and general manager. We worked closely with Charles Kamp, our Milwaukee-based legal counsel on environmental matters, to straighten out pollution-control difficulties. After negotiating specifications and deadlines with the Wisconsin DNR, we immediately began engineering a new $4-million water treatment plant.

The Flambeau subsidiary became a significant addition to Pentair's operations, but over the next several years it was a demanding business fraught with knotty problems and offering very cyclical profitability. For example, a large portion of its process steam came from a cogeneration gas turbine, electric generating plant owned by the local power company. Not long after we purchased the mill, the price and availability of natural gas made the use of that power plant impractical, if not impossible. Thus, we had to build a new coal and waste wood-fired steam plant of our own. Further expansion of the plant's water-treatment facility and the complete rebuilding of its sulphite-pulp mill also became necessary.

Our other mills were doing well. Niagara continued to enjoy the fruits of a seller's market for its groundwood publication-grade paper. Productivity remained high, and the plant continued to be Pentair's largest single contributor to both sales and earnings. By 1978, we had begun spending $9 million on a new groundwood pulp facility, warehouse, and roll-wrap line, which represented our largest capital investments to date. Fortunately, Niagara's pollution control equipment was in place, so we could spend that kind of money on more and better product, improved quality, and expanded grade mixes.

Despite a two-week strike in October, the Miami mill also reported a profit in 1978. Though it was difficult to identify the real issues involved in the strike, it seemed to focus on the switch from a three- to a four-shift work schedule. Similar to an experience at Niagara, once the four-shift schedule was adopted, no one wanted to go back to three. We had invested $3 million in a new secondary fiber plant and updated machinery at the plant that year. A new paper grade called Master-Matte, which employed a unique film-coating technology developed by Miami's technical staff, accounted for 35 percent of the plant's production in 1978. Quickly accepted by the industry as a premier film-coated paper, Master-Matte would be important to Miami's sales for the next several years.

At Conserve, sales volume continued to improve despite an ongoing shortage of raw material. While shareholders and financial analysts still questioned how the subsidiary fit into Pentair's overall operations, it continued to generate acceptable earnings. Although we received two serious inquiries into the sale of the business, we did not think that a divestiture would be beneficial.

We had now reached another moment of decision at Pentair. The Flambeau acquisition had given us three paper-manufacturing subsidiaries providing solid and diversified operations. We were annually producing 350,000 tons of paper for the magazine, book, commercial-printing business, and specialty-paper markets, and we were recognized as a small but reliable supplier of quality product. By the end of 1978, our position in the paper industry seemed solid enough to think about diversifying into other businesses.

Besides our status in the paper industry, there were two compelling arguments to consider further diversification. First, my interests and experiences and those of Gene Nugent were centered on the engineering, design, manufacture, and sale of industrial products. Despite our success in the paper business, most of us were hankering to develop and produce something more distinctively proprietary to Pentair. Second, the cyclical, capital-intensive nature of the paper business was a strain for a chronically under-capitalized company such as ours to support and to manage, and there was nothing to suggest the job would get any easier or less expensive. If anything, the prospects were more daunting than ever. New paper mills with improved technology would soon spell the end of the seller's market for Niagara's paper, and all of our paper mills would require our investing additional tens of millions of dollars to remain competitive. Diversification into less capital intensive businesses could soften the demands on our cash and perhaps offset the industry's cyclical characteristics.

The arguments to diversify were ultimately convincing. The next question: What kind of business (or businesses) did we want to enter?

After much discussion, we began to enumerate those businesses in which we were not interested, businesses where we had no experience or qualifications or, for one reason or another, did not seem appropriate. Consumer products, retail and service operations, high technology, recreational products, finance, distribution, and transportation were ruled out. That left industrial products, which we defined as products manufactured and sold to industrial users as opposed to the general consuming public.

We also decided that whatever new business we entered would have to be one in which one or more of us had a strong personal interest. Our positive experience with underperforming paper mills gave us the confidence to focus our attention on industrial-product companies that were not turning acceptable profits for their current owners; in other words, companies in distress. However, we would have to identify specific reasons why we could expect the operation to perform better under our guidance than under the guidance of its previous owners.

With this in mind, we aggressively began looking for an industrial products business that we might acquire. We had to be successful on our first venture because the investment community was skeptical of our ability to expand beyond paper. A failure on our first try would damage our credibility. With that in mind, we began to look for a company with annual sales of between $25 million and $100 million, and we set year-end 1980 as a target date for buying it.

The task proved more difficult and time consuming than we imagined.

Having decided to expand into another area, we had to wrestle with the ongoing challenge of financing the company's growth. We were as committed to expanding and developing our existing subsidiaries as we were to making another acquisition, but as usual, our capital resources were tight. Pentair's credit rating was high, and we were able to obtain our bankers' support for the Flambeau acquisition. By year-end 1978, however, we needed to sell additional equity to further strengthen our balance sheet.

Early 1979 seemed a good time to push an equity offering for additional capital. Our new Flambeau subsidiary was already contributing to the overall business, and we were reporting another record year in both sales and earnings. Given the good news of the past year, we were certain the investment community would support a new stock offering, and we set out to make it happen. This would be our first offering since the sale of those initial 200,000 shares in 1966, and we believed a New York investment firm should be retained to give us maximum nationwide distribution and market support. We also wanted a local brokerage firm to assure as much regional distribution and support as possible.

We selected Dain, Kalman & Quail, a Minneapolis-based firm, to be our local representative. For some time Dain had shown a keen interest in Pentair, becoming quite knowledgeable of and writing regular research reports about our various operations. For New York-based assistance, we looked closely at two firms: Paine Webber and Shearson Hayden Stone. Paine Webber had managed our $5-million debt financing in 1976 and had the inside track on the business.

On January 9, 1979, Jack Grunewald and I were in New York to visit Paine Webber in the morning and Shearson in the afternoon; by the end of the day we hoped to have learned enough to choose one firm or the other. To our surprise, there was a great deal of difference between the two firms, at least in their attitudes. The Paine Webber people were stuffy, egotistical, and condescending to us bumpkins from the Midwest. They spent a lot of time trying to impress us with their knowledge of the ins and outs of stock offerings and, despite our wishes, they made it very clear that they neither wanted nor needed a local firm as a partner. (They would not consider using a Twin Cities law firm for underwriting counsel, although I clearly presented that as a requirement.) In contrast, the Shearson officials were not only well prepared, they treated us as valued prospective customers and seemed sincerely interested in our business. Unlike Paine Webber, Shearson was agreeable to working with a Twin Cities brokerage and a Twin Cities law firm. Sandy Weill, Shearson's flamboyant chairman, personally took the time to greet us and express interest in our plans. Weill's attention to details made an important difference.

The choice of New York brokerages thus turned out to be an easy one. When dealing with an institution, you are really dealing with individuals. If the chemistry is not right, the relationship is probably not going to be happy or productive. The chemistry between the Shearson people and our people was better in that instance, even though we had worked with Paine Webber in the past. Perhaps it was just a matter of timing.

The initial objective of the offering was to sell common stock priced at $20 a share. To our disappointment the market price, despite an annualized earnings rate of $4.19 per share and a price/earnings ratio of less than five to one, was staying below the $20 level, making such an offering price impossible. We finally agreed to offer 400,000 shares of convertible preferred stock at $25 per share and an 8¼-percent interest rate. The conversion premium was about 25 percent. Thanks to our management staff's experience in communicating the Pentair story to investment bankers and brokers across the country, we achieved a wide distribution of those preferred shares and limited institutional purchases to less than 25 percent of the total.

On May 1, 1979 we agreed on the issue's pricing and the next day all 400,000 shares were sold, for a total sale of $10 million and a net to Pentair of $9.2 million. The offering was gratifying not only in dollar terms but in the sense it gave of the company's standing in the marketplace. The offering also provided welcome confirmation that our investor-relations program was effective and bode well for future financing attempts.

———————

Meanwhile, our attempts to acquire an industrial products company were not proceeding so smoothly. Part of the problem was that we were not fully aware of the possible opportunities in that industry. While we were a known and respected participant in the paper business, we were outsiders in the industrial-product business, and our acquisition targets were not clearly defined. The candidates we did manage to identify through personal contacts, industry press and other diverse sources were relatively few.

Eventually, we added a wide array of investment-banking firms to our information sources. Investment bankers, while eager to help, would not be able to help us overnight. Indeed, we realized that it would take months, even years, before we developed a mutual understanding with the investment-banking community, before we were accepted as a qualified buyer outside the paper industry, and before the quality of the leads bankers sent our way would be high enough to be worth our time.

Throughout 1979 we investigated many acquisition opportunities, all of which sooner or later were rejected. Three possibilities were seriously considered, and two of them were not even industrial product companies (one made toys, the other built furniture), but we were sufficiently anxious that we were willing to look hard at opportunities beyond the scope of our criteria. In both cases, we concluded that Pentair was not the logical buyer.

Complicating matters was the loss of our vice president for corporate development, Jim Kaufenberg, whom we named president of our Miami subsidiary. That left Gene, Jack Grunewald, and me to run the acquisition activity until we filled the corporate development slot the following year. Nevertheless, with the support of Dick Jost in personnel and labor relations and Roy Rueb in finance, we were becoming quite capable and confident in candidate review, evaluation, and negotiation. There is no substitute for experience in acquisition matters.

Despite the frustration and extra-heavy workload we began making progress in 1979. Through intensive practice in the acquisition game, we were honing our evaluation and due-diligence skills. At the same time, the investment bankers were becoming increasingly familiar with us and our acquisition criteria, thereby becoming more bullish on our qualifications as an industrial products buyer.

Also in our favor was the continuing success and relatively smooth operations of our existing businesses. Like everybody in industry at the time, we were watching the escalating costs of energy, and we had to install new equipment or adapt current operations to make the most of our energy expenditures throughout our businesses. Still, those businesses, including the Flambeau paper operation, were doing well and allowed us the time to further expand the corporation.

On October 17, 1979, we elected George Butzow to our board of directors, replacing Don Roberg, who resigned in April 1978. As CEO of MTS Systems Corporation, George brought knowledge and experience in industrial manufacturing companies that would be valuable to us.

———————

Earlier in 1979, two developments gave us cause to look back on our past, even while we faced eagerly toward the future. In April, following the mailing of our annual meeting announcement, we received a call from an attorney wondering if there was some value in the Pentair shares held by one his clients. The client was a Chicago woman whom none of us had ever met, but who in the formative days of the company (and against the attorney's advice) had invested $5,000 in our $1 stock. She had since not paid any attention to her investment. With no small amount of pleasure we could tell her that her 5,000 shares had grown to 30,000, with a market value of $600,000. In addition, she had earned an extra $40,000 in cash dividends. What a surprise that must have been for her, not to mention her attorney! What a delight it was for us to provide the good news!

The other development that April was Irene Roettger's retirement. She was the last of my entrepreneurial associates from the early days of Pentair. Irene, our corporate secretary since May 1972, held the home office together during some very turbulent times. She played an invaluable role in Pentair's development, and we were very sorry indeed to see her go. Irene's departure was yet another break with our past as we continued our march into the future.

Chapter Seven

Diversification 1980-1981

Our corporate focus in 1980 was to add an industrial-products company to our group of businesses. The previous year we had begun protracted and ultimately frustrating discussions with General Electric about purchasing its Wire and Cable Division. Those talks continued into late winter 1980 before breaking off just shy of a formal agreement.

In the months that followed, we looked very seriously at half a dozen acquisition possibilities, visited plants and pursued negotiations. These prospects included a manufacturer of school buses and special vehicles, a manufacturer of school class rings and awards, a maker of refractories for the steel industry and of wood pencils and crayons, a small Wisconsin rendering plant, and a large Canadian forest-products manufacturer. Obviously, we again were willing to expand our stated criteria regarding the nature of the business we would be willing to acquire.

Among those possibilities was an industrial-products manufacturer, and a large one at that. The company was Steiger Tractor, Inc., based in Fargo, North Dakota. Steiger produced large, four-wheel-drive farm tractors under its own name, as well as a similar line of tractors for the International Harvester Company (which owned 35 percent of Steiger's stock). Steiger also manufactured under contract for both International Harvester and Caterpillar. In 1979 the company earned almost $7 million on sales of $115 million.

Steiger intrigued me because of my own background: I had grown up on a farm. More important from the corporate point of view, the company had been doing well on the strength of a robust agricultural economy during the past several years and seemed to have a bright future. A large percentage of its stock was held by individuals and families who had been involved in the company from its earliest days and now wanted to cash out and pursue other interests. Our initial investigation and early conversations with the company's principals were encouraging. We agreed that International Harvester would retain its Steiger holdings while we would try to buy the rest. The cost of acquiring that 65 percent of the company would be about $20 million.

However, as our talks progressed, a number of warning flags caught our attention. The farm economy was rapidly deteriorating, and Steiger sales were dropping accordingly. Several agricultural economists suggested that the ag-economy decline was not a mere blip on the screen; it would probably continue into the foreseeable future. Our directors also recommended caution. Still more troubling to us was Steiger's management style. The company's plush office appointments, expensive leased cars, and other similar elements were extravagant, to say the least. I had seen the same signs earlier in the USI episode. Moreover, Steiger's CEO insisted that Pentair's role in the company's management be limited and very much under his direction. He also demanded a rich employment contract that would protect his position or assure him a healthy severance package if he was removed by the new owners. Even when his demands were modified during subsequent discussion, serious philosophical differences remained.

Doubts and misgivings grew even during our final negotiations with the Steiger board of directors in June 1980. Though we had reached a general purchase agreement with the Steiger board, I spent most of that day and the following night examining and re-examining our position. By morning, I concluded that the deal would not be a good one for Pentair. In a hastily prepared memo to our board, which was meeting that morning to approve the agreement, I expressed serious reservations about both Steiger's management and the farm-economy forecast, and I strongly recommended we not proceed any further. This was not an easy decision, and there was strong dissent on the board. We had already spent considerable time and effort on due diligence, and the final agreement was ready for our signature. After a lengthy review and discussion, however, the board agreed that we should terminate further consideration of acquiring Steiger. The decision was another blow to our plan of adding an industrial business.

Our board's decisions have not always been unanimous. Divided opinions combined with a healthy give-and-take around the table have strengthened the board's ability to make sound, well-reasoned choices. In the case of Steiger, the decision to step away from the deal ultimately proved positive, as the farm economy did slip and International Harvester discontinued its agricultural equipment business.

The stress of such activity was enormous, though, and it took its toll as 1980 progressed. While we learned a great deal about the acquisition process and refined our techniques and procedures, it was terribly frustrating to come so close to making a deal only to walk away empty-handed. During that period we reviewed our approach and procedures, but after some heated discussion we reminded ourselves that we had to be patient, continue our search and investigations, and resist the temptation to buy something that might not be right for Pentair. I was convinced we were going about the job in the right way and that our growing proficiency and expertise would eventually get us exactly what we wanted.

We needed a well-qualified replacement for Jim Kaufenberg, our former vice president for development, to help with acquisitions and corporate development. After a year's recruiting effort, Henry Conor steered us to Ronald Kelly, a bright and experienced young man we had known for some time. He began work January 1, 1981. Ron not only provided much needed assistance to our acquisition program, but he became a long-term executive with major operating responsibilities. Ron was another excellent addition to our corporate management staff.

———

Pentair's existing businesses continued to run well, requiring little corporate office time and attention, during 1980. Business slackened a bit because of a softening economy, but our earnings remained steady. Because we carried only a small amount of debt, the nation's rising interest rates were not a major problem. In the meantime, our aggressive capital and investment program benefitted us in two ways. Productivity and total production was up, and our investment tax credits reduced our total tax expense. Niagara continued to be our primary profit maker, though competition was increasing and the economy was beginning to cut into those earnings. Clearly, the years ahead were going to be even more challenging than past years had been.

Pollution control was a never-ending challenge despite the sizable amounts of money we had been spending on equipment to meet environmental requirements. Day-to-day concerns were handled by our on-site personnel; however, corporate staff oversaw these activities owing to the expense of installing the control equipment and the negative consequences of not complying with the rules. We were sincerely concerned about protecting the environment, yet mindful of the need to remain competitive in the market. Pollution-control procedures and technology were not well understood at the time, resulting in occasional upsets in our systems and minor permit violations. Both the paper industry and the regulatory authorities were pushing the limits of technology to protect the environment and to meet the demands of our separate constituencies. This created occasional conflicts between us and the regulators, exacerbating the dilemma of trying to do what is legally and morally right and also what is necessary to stay in business.

We met frequently with Wisconsin DNR officials and were occasionally either the plaintiff or the defendant in lawsuits involving the DNR. For example, in November 1980, Niagara personnel and I spent two days on the witness stand in a Marinette, Wisconsin courtroom. At trial's end, the DNR maintained its standing as a protector of the environment. We were assessed a nominal penalty for a system upset that caused an excess effluent discharge from our Niagara mill. We did not have to curtail operations. This permitted us to fine-tune our treatment plant, and we soon achieved consistently good control of mill effluent. Improvements in pollution-control technology and continued tightening of regulations over the next few years resulted in more than a hundredfold reduction of our environmental pollution. Continuing capital investments and operating expenses for environmental protection are yet another cost of doing business responsibly.

Fuel costs, on the upswing during the late 1970s, continued to rise in 1980. At our Flambeau mill, we hired an engineering firm experienced with wood-fired boilers to design a new waste-wood power plant that would help reduce both energy costs and air-borne pollutant emission. To cover the estimated $20-million cost of the power plant and related construction, we arranged to sell tax-free industrial revenue bonds. Because we would be burning wood waste procured from forest-product companies in the area, we were able to classify the new boiler as a solid-waste disposal unit, enabling us to put together a financing package using tax-free bonds for the entire project. In a period of extremely high interest rates, tax-free bonds afforded us a manageable debt service option. As construction progressed, we were able to restructure its financing in a favorable sale-and-leaseback arrangement. Nevertheless, the large capital expenditure required by paper mills was a topic of discussion for our directors who desired assurance of an acceptable return on those investments.

———

By late 1980, we had been relatively untroubled by inquiries or out-and-out attempts to take Pentair private or otherwise wrest control away from our management. On November 17 that respite was shattered by a man named Peter Wray.

Wray introduced himself to Gene as a Pentair investor and admirer. A founder of the Steak and Ale restaurant chain, he was now a major shareholder of The Pillsbury Company, which had bought the restaurant chain, and chairman of The Victorio Company (TVC) of Phoenix. Wray told Gene that TVC's business was investing in land and cattle operations, as well as in promising corporations like Pentair. In fact, TVC already held 135,000 Pentair shares.

Wray got down to business. TVC wanted to take our company private. TVC would provide the financing and assure Pentair executives high salaries, robust incentive compensation, and large equity participation. (He enjoyed, he said at that point, making people millionaires.) In return, we Pentair executives would, of course, agree to cooperate in the transaction. According to Wray's plan, TVC would offer Pentair shareholders $24 a share for stock then selling at $16 a share. When Gene advised him of our policy of remaining independent, Wray made some not-so-veiled threats about TVC proceeding to increase its position in Pentair and then left. To that point, the Arizonan's visit was not appreciably different from the visits of other suitors.

But we had not heard the last of Peter Wray. On December 4, he called me from Phoenix. After profusely praising Pentair's management, he reiterated his plan to take the company private and asked for my support. I told him that we were not interested in his or anybody else's takeover plan, and I made it clear that we would aggressively oppose any such effort. While expressing disappointment, he repeated his compliments about our management, and said he would get back to us.

On December 22 he did—with a courier-delivered package carrying a Schedule 13-D filing informing the SEC that TVC had acquired 6.1 percent (166,000 shares) of Pentair's outstanding stock. According to the filing, the stock had been purchased for "investment purposes only," but TVC reserved the option to change its mind about those purposes later. Most disturbing, though, was that TVC was in partnership with the Pritzkers, a Chicago-based family enterprise known for taking control of companies by unfriendly actions. Coincidentally, that very day's *Wall Street Journal* reported on a lawsuit filed against the Pritzkers by a group of shareholders in a "going private, leveraged buyout" bid.

I was furious. Once again I saw the company threatened by a gang of greedy outsiders in a completely unfair, unethical, and immoral power grab. The next day, I told Wray that we considered his actions very threatening, particularly in view of his affiliation with the Pritzkers, and I repeated our intention to vigorously oppose any takeover plan. I wanted to meet as soon as possible to explain our position in detail and thus prevent either side from doing something we might later regret. He agreed to a dinner meeting in the Twin Cities on January 5.

The holidays were spent with corporate counsel Stan Efron, shoring up our takeover defenses. We chose as our defense team the investment-banking firms of Blythe, Eastman, Paine Webber in New York and Dain, Bosworth in the Twin Cities and the law firm of Foley and Lardner in Milwaukee, with an experienced anti-takeover attorney Ben Garmer. The defense team was in place by January 1.

By that time we saw increased trading in our stock and a rising market price. That together with information that arbitrageurs and speculators were buying up Pentair shares reinforced the idea that the company was in genuine and imminent danger of falling into the hands of people interested only in a short-term profit. Thankfully, Pentair had few institutional investors; many of our stockholders had been with us for some time and were not likely to make a quick sale. Still, we had to move fast.

The differences between long-term, friendly investors and the institutions were striking. A typical long-term holder called to confirm support for management and urged us to get pension and compensation agreements to protect ourselves in the event of a takeover. Two institutional holders inquired about the state of the takeover action, saying they deplored the action but that their fiduciary responsibilities required that they sell to the highest bidder. Fortunately, only 10 percent of our stock was in the hands of institutions. That percentage increased to 60 percent in five years, however, with institutions focusing on short-term profits.

When Gene and I sat down with Wray on January 5, 1981, we were not convinced of the real effectiveness of our hurried defensive preparations. However, we pointed out in no uncertain terms that we would go to almost any length to thwart his takeover attempt, and we urged him not only to stop buying additional Pentair stock but to give serious thought to selling TVC's Pentair holdings either back to the market or to the company. Wray said that while his intentions were strictly friendly and constructive, he might want to sell his shares to someone who might be less congenial. In any event, he wanted to talk with the Pritzkers before he made his next move. We agreed to talk again on January 19. Gene and I left the meeting even less comfortable than when it began.

Back on our turf, our investment-banking team conducted a painstaking top-to-bottom analysis of Pentair to determine a definitive value of the company by which we could accurately evaluate a tender offer and appropriately respond. At the same time, our attorneys developed a plan of action on the legal front. Our objective was to get control of the situation, remove TVC as a shareholder, and put an end to speculation in our stock. We went so far as to retain the services of a private investigator who might expose unsavory or illegal activities on the part of Wray or any of his associates.

Thanks to the policies we had put in place during previous takeover attempts, there was no internal debate about our intent to remain independent. Management and the board of directors were unanimous in reconfirming their support for our policy position, and we believed we had the backing of the majority of our shareholders as well. While the defenses built into our corporate charter were limited and the State of Minnesota provided little statutory help at that time, we were determined to do anything and everything we could to prevent a takeover.

Wray asked to postpone our meeting for a week. The TVC board had not yet made up its mind about proceeding further with the acquisition of Pentair shares, and once more he urged me to go along with his plan. He also repeated his threat to bring a more hostile third party into the picture if we did not listen to reason.

On January 27 a Paine Webber representative and I flew to Phoenix to meet with Wray at his TVC offices. He was completely contradictory in his statements, insisting in one breath he would do nothing unfriendly, then in another threatening to buy more of our shares and bringing in a less-friendly outsider. As he had from the start, he insisted that he was in complete control of the TVC plan, then said he would have to check with the Pritzkers. None of what he said was very comforting. Before we left I offered to buy back his stock at the current market price of about $19 a share. Wray refused, saying he did not have the authority to sell the stock, and suggested we talk yet again in three days.

On January 30 we spoke to each other on the phone. Though still threatening in tone, Wray seemed agreeable to selling his shares to Pentair if we could agree on a price. He refused to accept an offer of $400,000 profit over his acquisition costs. We agreed to continue the discussion in New York on February 4.

On that day Gene, a Paine Webber official, and I sat down in New York's Knickerbocker Club with Wray and Melvyn Klein, a TVC director and member of the Pritzker organization. Klein played the role of the heavy, saying he did not like what he was hearing and was disgusted by the thought of negotiation in this case. He said if it was his deal, he would ignore Pentair's current management, acquire a majority of the company's stock on the open market, and then throw us all out. With that last pronouncement, he stomped out. Wray stayed put, finally agreeing to a plan by which we would buy TVC's Pentair shares for $23.75 apiece. That amounted to a payment of more than $4.25 million and gave TVC a tidy million-dollar-plus profit on its short-term holdings.

The following day our board of directors, reassured by our investment-banking and legal advisors that such a buy-back was appropriate, approved the Knickerbocker Club agreement. Within a week our attorneys had hammered out the terms. In return for our payment, we got our shares back and received a standstill agreement prohibiting TVC and its associates from further action against Pentair. I felt we had done what was necessary to protect the long-range interests of Pentair and its stakeholders. At the same time, buying back those shares and paying the attendant greenmail was one of the most distasteful things I had ever done. As far as I was concerned, that money had been extorted by a group of selfish opportunists who had been hell-bent on destroying a healthy and successful company for their own short-term gain.

Lesson learned: A corporation has few shareholders who can or will effectively help prevent a takeover. The responsibility lies with management and directors to prepare and to maintain the best practical defense, to manage the company effectively, and, in the event of a takeover attempt, to respond immediately. Constant preparedness is essential, and intense and unequivocal defensive action must start within minutes of the initial threat. If there is any delay or hesitation, the battle will soon be lost.

That unpleasant episode in the Pentair story was not quite over. On April 20 and 21, Pentair and its directors were served with a summons and complaint alleging that we had squandered the company's money in buying back those TVC shares at an amount above the existing market price. The suit was filed in the name of an individual holding 100 shares on behalf of all Pentair shareholders, and damages were defined as those damages suffered by Pentair as the result of management's wasteful actions and included accounting and legal fees. We soon learned that the shareholder bringing the suit had three other such suits pending and that the same law firm was handling all four of the actions.

The litigation had been initiated by a group of legal parasites who fed off corporations by extorting legal fees. Though some of our costs were covered by our officers' and directors' liability insurance, we decided to fight the case tooth and nail. Two years later, we finally reached a settlement that involved paying the plaintiffs about $60,000 as reasonable legal fees and expenses. In addition, we spent more than $50,000 on our own lawyers' costs, not to mention hours of management time and energy.

Altogether TVC's takeover attempt cost us roughly $5 million in terms of buy-back and expenses and diverted countless hours of our time from legitimate corporate business. The whole sorry episode resulted in delaying various facility improvements and retarding new-product development by one full year. What an egregious waste of precious resources for the gain of a few!

Pentair's performance was not as strong in 1981 as it had been in the preceding few years. The sluggish national economy had resulted in a decreased demand for our products, and we were faced with a number of operating problems in our subsidiaries. While our financial condition remained strong, earnings for the year fell from $12 million to $8 million on flat sales of about $220 million. Despite the decline, however, we maintained our annual capital-investment level of about $20 million.

In 1981, our operating challenges included environmental problems and upgrades at our various subsidiaries, as well as a three-day strike at the Flambeau mill and a nineteen-day strike at the Miami mills.

The environmental issues had become a continuing challenge which we had grown accustomed to handling. At the same time labor relations were becoming increasingly worrisome. From my perspective, our corporate attitude, following the lead of labor counsel, grew less professional and more dogmatic and confrontational. Contact between managers and workers was more formal, and the one-on-one communication we had established was diminishing. As a result, relations were becoming more strained, mutual trust was weakened, and both spirit and performance were falling off.

The faltering economy placed considerable strain on labor relations. In the face of foreign and domestic competition, companies had to adjust their operations to reduce costs and improve efficiency, which meant making changes in work practices and in staff reductions. In our case, the situation was aggravated by less than competent and constructive leadership among a few local and international union representatives. However, we were not without blame. In my opinion, we had lost some of our objectivity and professionalism, becoming more emotional and personal in discussions and negotiations. In part, this was the result of our turning over too much responsibility to an occasionally vindictive, disrespectful, and unprofessional labor-relations counsel. Labor relations and particularly negotiations are difficult. I believe that management has a great responsibility to maintain objective and professional standards out of firm and sincere concern and respect for its workers and for the business. I take much of the blame for management's position. I should have been more aggressive in correcting the situation. In retrospect, it is easy to understand and empathize with our occasionally unhappy and uncooperative workers.

The Miami strike was inevitable, but we could have handled relationships and negotiations more respectfully and professionally. The strike began on October 4, shutting down operations. There was picket-line violence, intimidation of nonstriking employees, and damage to plant and employee property. We hired an outside security service to help control the situation. On November 2 we resumed operations with salaried and supervisory personnel and were able to fill critical orders. The resumption of productive activity was slow, though, and earnings turned negative pending an end to the strike on December 6.

While there was no evidence of overt ill will when union employees returned to work, it took time for the plant to get back to capacity operations. Furthermore, the tensions at the core of the strike and the need to strengthen operations led us to replace the plant's president and general manager. We later concluded that the labor contract we had agreed to was noncompetitive and unworkable. Less than a year later the contract had to be renegotiated.

On a more positive note, acquisition activity picked up momentum with the hiring of Ron Kelly as our vice president for corporate development early in 1981. The world gradually accepted the idea that Pentair was serious about branching out beyond the paper industry, and more and more prospects were being presented to us. Simultaneously, we were becoming better and better prospective buyers.

During the first eight months of the year we seriously considered seven industrial-product prospects that ranged between $25 million and $100 million in sales. All seven were underachievers whose performance, we believed, could be improved significantly under our management. In each case, though, we were unable to reach mutual agreement on the company's values and never got as far as a purchase agreement. By that time, we had considered more than 125 nonpaper-manufacturing possibilities.

Then in August, we picked up a tantalizing bit of intelligence on a golf course. Jim Grove, vice president of sales at the Miami mill, was out on the links with a friend who had a business in the power-tool industry. He mentioned a rumor that Rockwell International Corporation might be interested in selling a division that manufactured portable electric power tools. Aware of the corporate office's interest in diversification, Jim immediately advised us of the rumor. Telephone calls to Rockwell resulted in arrangements for Ron Kelly to visit the company's Pittsburgh headquarters.

Ron learned Rockwell was keeping its divestiture plans close to its vest, wishing to select and to negotiate quietly with potential buyers of its power-tool division. Its management had decided to sell the operation in order to concentrate more closely on its aerospace and high-tech businesses. The power-tool operation had not been very successful for the corporation. Rockwell acquired the Porter-Cable professional power-tool company some 20 years earlier, changed the product name to Rockwell, opened a new factory, and created a lower-priced product line for the high-volume consumer market. But fierce competition and product deficiencies in the division's consumer business (which was in the process of being shut down) had caused operating losses.

Rockwell had set a selling price about equal to book value. The company was determined to find a buyer that would commit to a long-term operation, not tarnish Rockwell's good name, and treat its customers and employees fairly. We saw the business as a very appealing opportunity. Once the consumer-product line had been eliminated, the professional power-tool business would be an excellent fit with our objectives and operations. We provided Rockwell with a complete rundown on our company.

By the end of August, both Rockwell and Pentair decided to proceed with serious negotiations. Both managements met several times during the next several weeks in Pittsburgh, St. Paul, and Jackson, Tennessee (where Rockwell's professional-product plant was located). Rockwell generously provided its corporate jet for our convenience. Our respective policies, procedures, and personalities were compatible, and we believed an agreement could be worked out with reasonable haste. Our visit to the production plant in Jackson made a very positive impression. It was a solid facility with obvious potential for development, but the organization needed direction. In spite of the pending sale, the facility's workers were genuinely friendly, enthusiastic, and industrious. Their pride was reflected in their dress and demeanor, as well as in the plant's excellent housekeeping. The quality of the staff was no accident; personnel were supported and encouraged by the advocacy of a competent director of human resources, John Ulmer, and by Bobby Parker, director of manufacturing.

Among the Rockwell management group was Tom Ryan, who had made his career in the Porter-Cable and Rockwell power-tool operations. He had held several key positions, most recently in marketing. Tom, a hearty Irishman, was dedicated to power tools and was particularly enthusiastic about the Porter-Cable product line. He was a natural choice to head the operation, and he was eager to accept the challenge. Tom became the president of the Porter-Cable subsidiary, and he remains in that position today. His savvy on both the operating and marketing sides of the business, both domestic and foreign, his fine reputation in the industry, and his general management abilities have been a key to Porter-Cable's success.

By October 19, exactly two months since Ron Kelly's first visit to Rockwell, our due diligence had been completed and, after strenuous but congenial negotiations, the deal was formally consummated. Pentair, having paid $16.5 million for its latest acquisition, was now in the industrial-products business.

Right from the start we felt a great deal of confidence in the acquisition's soundness. That confidence was shared by our shareholders and the investment community. The new business, which we decided to call by its original name, initially provided sales of only a modest $45 million, but it offered proof that Pentair could acquire, assimilate, and manage a subsidiary outside the paper industry. Among management it reinforced the conviction that we were continuing to make progress toward our goal of becoming a major American corporation.

In 1981 Pentair completed its 15th year in business. Our anniversary celebration was expanded to include more than the four surviving company founders and others who had played key roles in our formative days. The recognition party at Midland Hills Country Club was a festive occasion and included our directors, corporate staff, and subsidiary executives. We made prominent display of balloons and inflatable systems, a canoe, several pairs of moccasins, leather vests and skirts, and assorted tissue-paper products. Aside from the camaraderie, there were feelings of wonder and respect as the founders considered the current size and complexity of the company while the newcomers marvelled that it ever survived.

It was very satisfying to look back over those 15 years. We had come a long way from our original business idea and five founders to a multifaceted corporation boasting 1,800 employees at several locations around the country, $200 million in annual sales, and $12 million in earnings. Even more important, we had been able to establish a way of doing business, and it was working. We now had a hard-working, smooth-running organization of talented and committed people in whom I had great confidence and trust. The nightmare that characterized our early years proved to be a prelude to the American dream.

Nineteen eighty-one was a particularly momentous year for Pentair. While maintaining strong existing operations, we had diversified into the new field of industrial manufacturing. We had survived an aggressive takeover attempt and reinforced our ability to remain an independent public corporation enjoying the enthusiastic support of its various stakeholders. The Pentair Approach to Business statement I had written for our 1980 annual report became a tangible guide to our corporate philosophy and policies that would evolve into our formal Code of Business Conduct.

Pentair also solidified its position for long-term growth with bright prospects for the future. For the first time, I was convinced that Pentair was destined to survive its last remaining founder and subsequent managements, and I was determined to do everything possible to make certain that happened.

I was determined to prevent the breakdown apparent in other companies of similar size and longevity that had not been able to make an orderly transition from the company's founder to its subsequent management. I had seen the sad spectacle of successful company founders refusing to relinquish control even though their effectiveness had long since faded. Younger, more competent replacements became discouraged and left the company for lack of opportunity. That should not be allowed to happen at Pentair.

Accordingly, in 1978 I advised Pentair's management and directors that I would turn over CEO responsibilities to a successor in 1981, provided that Pentair had reached annual sales of about $250 million, that it had added a significant acquisition in the industrial-products business, and that there was a logical successor in place. By 1981 I would be 60 years old. I would have spent 15 years as the company's CEO, surely a longer period of time than a person could reasonably expect to be motivated, competent, and creative in any single job. By announcing my intention early, I hoped to eliminate surprise and to give management time to identify and to highlight promotion opportunities within and outside Pentair.

With the completion of the Porter-Cable acquisition, I reiterated my intent to step down as Pentair's chief executive and named Gene Nugent my choice as successor. Gene had been with the company for six years, five of those years as president. He was a highly skilled and principled executive, and he shared my commitment to the long-term health and growth of the company. I firmly believed that Gene was the right person for the job. Our board of directors agreed.

The formal announcement was made December 15 during a business and profit-planning meeting at our recently acquired Porter-Cable facility in Jackson. Beginning with the new year, Gene would be Pentair's president and CEO, while I would serve as chairman of the board.

Pentair acquired the Niagara, Wisconsin paper mill from Kimberly-Clark in
1972. The performance of Niagara of Wisconsin Paper Corporation (NOW), as
it was officially known, improved dramatically as employees responded
positively to Pentair's management style. Stronger demand for coated paper
resulted in a seller's market within a year.

Niagara executives in 1976 included (left to right): Bill Beerman, executive vice president; Tharlie Olson, senior vice president; and Ken Wallace, chairman and president.

Martin V. Ponzio, local union president at Niagara. The burly labor leader, known to all as "Pope," was fond of saying "We're all in the same canoe."

Niagara mill's main machine room with number 3 and number 4 paper machines.

The New Yorker magazine, long-time Niagara customer. New Yorker vice president Sam Spoto (left) and Tom Thomsen, Pentair vice president, review paper performance and discuss contract requirements.

Jim Winn, executive vice president and general manager (left), and Jim Grove, vice president, sales, led the Miami turnaround.

When D. Eugene (Gene) Nugent joined Pentair in 1975 as vice president for operations, he brought with him skills in planning, marketing, and external relations. He later became chairman and chief executive.

Awash in waste. The Miami paper mill was a pioneer in recycling wastepaper, and this greatly contributed to the success and profitability of its business.

*In addition to Murray Harpole and Gene Nugent (not pictured), the 1977
corporate management staff included (left to right): Richard Jost, Jim
Kaufenberg, Jack Grunewald, Gary Burwell, and Irene Roettger.*

Pentair's acquisition of Delta in 1984 was celebrated with the cutting of a wooden ribbon. Left to right: Larry Poe, Pentair executive vice president; Gene Nugent, Pentair CEO; Joe Collins, Delta president.

The product line of Delta, the number one producer of woodworking machinery in the United States, reflects unprecedented product innovation.

The Jackson, Tennessee location of Porter-Cable was home to the manufacturing, management, and service functions.

Pentair entered the paper business just as states were pressing for strict environmental regulation. The cost of compliance: $4.5 million for the Flambeau water treatment system.

John H. (Jack) Grunewald was hired as vice president for finance in 1977. He has made important contributions in finance, financial control, and investor relations and became chief financial officer for Pentair in 1981.

The 1980 board of directors included (left to right): Quentin Hietpas, Kenneth Wallace, Dr. John Baird, D. Eugene Nugent, George Butzow, Henry Conor, and Murray Harpole.

Chapter Eight

Expansion 1982-1984

By Pentair standards, 1982 was a relatively quiet year, with no acquisitions, divestitures, major takeover attempts, or other precipitous corporate developments.

Though the national economy remained soft, it was stronger than in 1981, and our sales and earnings rebounded accordingly. Pentair's gains were enhanced by a stronger market for Niagara's product and increased production resulting from a $10-million modernization of the mill's number three paper machine in 1981. Our new Porter-Cable subsidiary added modest profits on nearly $50 million in sales for the year. Net earnings got an additional boost from a 50-cent-a-share investment tax credit on the new power plant at Flambeau.

The relative calm of that year gave Gene and me the time and opportunity to further settle into our roles as chief executive and chairman, respectively. Our workload and streamlined corporate staff did not give us the luxury of a lot of fine-tuning or nitpicking as we worked out our new responsibilities, but we did smooth out some of the rough edges of the corporate transition we had set in motion at the end of 1981. I had proceeded with that transition without first having written formal job descriptions for the two top management positions, or for that matter, without extensive discussions about the specific responsibilities and authority that go with those jobs. Fortunately, our personal relationship was such that we could work out the details as we went along. The comparatively uneventful year helped by keeping distractions to a minimum.

My principal responsibilities as chairman were long-range planning, establishing and codifying corporate policy, developing strategy, and chairing meetings of the board. On a less formal level

I maintained my practice of visiting subsidiaries, talking with personnel at all levels of the organization, and staying in contact with the company's various constituents—keeping Gene and our supervisors informed in advance of such activities. I would turn over general management, operational policy-making, and shareholder and financial-community relations at an appropriate pace.

It did not take long, though, for the dynamics of the situation to become obvious. Despite our friendly and pragmatic relationship, Gene was trying to acquire as much power and authority as he could while I was stubbornly trying to hang on to it. For the first two or three months we gingerly danced around some issues, calmly discussed others, and heatedly debated still others. However, we were always able to lay our cards on the table and hash out our differences.

Sometimes our discussions included one or more of the company's directors, but we were careful not to distract or bother others in the organization. I did my best to restrain a temptation to dictate terms, and I made sure not to encourage operating personnel to go around Gene for information or decisions. Our operating personnel respected the need to work through the new channels of authority, and the board had both the tact and the good sense to let Gene and me work out our differences without undue interference. Everybody's goal was to ensure as smooth and effective transition as possible.

By year's end, Gene and I had established an effective working relationship under the new arrangement. Differences would arise from time to time, of course, and there continued to be strains and frustrations. But our comfort with each other and the new order of authority was such that we were always able to work things out for the greater good of the company.

I became more involved with some outside activities that I had steadfastly avoided during Pentair's developmental years: service club memberships, directorships at other corporations and charitable or civic organizations, service on advisory committees, fundraising, and so forth. For the first 15 years of the company's life, I felt these activities would take my eyes and mind off the job at hand. However, having begun to turn over day-to-day management responsibilities, I could look beyond our own corporate boundaries. Thus, in early 1982, I began to advise start-up companies and became active in Rotary International, the YMCA, various charities, Iowa State University (my alma mater), and other worth-while groups and causes.

Such outside activities did not become all consuming, by any means, but they did allow me to help repay society for some of the guidance and assistance I had received in the past. They also helped balance the time and attention directed toward Pentair, making the transition easier for both me and the company.

Our Niagara subsidiary continued its valued role as Pentair's primary profit contributor. At the same time, as competitive companies added to their own production capacity, we were seeing the end of the seller's market in coated groundwood paper. It became increasingly necessary to boost the levels of our capital investments to assure our standing in terms of both quality and quantity. Market pulp costs were a sufficiently pressing long-term concern that we seriously pursued the acquisition of the Marathon pulp mill, situated on the Ontario shore of Lake Superior, from American Can Company. We also investigated a joint venture with General Electric Credit Corporation in an alcohol process to obtain cellulose fibers from wood. Both initiatives were eventually dropped for economic or technical reasons.

The new, $21-million power plant at Flambeau, the largest single capital investment Pentair had made to date, began service in October. Financed in part by solid-waste disposal bonds and a lease-back arrangement, the plant would assure the Flambeau mill of adequate process steam and help contain our energy costs. Gene proposed and the board concurred that I be recognized by having the new facility designated the Murray J. Harpole Power Plant. The facility's dedication luncheon and ceremony on October 18, 1982, was attended by 120 persons, including my wife, my mother, and two of my children and their families. That was a very thoughtful honor; I could not help but feel almost embarrassingly pleased.

Meanwhile, the integration of the new Porter-Cable subsidiary proceeded smoothly, which spoke well of our due diligence prior to its acquisition, the cooperation from Rockwell, and the compatibility and cooperative competence of the Porter-Cable and Pentair organizations. That first year as part of Pentair, Porter-Cable exceeded plan in both sales and earnings despite a soft market. (Housing starts, a traditional indicator of the strength of the electric power-tool market, were at their lowest point in several years.) That initial success bolstered our confidence in the Porter-Cable name and reinforced our belief that Pentair could compete in industrial products as well as in paper.

At our annual meeting of shareholders in April, H. William Lurton, CEO of Jostens, Inc., was elected to our board of directors. Bill's election was especially significant to me. I had looked up to Jostens since I was in high school. One of the Minneapolis-based company's salesmen had made a strong impression on me when I was purchasing a class ring. Now we had on our board that company's chief executive, a man of exemplary qualities in both business and the community. Bill replaced Dr. John Baird, a former vice president for research at Control Data Corporation, who died in August 1981.

Following an extended recruiting effort, Larry Poe was hired in September 1982 as executive vice president for operations. Larry's hiring not only filled a key opening in the company's new management structure but added another experienced manager to our corporate staff. As part of the recent management transition, we were already beginning to think ahead to our succession needs when Gene would reach retirement age in 10 years.

At the beginning of the year, our immediate concerns about the management transition had been accommodated and were behind us. While making the change in our leadership structure, we were also changing the very nature of the company, becoming an industrial products manufacturer as well as a paper-maker. Financially, our cash flow was strong and our debt-to-total-capital ratio was below 20 percent.

We could not only look back on a strong year, but look forward to continuing growth in both sales and profits.

But no two years are alike, and 1983 was anything but a tranquil year. In fact, 1983 was highlighted by greatly increased acquisition activity, another significant sale of common stock, and the divestiture of one of our long-standing subsidiaries.

Overall performance during the first half of the year was slower than the previous year's, but as the national economy grew healthier, our sales and earnings gathered steam, too, with sales, earnings, and earnings per share all exceeding 1982 levels by year-end. Net sales for 1983 were more than $300 million, and earnings were nearly $12 million. We declared a 25-percent common stock dividend in November. Niagara continued to lead the way, enjoying a greatly improved market, and Porter-Cable made hearty advances in both sales and profitability in part on the strength of aggressive new-product introductions. Looking ahead, we believed it increasingly probable that Pentair sales would break the $1-billion mark by 1990.

We considered more than 100 different acquisition prospects during 1983. One of the first was the Lynchburg Foundry Company (LFC) of Lynchburg, Virginia, which was being divested by the Mead Corporation at a selling price of about $50 million. LFC was a large, modern foundry annually selling about $120 million worth of gray and ductile iron castings to industrial giants such as Ford, Chrysler, Cummins, and Caterpillar. As such, LFC was viewed as a highly desirable addition to our industrial-products business. We eagerly proceeded with our due diligence and negotiated what we believed was a winning offer comprising both cash and a limited number of Pentair shares. However, much to our dismay, the Mead board of directors decided, for technical reasons we found questionable, to sell to another bidder.

Despite the disappointment, what we had learned about LFC's business intrigued us enough to look closely at three other foundries over the following several months. The more we looked, the more we became convinced that LFC was probably a one-of-a-kind opportunity. The U.S. foundry industry was in serious trouble on account of foreign imports, pollution-control pressures, and a reduced demand for castings. In fact, none of the three foundries we looked at after LFC appeared to be sound long-term investments. We concluded that we would not be adding a foundry to our businesses in the foreseeable future.

Foundries were not the only operations we investigated in 1983. While working on the LFC deal, the Port Huron Paper Company also became a serious acquisition candidate. Gordon Morseth, the company's president, reluctantly introduced the subject to Gene and me at a breakfast meeting during the American

Paper Institute convention in New York City. Five years earlier we had talked to Port Huron about acquisition or affiliation. At that time, the interest was not strong enough on either side to reach an agreement on values. An old-line paper manufacturer based in Port Huron, Michigan, the company had, since our 1978 discussions, acquired an older tissue-paper mill in Detroit. The company also owned a small paper-converting operation in Leitchfield, Kentucky, and was in the process of setting up a similar facility in Los Angeles.

In 1983 as in 1978, Port Huron's performance was on the decline, and the company was unable to obtain the capital necessary to stay competitive in its businesses. This posed a difficult problem for the 100-year-old publicly owned company, much of whose stock was controlled by local families going back two or more generations.

From Pentair's perspective, acquiring Port Huron posed several sizable problems. Despite our familiarity with the company, we needed to know much more about its current operations and prospects. Furthermore, acquiring a public company through a tender offer and merger would be more complicated than the cash acquisitions we had made up to that point. Of still greater importance was the question of whether we should be thinking seriously about buying the operation in the first place. Our management and board of directors had difficulty reaching a consensus.

Port Huron's annual sales were about $110 million at the time, which meant that despite its age, it was still a fairly large-scale player in its segment of the industry. Nonetheless, there were several sticking points when considering its acquisition. One was that the company was wholly dependent on market pulp as a fiber source, which ran counter to Pentair's objective of being at least 50 percent self-sufficient in its fiber supply. Other such points included Port Huron's high energy costs, expensive pollution control concerns, significant capital-expenditure requirements, and growing need to develop new products and markets to replace its fading primary product, one-time carbonizing paper.

These serious concerns were eventually offset by the belief that Port Huron's unique capability to produce high-quality lightweight papers could be successfully applied to new paper grades, which, when combined with an expansion and upgrading of facilities under Pentair management, would create a profitable new subsidiary. Thus, Pentair decided in late August to acquire Port Huron through a tender and merger agreement by which we would pay 0.65 Pentair common shares for each Port Huron share tendered; we would pay cash to those Port Huron stockholders who chose not to tender their shares. The total purchase price was $15.6 million, which included the market value of 540,000 Pentair shares plus our additional commitment to assume Port Huron's long-term debt of $15.7 million. The merger was completed October 17, 1983.

Once Port Huron was formally part of the Pentair family, we named Jim Winn the subsidiary's president and general manager, replacing the former manager who had reached retirement age. We also initiated meetings with employees, customers, and suppliers, making it a point to assure one and all of our commitment to the business and its various constituents. We would still have to negotiate a new labor contract, but other than that, our immediate concerns there were straightforward and familiar, and Port Huron's assimilation went ahead as smoothly as could be expected.

As we were adding Port Huron to the corporation, we were preparing to divest one of our long-time subsidiaries, Conserve Industries.

Conserve had been a continuing source of concern among investors and financial analysts. It offered steady, if unspectacular, profit with precious little bother. However, on the downside we had not been able to substantially expand its business, and as Pentair grew larger, Conserve became a relatively small unit. Because of this, we were not providing the business the attention and support it deserved. Thus, in 1983 we decided to divest. After discussions with several potential buyers, we finally sold the business to its president and general manager, Ernest Roberg, in partnership with one of his larger customers. Ernie was a member of the family from whom we had bought it in 1972. The sale price amounted to slightly more than book value, and we retained possession of a tract of land associated with the original purchase. The transaction was closed October 18, 1983.

While never a very large component of Pentair's business, Conserve played an important role in the corporation's development, so it pleased me to see the operation continue successfully under its new ownership. The divestiture was a satisfactory outcome to that chapter of the Pentair story.

In September 1983 I submitted to our board of directors the draft of a policy statement that would prohibit any Pentair executive from continuing in office beyond the age of 65.

The statement codified my belief that companies were ill-served by founders and other top-level officers who stayed in office too long. Pentair would have the competent, creative, and committed leadership it required only if there was meaningful opportunity for advancement within its executive ranks. I felt that opportunity would be defined and enhanced by a formal policy dictating the retirement of its senior officials. The board accepted the statement and adopted it without substantial change in January 1984. Among other benefits, the new policy allayed any lingering concerns about the sincerity of my intentions and added a further degree of certainty to the management transition we had already initiated.

The workload during 1983 had been such that Gene and I shared much of the responsibility and authority in acquisition and divestiture negotiations and other key company business. I was comfortable with Gene taking a leading role in business investigations and decisions, especially in view of the fact that Gene, more than I, would have to live with the long-term consequences.

Yielding more and more authority to Gene was made easier by the new retirement policy and our good personal relationships, but it was never an entirely simple or painless proposition. I was sometimes surprised by my irritation regarding even some relatively minor items. Differences in management styles, in employee relations, in expenditures and allotment of time—at one point or another all of those things angered and frustrated me and sometimes led to heated exchanges with Gene. Intellectually, I knew that there would always be different ways to doing the job and that one way (his) could be just as effective as another (mine). But emotionally those differences were extremely difficult to accept, and at times even small things contributed to a stressful environment.

Slowly, I learned to accept the various differences, but my concerns about those differences would never entirely disappear.

Among the many acquisition possibilities we considered in 1983, one of the most desirable prospects was Rockwell's stationary power-tool business. The business was a logical complement to the portable power-tool operation we had purchased from Rockwell in 1981, and it would add more than $100 million in annual sales to our industrial-products diversification.

As a matter of fact, we had informally discussed purchasing the stationary business when we were negotiating for Porter-Cable. But, at that time Rockwell was not quite ready to sell, and we were reluctant to take on another industrial-products operation until we had assimilated the first one. In addition, Rockwell's stationary business included a large factory in Brazil, where unstable politics, a volatile economy, and a high inflation rate posed constant problems.

However, by January 1984, Rockwell was ready to sell its stationary tool operation. For our part, we had more than two years of experience with Porter-Cable and had become more comfortable with the idea of doing business in Brazil. Because of our congenial relationship with Rockwell officials, discussions proceeded swiftly (Rockwell negotiated exclusively with us), and in mid-January we signed a letter of intent to purchase the available business. A definitive agreement was signed April 2, and the deal was closed April 12. In exchange for the $45-million purchase price (which included the lease of some equipment), Pentair added more than 1,400 new employees, as well as facilities in four U.S. locations and in Canada and Brazil. The acquisition also doubled our industrial-products business to roughly $200 million a year, or one-third of our total corporate enterprise.

Our friends at Rockwell, tough but fair negotiators, were again very helpful both during and after the acquisition. Among the kindnesses shown was the availability of the Rockwell jet, which allowed us to meet very quickly with the business's scattered employees and thus help minimize the uncertainties and concerns that always accompany an ownership change. In addition, we needed to integrate the facility as swiftly as we could into Pentair processes and procedures and to implement a capital-investment program that would upgrade its facilities. We also expedited engineering and development work on product-design improvements and product-line expansion.

As we had after the Porter-Cable acquisition, we decided to change the name of both the business and the product line. The product line included table saws, band saws, drill presses, jointers, planers, and sanders. Those basic products had been part of the Delta Manufacturing Company prior to its acquisition by Rockwell, and there was still a lot of good will toward the Delta name. Thus, we renamed the entire business (established, like our other businesses, as a wholly owned subsidiary) the Delta International Machinery Corporation and called the basic product line Delta. Canadian operations would be known as the Beaver Delta Machinery Corporation, while in Brazil we would be Invicta-Delta. Pentair now owned the largest U.S. manufacturer of general purpose woodworking machinery, plus substantial operations both north and south of the U.S. border.

As at Porter-Cable, we benefitted by acquiring an experienced management team. The Delta team included Joe Collins, whom we named president of the Delta subsidiary. Joe came out of a finance background with career experience in several management areas at Delta. He was young, eager, and challenged by the opportunity to master all phases of the business. The result of Joe's appointment has been continuing growth in sales and profitability as he has expanded markets and product offerings while applying excellent general management and marketing direction.

Our new business in Brazil, while comparatively small, posed special challenges right from the beginning. Though we had to be cautious, we could not waste time making the capital investments deemed necessary. We minimized our exposure to currency exchanges and devaluation, aided by the fact that Invicta's products were transferred into our United States distribution at a nominal price above cost. This allowed us to realize earnings in U.S. dollars as we went ahead with our improvements.

Operating in the Brazilian economy was interesting. We had to give our local employees pay raises every week to compensate for inflation. We maintained a bank on the factory premises so employees could deposit their checks as soon as they received them and begin drawing interest as a means of curtailing inflationary losses. Our Brazilian workers were accustomed to their wild economy and performed well under the circumstances. The Invicta operation was generally successful for the next several years, despite significant economic and political problems that made doing business there always unpredictable, often frustrating, and occasionally downright unnerving.

———————

Over the previous several years, Pentair had achieved a lion's share of its growth through the acquisition of businesses that were underperforming for their previous owners. While the results of those acquisitions spoke for themselves, Gene and I, by the early 1980s, increasingly wanted the chance to build a business from scratch. The only opportunity we could realistically identify was a new paper mill. After all, papermaking was the business in which we were most firmly established.

In late 1983 we commissioned an engineering firm to study the feasibility of adding a new paper machine, associated buildings, and support facilities adjacent to our mill in Niagara, Wisconsin. Completed in May 1984, the study suggested that a competitive-sized, state-of-the-art paper machine and accompanying facilities would cost more than $400 million. Although only an estimate, the figure was greater than we could finance, and, to the relief of our bankers, we dropped the project from further consideration. Still, the investigation of such a project added to our knowledge of design and cost, and it by no means dampened our desire to build something from the ground up somewhere, sometime.

Then in mid-1984 we were contacted by the economic development staff of the city of Duluth, Minnesota, who urged us to consider building a new paper mill on the city's West End. On August 22, Gene Nugent, Ron Kelly, Tharlie Olson (senior vice president, paper group), and I drove to Duluth to investigate the idea. A meeting at city hall with Mayor John Fedo and his staff was also attended by representatives of Minnesota Power Company. Minnesota Power, based in Duluth, was represented at the meeting for reasons of civic responsibility and because it had an interest in enhancing its electric-power service area. We listened to their proposals, visited the proposed site, and returned home to analyze the situation.

The city would make available a tract of land not currently in productive use and provide both limited financial support and favorable financing guarantees. Intrigued by the idea, we duly investigated the possibilities, but we decided that the job of financing such a project, even with community help, was more than we could handle. Representatives from Duluth made a follow-up visit to our offices, and late in the year Minnesota Power tentatively suggested a joint venture. But for the time being, the prospect was dead.

Later in the year we were approached again, this time by the Prince Albert Pulp Company of Prince Albert, Saskatchewan. The company produced market pulp for the paper industry, and we were that mill's largest single customer. Now its owner, the Saskatchewan provincial government, sought to turn it over to private operators and coincidentally increase employment in the region. As a first step in that process, the government wanted to recruit a partner to build a new paper machine next door to the pulp mill.

As a major customer, we had visited the Prince Albert facility on several occasions. It was a solid operation, and the proposed plan was interesting in its own right. By that time we knew the costs involved in building such a paper machine, and by sharing those costs with the Canadian government we could reasonably expect to accommodate the financing. So, working with Canadian representatives through the first few months of 1985, we seriously investigated the possibilities. Our study suggested that we make a supercalendered grade of paper that was becoming increasingly popular for newspaper advertising inserts throughout the United States and Canada. Further, the machines necessary to make such a grade of paper were readily available from Europe, where the paper grade had been developed. We established the preliminary design for a suitable facility.

Unfortunately, as the project progressed, it became increasingly difficult to work out a satisfactory relationship with our prospective Canadian government partners. Their thinking was dominated by political concerns, with issues involving jobs and regional social needs, while the need to run a profitable business was secondary. Eventually, our talks broke down, and we all agreed the timing for such a venture was not right.

From our point of view, the study and discussions had not been a waste of time. We came away with a solid sense of the kind of paper machine we would want to procure if and when we went ahead with a new plant and the market that plant should serve. Furthermore, we were convinced that with an equity partner we could secure the necessary financing and build a world-class mill.

It was ironic that while we explored one new paper-making prospect after another in 1984, I was increasingly troubled by the outlook for our existing paper businesses.

To all appearances, we were doing nicely, owing largely to the continued positive performance at Niagara. In fact, though, our other paper subsidiaries were not performing very well. The first half of 1984 had been reasonably good, but the last half was battered by a deteriorating market. After our first two years of ownership, Flambeau had become a highly cyclical operation with an overall marginal performance. To make matters worse, the plant needed significant capital improvements to remain competitive in its appropriate markets. For its part, Port Huron required capital improvements and product-development activity at a rate faster than we had anticipated. Even taking those improvements into account, its short-term profit outlook was modest at best. Meanwhile, at Miami our ongoing program of capital investment, organizational improvements, and product-mix upgrades resulted in small, gradual profitability gains. But labor relations at the Miami plant eventually overwhelmed everything else.

There seemed to be several causes. Many of the plant's employees were from coal-mining families, whose experience with management had been historically bitter. Many had only limited schooling, relative to our workers at other locations. In the meantime, their international union representatives had their own agendas that were directed more toward personal advancement than toward the good of either the company or work force. In any case, Pentair had not been effective in dealing with Miami's restive workers, and our negotiating stance was becoming more emotional and confrontational. During the second half of 1984, we were trying to renegotiate changes in a two-and-a-half-year-old contract we had hammered out following the nine-week strike of 1981. We were unable to get the union's support for those changes, and the inability to come to terms on the issues made a bad relationship even worse. Divestiture was discussed as an alternative. We had to close, fix, or sell the mill.

Disturbed as I was by its immediate prospects, I was opposed to selling only Miami. Its performance was at least as good as or even better than Port Huron's and Flambeau's, and it did not require nearly as much in the way of new capital improvement. The biggest problem involved our relationship with labor, and we could surely find a way to straighten out that relationship. I believed that Miami could and should be both a productive facility and a desirable place for people to work. It was neither.

The paper business had been good to Pentair; indeed, it had been the foundation on which the company had developed into a major American corporation. Furthermore, I found the paper business fascinating and enjoyed the people who worked in it. For the year 1984, sales were $390 million in our paper group and $156 million in our industrial group. Now, however, we questioned the suitability of the business, or at least some parts of it. More and more I viewed the problem as one of corporate culture. Paper and industrial businesses required different management philosophies, attitudes, and styles. I saw a growing shift of emphasis within our management team from paper to industrial products. Of course, there were basic differences between the two businesses. Paper mills were in a process industry producing commodity products. They required large and ongoing capital investments regardless of the short-term profit outlook. Its practices and procedures were unique to a process industry. On the other hand, industrial-product manufacturing produced more proprietary goods and was far less capital-intensive; its practices and procedures differed widely from those of the paper business. Moreover, the paper business was cyclical, with dramatic fluctuations in profitability; industrial products were steadier and more predictable. Such differences were difficult to reconcile.

If anything, our management was biased by interest and experience toward industrial products. What troubled me, though, was the belief that we could succeed in any business only if we ran it with a total, wholehearted commitment. After giving the matter a lot of thought, I concluded that the piecemeal sale of our paper business was not the appropriate response to the challenges we faced. At the same time, I questioned whether Pentair was either large enough or integrated well enough into the paper industry to achieve a competitive return on investment. I was concerned, too, that Pentair could not overcome the cultural differences and successfully manage a paper business and an unrelated business under the same corporate structure. In short, I had come to believe that we should sell our paper operations in toto. Such a sale would not only provide the company with the greatest long-term benefits but would also be in the long-term best interests of our paper business employees and other stakeholders. The proceeds could be used to significantly strengthen and expand our industrial products business, reduce debt, and pay a special dividend.

Late in 1984 I discussed these thoughts with Gene and informally with each of our directors. Such a divestiture would be a major event for Pentair and its planning would have to be thoroughly developed. The directors did not oppose further development of the plan. I scheduled a meeting for early 1985 with the CEO of a major paper company who had previously expressed interest in our paper businesses and who would respect my confidence. Meanwhile, Gene and I continued to talk about the matter; he did not share my concern about Pentair's future in paper. Since I would be retiring in little more than a year, he was eager to have the opportunity to continue the successful development of both of the company's business areas.

Respecting his enthusiasm and commitment, I agreed to stop our divestiture discussions. I supported his efforts to develop the paper business and did not bring up the matter of divestiture at the scheduled meeting with the paper company CEO, which Gene and I both attended.

———————

My relationship with Gene continued to evolve as we became more accustomed to our respective roles. We still got on each other's nerves from time to time, as Gene was eager for more power and authority than I was yet willing to yield, but our differences did not derail our day-to-day compatibility.

Major staffing concerns required our attention. We needed to recruit candidates for the executive vice president and chief operating officer's post. Larry Poe, whom we had hired for the job, did not prove to have the compatible management style required for Pentair's long-term best interests, and Larry was given the role of senior vice president for industrial operations. The EVP-COO's position was particularly sensitive, because the person who held that job would be groomed to fill the chief executive's job when Gene retired. We wanted to be certain to get the right person in place. At the same time, we were recruiting a vice president for human resources. We needed a seasoned individual, someone who could bring us a new, less confrontational approach to labor relations as well as handle the ever-increasing demands in benefits, pensions, training, organizational development, and other matters related to a growing corporation. In view of the importance and sensitivity of these positions, for the first time we made use of an industrial psychologist.

During that time Gene, the management team, and I expanded, formalized, and submitted for the board's approval the Pentair Code of Business Conduct that I had originally written for our 1980 annual report. The board approved the code in July, and in January 1985 it was officially published.

The code simply documented the way of doing business that had evolved through experience and practice over the previous 18 years. The philosophies, policies, and practices we had established during the company's development were sound and resulted in a successful and respected corporation. To assure that those policies and procedures were followed by our steadily growing organization in the years ahead, we decided they needed to be set down on paper. By officially codifying the "rules," we not only provided for their continuity but also gave our employees, suppliers, customers, and other constituents the stated means against which to measure our ongoing performance. The code would tell the world what it should expect of Pentair, now and in the future.

As problem-plagued as it seemed at times, 1984 turned out to be yet another year of record financial performance. Net sales of $545 million were up a whopping 71 percent over those of the previous year, while our net earnings of $21 million were 78 percent ahead of the last year's number.

A large share of the credit for those improved figures was due to the past five years of capital improvements, which totaled more than $115 million. Capital improvements in 1984 alone were $36 million. Credit was also due to the continued strong performance at Niagara and the contributions of our newest subsidiaries, Port Huron and Delta. Despite the two acquisitions, aggressive capital investments, and mediocre performance at Miami and Flambeau, we were pleased to be able to retain a very strong balance sheet.

Taking the long view of our situation, at the end of 1984 I had no doubt that our expanding volume, increasing diversification, and forthright management decisions were combining to make Pentair a stronger and better company.

Chapter Nine

Satisfaction 1985-1986

My retirement at the age of 65 had been firmly established when, in January 1984, our board of directors formally approved the retirement policy I had proposed the previous September. My plan was to step down as Pentair's chairman on July 6, 1986, exactly 20 years after the company's founding. Besides the anniversary significance, a July 6 retirement would allow me four months to tie up loose ends prior to my leaving as a company employee on my 65th birthday October 31.

It was important to articulate my retirement plans well in advance of the actual event and to announce that Gene Nugent would succeed me as corporate chairman. Surprise is often the bane of corporate decision making, and this announcement was intended to assure that no one would be caught off guard by an unexpected management transition. At our periodic visits with the investment community beginning in the spring of 1985, I made it a point to state my plans and to give Gene a greater role in those meetings. The planned changes were also announced at key employee meetings at our annual meeting of shareholders in April, and to both the local and financial press. Well before my retirement was a fait accompli, the decision was widely known and accepted.

It was now important to do those things that would facilitate Gene's move into the role of corporate leadership. Because I was the founder and long-time chairman, many people in the organization still looked to me for advice and direction; in fact, that reliance had continued even after Gene had taken over the chief executive's role. I had made an earnest and significant effort to transfer authority and responsibility, but it had been more difficult than I had expected. I had become accustomed to thinking of the company as mine.

However, once we had gone public with our transition plans, the situation clarified itself. People within and outside the company now knew that I was retiring and that Gene would become chairman in July 1986. I dropped out of meetings and decision making and gave Gene more room to operate on his own. I removed myself from a leadership role in matters where he would have responsibility long beyond my tenure; for example, negotiations regarding acquisitions and joint ventures, large capital-investment projects, executive recruitment, and investor relations. My role was increasingly one of coaching, advising, and assisting during the transition and making sure that essential policies were securely in place. It was also important to have enough outside activities to minimize free time and to help me avoid the temptation to meddle.

An immediate concern was for the future—specifically 1992, when Gene would retire. In view of our small number in the corporate office, it was important to plan for a successor and to have a supportive staff in place ready to lead the company through the 1990s. A nine-month recruiting effort brought us S.A. (Tony) Johnson, who was named president and chief operating officer in March 1985. Tony was a mechanical engineer with an MBA degree and marketing, operations, and general management experience that had led to a vice presidency of Cummins Engine Corporation and more recently the CEO's job at the Onan Corporation. He was intelligent, personable, and highly motivated; a great fit for the position at Pentair. That same month, Allan Kolles was hired as vice president for human resources. Al brought a wealth of experience in personnel management and benefit programs as well as a professional approach to employee relations and labor negotiations.

In addition to these two major management changes, the sudden death of director James Hoaglund on February 9, 1985 left a vacancy on our board that I wanted filled before my retirement. After Gene and I interviewed several candidates, James Thwaits, president of International Operations and Corporate Staff Services of the 3M Company, was recommended and elected to the board in October. Jim's appointment added a very experienced and objective member to an already competent board.

On another front, now that a long-term commitment to the paper industry had been affirmed, our efforts to find a way to build a new paper mill finally yielded success in 1985. We had maintained contact with the city of Duluth since our initial discussions in 1984. In May of 1985 Minnesota Power Company offered to participate with us in a joint venture to build a mill in the port city. Our first step was to investigate the possibility of bringing in a third partner. Unsuccessful discussions with Japanese and Norwegian firms led us to discard that idea. By now our two companies had developed mutual respect and compatibility such that we were ready to proceed without additional help. On May 14, Pentair formally abandoned further consideration of the project in Prince Albert, Saskatchewan, and decided to go ahead with one in Duluth. In early June, Pentair and Minnesota Power agreed on a memorandum of understanding to proceed as equal partners in the venture. By the end of the month, we agreed to invest $1.5 million each in a wide-ranging feasibility study that, if it proved positive, would lead to a definitive pact.

One of our primary concerns was the availability of suitable wood supplies to make the grade of supercalendered paper we wanted to produce in a new facility. The particular paper was at that time produced in Europe using European wood species. As part of our feasibility study, we airlifted North American logs to Finland, where the wood was processed by the pulp-making machinery we intended to purchase. The groundwood pulp was then transported to Germany and processed on a pilot plant paper machine like the one we planned to buy. The results of that part of the study were positive. It would be possible to proceed using domestic wood supplies.

We also assembled a task force comprising engineering and technical personnel from our existing paper mills and put them together with Minnesota Power specialists in large-facility construction. That group, with corporate staff from both partners, worked with engineers from Rust Engineering Company of Birmingham, Alabama. These consultants, who had done much of the early research into a new facility, confirmed costs and technical features.

By early October 1985, the overall feasibility of the project was established to our joint satisfaction. On October 21 we made the official announcement: Pentair, Inc., and Minnesota Power Company would engineer, construct, and operate a paper-manufacturing facility in Duluth. The new business would be called Lake

Superior Paper Industries, Inc. (LSPI). The project task force, headed by Ron Kelly, vice president for corporate development, estimated the cost of the new plant at $400 million and set the target date for the mill to be up and running at December 15, 1987, only two years away.

As we planned to begin a new venture, we also divested one of our businesses in 1985.

Our acquisition of the Port Huron Paper Company in 1983 included its Huron Office Products Division, which we included in our industrial-products group. Though we had made capital investments in this office-products business and it was profitable, it neither controlled a large share of its market (business forms, memo pads, carbon paper, etc.), nor fit very well with our other industrial activities. Thus, we were receptive to discussing a sale after receiving an unexpected call in January 1985 from Francis Guiliano, CEO of the Ampad Corporation, expressing interest in the business.

By April, following weeks of frustrating negotiations, we had worked out a deal whereby Ampad would purchase Huron Office Products for $13 million, or slightly more than book value. With Ampad's position in the office-products market, we felt the sale was logical for everyone.

Labor relations reached the crisis point at our Miami subsidiary in 1985. We were no longer able to generate a meaningful profit at the Miami mill, and the outlook was so poor it discouraged the initiative and the capital investments necessary to achieve competitive operations. The mill had to be fixed, closed, or sold. Fixing the situation required first establishing a total work environment that provided for competitive productivity. We chose to try this and, in so doing, unknowingly set the stage for a new work force and a management-employee relationship that would eventually provide satisfaction, productivity, and benefits beyond all expectations.

Our labor contract at Miami expired in April 1985, ending the three and a half year agreement whose wages, work practices, and medical benefits had put us in a noncompetitive position in the industry. From time to time during that period, we had negotiated minor modifications in the contract terms and delayed wage increases as a means of controlling costs, but those steps only exacerbated our ongoing problems with the union. However, we had no doubt that we had to have a new contract that would make us more competitive. More important, we needed improved work practices and relationships.

At that time we were paying our Miami workers wages that compared very favorably with those of our competitors. We were also one of the few companies in the region, if not the only one, to provide fully paid medical benefits. Still more troublesome were the work practices and rules, which were truly killing us. For example, under the existing practices and rules, the facility was over-staffed to assure continuous coverage of all tasks. No task, no matter how small or short term, could be handled by any worker whose job description did not include that task. In the event of an equipment failure, work would stop until the proper worker was found to fix it; if such a worker was not on the premises, an off-duty worker had to be located and called in following a complex procedure involving seniority, previous overtime assignments, and job classification. It did not matter if the equipment problem could be resolved by a minor adjustment or repair—the rules were the rules.

Such practices and rules had been developed over the course of many years (and at least two different owners). Low productivity and poor quality as well as continual conflict among employees and between management and the union was the result. Formal grievances, most of them petty, were filed at a rate of about one per day and their resolution often took several months. Most of the problems involved negative and counterproductive attitudes, prejudices, and a lack of confidence and trust. Sometimes the problems were made worse by our own increasingly confrontational posture. In any event, we sincerely believed that the survival of the plant was at stake and that the problems were creating severe strains on the entire corporation.

Negotiations on a new contract continued beyond the April 5 expiration date to July 8, at which point we had reached an impasse. Under the law, we were able to implement a contract containing the terms on the table when the stalemate was reached. We believed those terms provided wages, benefits, and work practices that were competitive in the industry and appropriate to the effective operation of the plant. For its part, the union stayed on the job through the negotiations and under the terms of the implemented contract. Despite occasional interruptions, quality problems, and minor acts of sabotage, production was reasonably good during the period. Then, during the night shift of August 29, the union members of the work force, without notice, walked out on strike.

The plant was shut down in an orderly fashion perhaps signalling the workers' desire to protect the business and their expectation of a quick resolution. However, the union then filed a series of unfair labor practice charges with the National Labor Relations Board. The situation dashed hopes of a quick settlement and diverted time, money, and attention from resolving the issues. It was the most serious labor-related challenge in our experience.

As soon as the workers walked off the job, we implemented plans to resume production using supervisory and management personnel. The mill's long-term survival depended on holding on to our customer base, and the staff of management employees had maintained acceptable production during the previous strike. Again, we contracted with an outside security service to protect our employees and property. Unlike our previous experience at Miami, though, we anticipated a fairly long strike and believed that we would need to bring in additional employees at least on a temporary basis. Accordingly, we hired about 250 persons (about 3,000 had applied) to work under the terms of the implemented contract. Most of those workers had little or no experience in a manufacturing plant, but they were enthusiastic and eager to succeed at such good-paying jobs. Our need for some experienced papermakers and tradesmen was filled by trained workers recruited from around the country. Some of the latter required temporary housing and expenses while they worked for us.

When the strike began, the union was confident that we would not be able to carry on with unskilled and inexperienced workers. In fact, it was the conventional wisdom throughout the industry that an apprenticeship of many years was necessary for a new worker to become proficient in a paper mill. We discovered that with the diligent efforts of our management, supervisory staff, and recently recruited experienced papermakers, new employees picked up the requisite skills rather quickly. Of course, our training costs were high, but we were delighted by the rapid learning ability of the new work force.

We were losing as much as $750,000 a month at the plant during the strike, not a great deal more than we were losing during the months immediately preceding it. The market for Miami's product was depressed at the time, too, which further affected our performance. Still, customers gave us every opportunity to fill their requirements; clearly they wanted the plant to overcome its problems and continue on as a reliable source of quality paper.

As the strike ground on, the union's position hardened. Increasing acts of vandalism and violence intimidated and discouraged the new employees. The rough stuff continued for about six months, but it reached its most frightening point on October 30, when Odos Banks, the local union president, was arrested after purchasing 40 pounds of dynamite from an undercover agent. Banks was accused of planning to blow up part of the plant. He was later tried, convicted, and sentenced to several years in prison. As distressing as those incidents were, I do not know how they could have been prevented short of closing down the facility.

Despite the violence, negotiations continued with the assistance of a federal mediator until the middle of November. After an occasional hint of a breakthrough, the talks fell apart. We repeatedly requested that the strikers return to work, but at that point we decided to convert the temporary employees into a permanent work force and hire enough additional personnel to staff the mill in full. (About 10 percent of the plant's union employees applied for the permanent positions.) We were now operating with a nonunion work force, even though our obligations under the union contract would not be resolved for the next several months.

Inside the plant, management initiated an extensive training program that covered all aspects of running the facility, safety, maintenance, and quality. The esprit de corps and general enthusiasm of both the salaried staff and the new workers were both amazing and rewarding. Incredibly, within six months of the new group's hiring, the plant was producing the same amount of paper as it had before the strike but with 10 percent fewer workers. By the end of 1986, the plant was setting production records and achieving an unprecedented level of quality. Most important, Miami was now an exciting and satisfying place to work. As a matter of fact, as time passed and the union was decertified, many former employees came back to fill vacancies. Almost without exception, those "old" workers were swiftly integrated into the new work force and were genuinely surprised by how good a workplace Miami had become. They discovered a new flexibility in work assignments and a team concept that empowered each employee to handle several different tasks. It was an entirely different environment.

The plant's new and improved attitude and performance allowed us to continue to develop new grades of paper and resume significant capital investment. Three years down the line, the Miami facility showed operating earnings of $1.5 million a month! We had transformed the mill from an unpleasant to a pleasant place to work for all employees and made it a consistently profitable performer.

It was a great shame that transformation could not have been accomplished without the strife and the loss of work for so many good employees, but such are the costs of labor discord. The transformation was nonetheless one of the most gratifying experiences of my career.

———————

The merits of our diversification into industrial products became clear in 1985. Both Porter-Cable and Delta turned in strong performances for the year, while our uncoated-paper operations encountered tough going. Port Huron, Flambeau, and Miami were forced to slog through depressed markets, especially during the first half of the year. Thankfully, Niagara had another good year and was again the company's primary generator of profits. Overall sales and earnings were essentially flat in 1985, ending the year at about $535 million and $20 million, respectively. Capital expenditures totaled almost $60 million.

Our acquisition activity started strong that year. In March we sold $25 million in subordinated convertible debentures in anticipation of making another large industrial-products company purchase. However, the Lake Superior Products project and the Miami paper mill strike effectively disrupted the acquisition hunt.

On the advice of the investment bankers who helped us sell the convertible debentures, we took our road show for the first time to Europe in 1985, visiting France, Switzerland, England, and

Scotland. It was an interesting experience and we met with receptive audiences wherever we went, but I doubt the visit was very successful. We decided we would have to make periodic visits and cultivate relationships over the course of several years before we could expect significant understanding and financial support in Europe.

Meanwhile, on this side of the Atlantic, unfriendly takeover activity was reaching epidemic proportions. Raiders, speculators, and opportunists were taking over more and more companies for their quick personal gain, with little regard for the company or its stakeholders. The attempted takeover of Pentair four years earlier had been etched in my heart and mind, and I had been speaking out against the practice ever since. In 1985 we engaged the investment banking firm of Kidder Peabody to review our takeover defenses, to provide guidance as to the fair value of the company, and to advise us on shoring up our antitakeover position. That same year my public statements against hostile takeovers led to a debate with Irwin Jacobs, a Minneapolis-based businessman who had developed a considerable reputation as a corporate raider. The debate was part of an economic/business conference for journalists sponsored by the College of St. Thomas in St. Paul. I was not conditioned for the management-bashing rhetoric of a corporate raider. I did point out that within three years following each of the three takeover attempts at Pentair, our shareholders had more than doubled the value of any premium offered by the raider and the company continued to grow thereafter. A few months after the debate, I became a charter member of the Stakeholders of America, an organization that counted among its members several CEOs of major American corporations who wanted to curb the abuses of hostile takeovers. The group's purpose was to educate the business community and the public in the dynamics and results of the takeover phenomenon and to lobby state and federal legislators on behalf of the antitakeover cause. I remained active in the group until its dissolution in 1989.

By 1985, Pentair was receiving regional as well as national recognition. Our participation in a plan to build a world-class paper mill in Duluth was hailed as a much-needed shot in the arm for an economically depressed part of Minnesota. *Fortune* magazine listed us as one of the 500 largest industrial corporations in America (440th, to be precise) based on our 1984 results. More important, the publication ranked us 199th in total investor return and 114th in return on equity. We had become a Fortune 500 industrial company in 18 years.

In 1985, I was honored by my induction into the Minnesota Business Hall of Fame. That award is given to four Minnesotans a year, citing them for their contribution to employment opportunities and economic and community development, as well as for their risk-taking, innovation, and ethical standards.

It was very flattering to receive the award as well as the congratulations and good wishes from friends and colleagues. The letters I received from each of the 19 pupils of Mrs. Blossom Romitti's fourth-grade class in Niagara, Wisconsin were among the most meaningful. Impressed by the several interesting ways the word "congratulations" could be spelled, I wrote to each of the students, which led in turn to an invitation to spend part of one school day sharing experiences with the combined fourth-grade classes, a rich and wonderful experience that I will not forget.

Although 1986 began like any other year, with a full complement of interesting and challenging activity, for me it would be the end of my formal involvement with the company I helped found. That alone made it a year unlike any other.

My attention turned toward the January board meeting that would set dividends and compensation, preparing the annual report and annual meeting of shareholders, securing additional financing for continued expansion, visiting subsidiary operations, evaluating capital projects, and further strengthening the company's defenses against unfriendly takeover attempts. I was continually aware that later in the year I would be turning over my activities to Gene.

Overall, 1986 was a challenging year for Pentair. The uncoated-paper market was recovering slowly from its recent doldrums. The market for one-time carbonizing paper declined faster than replacement grades could be developed. (We had already invested more than $35 million in new machinery and facilities at Port Huron, yet more would be required to restructure the mill for new paper-grade manufacturing.) At Miami, while reporting steady progress in the wake of the previous year's strike, we carried over a number of unfair labor practice charges and union lawsuits to wrestle with, besides the ongoing recruitment and training of a new hourly work force. Our Niagara mill continued to reign as the corporation's top profit-earner, but the mill experienced a lot of trouble because of poor performance on a major paper-machine rebuild.

As in 1985, our industrial-product subsidiaries provided a welcome counterbalance to paper. Porter-Cable and Delta were up once again in both sales and earnings. Our modest capital investments in those two businesses were showing healthy returns as both moved toward leadership positions in their respective industries with the introduction of several new products. (Delta's Canadian foundry, deemed uncompetitive and lacking much hope for improvement, was closed and later sold.)

Meanwhile, Pentair was being approached at least once a month with inquiries about selling out, going private, or otherwise changing its corporate control. Our policy remained unequivocal and our defenses were strong; still, the takeover environment was so hostile and abusive that we could not help but be concerned about the overtures and threats. The Kidder Peabody study commissioned in 1985 and reported to the board in early 1986 suggested our defenses were potent and up to date in all except a few areas.

One Kidder Peabody recommendation was to add a Shareholder Rights Plan, or poison pill, to our arsenal. The poison pill was relatively new at the time and being challenged in the courts, so we decided to await further rulings on its legality before adopting such a measure ourselves. Another recommendation was that Pentair change its state of incorporation from Minnesota to Delaware where stronger antitakeover laws were on the books. I was strongly opposed to the idea and was convinced that Minnesota's legislature was moving to improve the protection for corporations chartered in the state. The board of directors supported my point of view. Through the Stakeholders of America and other such groups, we were beginning to make headway against raiders and abusive takeover tactics.

Up in Duluth, we forged ahead with the LSPI project. The design and engineering work proceeded quickly in Rust Engineering's capable hands and groundbreaking was set for April 26. About a thousand persons showed up for the official public ceremony at the Duluth Arena. Minnesota Governor Rudy Perpich, Duluth Mayor John Fedo, and several other state and local dignitaries were among the guests. Although Pentair had been headquartered in Minnesota since its founding, the Duluth project was its first large-scale operation within the state's borders. For the first time the corporation was getting a lot of local recognition. Because the northeastern part of the state was suffering hard economic times, a major new operation like LSPI was more than a run-of-the-mill business-page story. It was front-page news.

While the engineering activities moved forward, we were busy putting together the project's financing package. By the time we broke ground in April, cost estimates for the facility had been confirmed at approximately $400 million. Only about $40 million of that amount would come from equity contributions from Minnesota Power and Pentair; the balance, about $360 million, would have to be financed. When the financing package was complete in late May, no fewer than 14 banks were participating.

Sticky problems remained even with the financing in hand. For one thing, soil conditions at the plant site were much worse than we thought. We discovered that we would have to drive roughly 150 miles of piling to support the structure—twice the amount we had planned. To make matters worse, a salvage operation had once occupied the site, and the soil had been tainted with PCBs and lead. We had been aware of the contamination from the start, however, the amount of contamination was worse in some places than we had feared.

The presence of an abandoned Chinese food-canning operation that occupied a portion of the construction site was another hitch. Though it had not been used for the past 20 years, the plant was still owned by the flamboyant former Duluth entrepreneur, Jeno Paulucci. We contacted Paulucci prior to committing to the project, and he expressed civic interest and feelings of cooperation and support in seeing that our paper-mill project move ahead as quickly as possible. After we had tied up $100 million in equipment purchases, he decided that maybe he would like to resume operations at the long-closed canning factory on the site. In light of those tentative plans, he determined the value of the factory to be about $25 million, though its appraised value was less than $500,000.

The Paulucci property was part of the 92 acres that were to be acquired by the city of Duluth under the right of eminent domain. Thus, Paulucci's dispute was with the city, not LSPI. But in the final analysis, LSPI would have to pay the cost of acquiring the property and would incur costly penalties if the proceedings were delayed. Because the old factory was located precisely where the new facility would be built, the building program itself would have to wait for the problem's resolution.

Litigation in the dispute progressed rapidly to the Minnesota Supreme Court, whose favorable ruling allowed work to proceed without more than a month's delay. But the matter did not end there. Paulucci launched a series of full-page newspaper advertisements arguing his case and initiated additional legal challenges to the project. It took four years and a payment of more than $3 million for the disputed plant site before the matter was finally settled. The episode was yet another reminder that there are a few bad apples in every bushel of business dealings.

————————

The acquisition of another large industrial-products business remained, through all the other developments of 1986, a high priority for us.

In March our efforts included hiring James Frank as vice president for corporate development, filling the post vacated by Ron Kelly, who was elected president of LSPI. In April we learned from Kidder Peabody that the McNeil Corporation, an old-line Akron, Ohio-based publicly held industrial company, might be available, and we authorized Kidder to explore the possibility on our behalf.

For many years McNeil had been very profitable in the manufacture of proprietary machinery for making bias-ply automobile tires. When the industry changed to the production of radial tires, the market for McNeil's bias-ply product collapsed. Though in a strong cash position, the company was ill-prepared to deal with such a major change in its business. Management's response was to acquire several unrelated businesses to replace lost tire-machinery sales, but none of the acquisitions performed very well. The new and competitive business environment stressed the company's management and its finances. Next, the company became the target of corporate raiders and was paying greenmail in an effort to buy off the raiders and retain control. Soon the company no longer had the financial or management strength necessary to continue as an independent company.

McNeil's chairman and CEO was Glenn Meadows, a career employee who had gained his management experience when times were very good and relatively easy. McNeil's executives had become accustomed to the good life, holding memberships in seven different country clubs and enjoying a plush company lodge in the Carolinas and two corporate aircraft. In fairness to Meadows, the lifestyle had been inherited from the previous management; in any case it was not very conducive to running a company that was fighting for its life.

Looking for another company to rebuild McNeil's business and protect the best interests of its employees and shareholders, Meadows and his staff were favorably impressed with the information they had received about Pentair from Kidder. They seemed to be particularly pleased with our Code of Business Conduct and our track record of dealing with acquired companies. With cordial feelings between us, due diligence and negotiations proceeded swiftly, and on July 21 the respective boards agreed on a tender offer to purchase McNeil's outstanding stock. On August 15, 1986, Pentair purchased the common shares and convertible subordinated debentures for $83 million in cash.

McNeil, now part of Pentair's industrial-products group, added annual sales of about $180 million in two principal businesses, Lincoln and F.E. Myers. Lincoln was a leading manufacturer of lubrication, lifting, and material-dispensing equipment for the industrial and automotive markets, with manufacturing facilities in Missouri, Arkansas, Canada, and West Germany. Myers, a 117-year-old company headquartered in Ashland, Ohio, produced water-system pumps, a variety of pumps and components for environmental systems, and a small line of industrial pumps. (The Myers operations also included a modern gray and ductile iron foundry.) A very small third business developed swimming-pool chemicals and equipment. Under Pentair, Lincoln and F.E. Myers were set up as two separate operating subsidiaries. The third business was sold, as were McNeil's lavish Akron headquarters, corporate airplanes, and Carolina lodge.

With the McNeil acquisition, Pentair had increased its industrial-products business to about $400 million a year, making it roughly equal in size to our paper business. McNeil had been an underperforming business with heavy overhead expenses and now provided us with another good opportunity to develop an excellent return on our investment.

———————

In April 1986 I presided over our annual meeting of shareholders for the final time, with a disquieting sense of my impending retirement. Looking over the crowd of more than 200 persons, I saw several who had purchased stock during our original offering back in 1966. Seeing those loyal supporters in the audience after 20 years of struggle and achievement gave me a great deal of satisfaction, and I was both touched and honored when the crowd accorded me a standing ovation at the conclusion of my remarks.

On July 6, 1986, exactly 20 years after the company's founding, I stepped down as chairman of the board. The directors gave me the title of chairman emeritus along with a bronze sculpture of 19th-century explorer, pioneer, and entrepreneur Joseph Nicollet and a formal statement of appreciation. As planned, Gene Nugent was elected Pentair's new chairman and would continue to serve as chief executive officer. Tony Johnson became president and chief operating officer.

During my remaining few months as a Pentair employee and as a director, I continued to take part in management meetings and decision making. I cannot say I was really needed to coach or assist Gene and our other top managers any longer; two years of transitional counsel had been sufficient. Now it was time for the new team to run the show, and for me to provide advice and support only when asked to do so. During those final months I finished documenting corporate policies and procedures, some of which had to deal with retirement. Since I was the first person to retire from corporate office at Pentair, new guidelines had to be formulated for that procedure, too.

Finally, on October 31, my 65th birthday, I officially retired as a Pentair employee (while continuing as a director). Gene kindly arranged for a gala banquet to mark the occasion, and more than 150 persons, including my wife and children, my mother, brothers, and sisters, and both corporate and subsidiary officials, were present. I felt both humbled and privileged by the attention.

For 20 years I had been living the American dream. I had lived the thrills and the satisfaction along with the hard work and frustrations of taking a company from nothing more than an idea to a major industrial corporation. Still, the measure of that dream was not yet complete. It was my belief, and it still is, that a successful, independent public company should continue in perpetuity and that every founder and chief executive is responsible for seeing that the company has the strength, direction, and management to carry on beyond the CEO's retirement. If the CEO has done the job well, the company should continue successfully for at least another five years. With that in mind, as a retiring founder I had to wait five years to know whether I had fulfilled the American dream and met its obligations.

I was confident that I was leaving Pentair as a stable, independent, and respected public company. That company had been profitable for the past 18 years; currently it was operating at an annual rate of $800 million in sales and $20 million in earnings, and there was plenty of potential yet to be realized. The company was satisfactorily diversified and employed some 7,000 persons in the United States and abroad. Its balance sheet boasted nearly $150 million in shareholder equity and $450 million in total assets.

Among other good things, Pentair was proof positive that the American private enterprise system could indeed work to everyone's advantage.

Chapter Ten

Carrying On 1987-1991

Though as of October 31, 1986, I was officially retired from Pentair as both an officer and employee, I had not separated myself from the company. I remained a member of the board of directors, chairing its Executive Committee and sitting on several other committees. I also retained the office and secretarial services the company generously provided me as chairman emeritus. True, the office was located out of the mainstream of management activity in our suburban St. Paul headquarters; but you cannot be too far away from the action in a command post that numbers fewer than 30 persons.

I could now look forward to nearly five years as a Pentair director before my official ties to the company would end. However, it is in writing about those last five years that I have experienced the greatest difficulty. While they are the freshest in my mind, they are also the most clouded and perhaps distorted by the emotional frustration of trying to serve as an objective, open-minded corporate director yet tending to think and feel as an operating executive. Accommodating that dichotomy was not easy for me; it must have been troublesome for Gene, too. My discomfort is undoubtedly evident in my discussion of the company's affairs. To the extent that I err through personal bias, I hope there is value in illuminating the dangers of a CEO and founder staying on too long.

I was determined to keep from interfering with the company's operations. I was retired, after all. But staying so physically and emotionally close to the action made that more difficult than I expected. While I had a sincere respect for Gene both as a chief executive and a human being, his way was different from my way; his management style and decision making were not mine. When we were working together, those differences produced compromise in the name of cooperation and congeniality. Now Gene had primary responsibility for and authority over the company's operations while I shared a constrained role with the other directors. I believe I have been successful in avoiding the temptation to meddle, but it has been tough watching my company (I still tend to think of it as my company) managed differently from the way I would manage it.

In retrospect, it would have been wise for me to physically remove myself from the operation and from the company's hometown itself. I thought hard about moving to another city, but at the time I had too many arguments against such a move. Of course, I was still keenly interested in Pentair's welfare. I felt a continuing responsibility to the company, having set it on its present course, and more than just an idle curiosity to see the results of my efforts. Finally, I was thinking about writing this book about Pentair's first 25 years, and I needed ready access to files and records. The board, mindful of our small corporate staff, had requested I be available to help out in case of emergency. So I stayed. With the benefit of hindsight, I recommend against such a decision to others in a similar position.

I immediately experienced physical separation. After retiring, Ruth and I took a month-long trip to sightsee and to visit friends in Illinois, Arkansas, Oklahoma, and Texas. The trip was my first extended absence from the company in 20 years, and we thoroughly enjoyed ourselves. At the same time, it was impossible to shake the sense that something very basic was missing from my life.

In December 1986 I took part in our annual business and profit-planning meetings and a meeting of our board of directors. It was odd, although not unpleasant, to be seated as a member of the board and not run the meetings. Management included me in some of their meetings through the end of the year and into the next. Gene and I continued to meet informally, often over breakfast or lunch, during the next several years, and while the meetings were infrequent, they were always open, candid, and free-wheeling.

During those early days of retirement, I took greater part in the outside activities I had begun during the past few years. I served on the boards of three small companies, a major trust company, and a variety of civic, charitable, and educational institutions. I also continued to speak publicly on the evils of hostile takeovers and to play an active role in the Stakeholders of America organization. Ruth and I traveled frequently, visited relatives and friends, took in the sights, and indulged in the thrill of downhill skiing.

Any thought that I remained in a preferred position as chairman emeritus, however, was summarily dispelled in March 1987.

Pentair had incurred about $60 million in additional debt when it acquired the McNeil Corporation in 1986, and its debt-to-equity ratio had increased to about one-to-one. The ratio did not seem uncomfortably high to me. We had always found ways to work out of large debt, and the lower equity offered the benefits of a good return for our shareholders while reducing our attractiveness as a takeover candidate. There had been a brief discussion of a $25-million equity offering at a board meeting in January, but the discussion concluded with a consensus that such an offering was neither necessary nor desirable.

Then, one afternoon in March, Gene called me in Montana where I was visiting my daughter and enjoying some skiing. He had scheduled a board meeting two days hence for the purpose of authorizing the immediate sale of $50 million of preferred stock. Management concluded that we needed the additional equity and should act while the price of our shares was strong. Our earnings outlook was slipping, and we needed to act fast to take advantage of the market. Delaying the board meeting might interfere with Pentair's participation in an upcoming American Paper Institute convention in New York.

I was not able to return home before the afternoon of the meeting day, and I was disturbed by what seemed a precipitous action and an unwillingness to accommodate my schedule. I felt totally frustrated. I had no information with which to develop anything but a negative opinion on the offering issue, and I could not return in time to attend the meeting. My feelings were decidedly hurt.

Two days later, the board, in my absence, approved the authorization of two-million convertible preferred shares at $25 a share. This drove home the fact that I no longer exercised any real control. While the experience caused me some long-standing re-sentment and suspicion, it is a good indicator of the extreme sensitivity I had to the loss of operating control.

———————

Pentair achieved record sales and earnings in 1987, without my active involvement. The company's results were bolstered by a full year's contribution from our Lincoln and F.E. Myers subsidiaries acquired in the McNeil Corporation purchase. Meanwhile, our paper businesses encountered soft markets and some operating problems during the first half of the year but recovered nicely during the second. Porter-Cable and Delta performed well all year.

In September 1987 Pentair divested its Port Huron Paper Cor-poration subsidiary for approximately book value. Port Huron had not been a good acquisition; it had never overcome the problems that predated its acquisition, and it had contributed only marginal profits at best to Pentair. The subsidiary's major facility in Port Huron, Michigan, was sold to a Canadian paper company; its smaller Detroit mill was sold separately to Kapaco Group, Inc. six months later.

We were continuing to grow as we moved into 1988, but the additional equity increased the difficulty of earning satisfactory returns on investment and gains in earnings per share. Our board had approved a Shareholder Rights Plan, or poison pill provision, in our bylaws that, together with the recent strengthening of Minnesota's antitakeover laws, greatly reduced the company's vul-nerability to raiders. Our challenge now was to continue to show a competitive return to our shareholders.

Meanwhile, Lake Superior Paper Industries took giant strides toward completion of the paper mill in Duluth. The project pro-duced its first reel of paper on November 4, 1987, under budget and ahead of schedule and was producing salable paper before the end of the year. To reduce our capital requirements, we were able to refinance the project through a sale-and-leaseback agreement, and we were looking forward enthusiastically to the plant contrib-uting significantly to the corporation's earnings within three years.

Personally, I was becoming more comfortable with my role as a retired founder. The company's sound financial performance in 1988 was certainly reassuring: record sales of $823 million, with earnings of $40 million. The industrial-products group continued to perform well, contributing, for the first time, more than 50 percent of the company's revenue and more than 40 percent of its income. LSPI had come on strong, reaching profitability almost a year ahead of expectations, and with the divestiture of Port Huron the outlook was positive again for our paper business as a whole. Pentair was not only performing well, but it was also a good place to work. It was the kind of company I had dreamed about.

During 1988, I spent more than a quarter of my time in leisure travel, including an African safari and a trip to Alaska by recreational vehicle. Here at home, I was busier than ever with my antitakeover activity as well as civic, charitable, and educational board involvement. The company's success while I was increasingly engaged in such outside work strengthened my confidence that we had indeed made an effective management transition.

———————

There were some developing concerns even in the shadow of the year's achievements. Our Niagara mill, one of the pillars of our success, was ironically the largest of these concerns.

Forty-five percent of our earnings were coming from Niagara at that time and the improvement in Pentair's earnings over the previous year was the result of greatly increased profits out of Niagara. Nevertheless, there was no denying that Niagara was a higher-cost producer and now needed to efficiently exploit market niches with high quality and superior service for the kind of return that would meet corporate objectives. In addition, large ongoing capital investment was necessary if the plant was to remain modestly competitive in the years ahead. Our management was forecasting capital expenditures of up to $300 million over the next three years to assure its competitive standing and reduce its dependence on market cycles.

Meanwhile, a report provided by Kidder Peabody recommended that Pentair strive to improve the financial return of its paper businesses. According to that report, the market value of the company's paper-making assets greatly exceeded their book value, and we were showing a poor return on them. That situation was getting in the way of a fair return on shareholders' investments and making the company vulnerable to unfriendly takeover. The report urged the company to take steps to recover some of its asset value or aggressively invest in new machinery and expansion, and consider vertically integrating, perhaps by acquiring a pulp mill.

As a result of the Kidder report, Pentair initiated parallel efforts to develop a joint venture that would recover some asset value and pursue ambitious internal-development programs. We explored a $300-million expansion at Niagara, we began serious investigations with an eye on acquiring an interest in a pulp mill.

. The handling of the possible investment program at Niagara was particularly troubling. Management warned that the proposed investments would depend on a change of culture at the plant, including the plant's union agreeing to greater flexibility in work assignments and the establishment of a work-team concept. The team approach had already proved successful at our Miami mill and LSPI, as well as at some of Niagara's larger competitors. Discussions with the union over the next several months did not resolve the issue, however, while work on needed capital improvements was delayed. The result was a frustrating stalemate and escalating tension.

By the end of 1988, it was evident that significant capital investments had to be made regardless of any work-rule changes if the mill was to remain competitive and maintain its productivity, quality, and service. So, in early 1989, new projects were authorized at the cost of reduced management credibility and respect and with the delay of important projects. To me, the entire episode was highly disturbing. I could personally identify with the work force as veiled threats of that sort have always made me angry. Also we were jeopardizing the performance of our major earnings contributor and reducing the trust, confidence, and quality of work life of our employees. My personal feelings aside, the fact is we did not fully recover from the effects of that action for several years.

Thankfully, very positive news was coming out of our Miami and Flambeau subsidiaries. All of our paper facilities had been steadily improved, Pentair having spent in excess of $220 million on Niagara, Miami, and Flambeau together. Then, in 1988, Gene and the corporate staff had made a bold decision to consolidate the Miami and Flambeau businesses into a single subsidiary to be known as the Cross Pointe Paper Corporation. Cross Pointe offices and a customer-service center were set up in the Twin Cities and a distribution center, warehouse, and converting facility established in Chicago. Robert Touchette, one of the architects of the project, was named Cross Pointe's president; Jim Winn, senior vice president for marketing; and Jim Grove, vice president for sales. All three were career paper people experienced at both Miami and Flambeau.

Why the consolidation when each operation made important strides on its own?

For one thing, the products of the two mills overlapped, so the merger eliminated competitive sales and marketing. The international distribution center in Chicago provided product delivery and service second to none in the country. For another, by combining production capabilities and centralizing marketing, sales, and service, and by capitalizing on paper made from recycled material, a consolidated operation met a genuine market demand. In any case, the proof was in the pudding. The new Cross Pointe subsidiary, with Miami and its exciting offerings of new paper grades as the primary contributor, immediately provided greatly increased earnings and stability. This would prove to be a very satisfying, long-range development in what had been promising but difficult businesses.

The ongoing progress at LSPI provided more good news. Because of the Duluth plant's smooth start-up and sooner-than-expected profitability, management began exploring the feasibility of adding a second paper machine at the site.

Pentair's industrial-products operations continued to look good. Their capital-investment requirements were comparatively modest, and the money we put into those businesses showed solid returns in terms of stronger organizations, increased productivity, and a stream of new products. Quality and service were on a steady incline, market share was growing, and sales and profitability were increasing apace.

———

A year earlier, Jim Frank, Pentair's vice president for corporate development, had actively resumed his search for a large industrial business.

By mid-1988, after reviewing a number of candidates, the most promising possibility was the Federal Hoffman Corporation in Anoka, Minnesota. The company, with $300 million in annual sales, was not unfamiliar to us. Quentin Hietpas, one of our directors, brought Federal Hoffman to our attention about three years earlier and introduced us to its principals. At that time it was owned by a charitable foundation that was being forced by tax laws to liquidate its holding. Our discussions were short lived, however; the company was purchased by a management group in a debt-heavy leveraged buyout. In 1988 the company was up for sale again because the management buy-out group needed to satisfy refinancing requirements of its debt and wanted to realize the profit on its investment. Through his contacts at the company, Quent again alerted us to the Federal Hoffman situation. The selling group liked the way we did business and appreciated our Code of Business Conduct. As a result, they negotiated only with Pentair and without auction or competitive bid.

Federal Hoffman comprised two unrelated businesses. Its Federal Cartridge operation manufactured ammunition for the sporting market, of which it controlled about 30 percent. Hoffman Engineering, the largest such manufacturer of electrical enclosures in the United States, held about 40 percent of its market. Both were quality producers that enjoyed excellent reputations in their industries. However, both were suffering from a dearth of capital investment and aggressive management. As a result, Federal and Hoffman, with $300 million annual sales, presented a genuine opportunity to increase their profitability through the application of increased investment and strengthened leadership.

Federal Hoffman differed from our previous purchases in one notable aspect: its purchase price was significantly higher than book value. Fifty percent of the $190-million acquisition cost was good will. We would have to substantially improve its profitability for it to meet our performance objectives. Management was confident we could do it, however, and the deal was closed November 11, 1988. The new businesses were set up as two separate Pentair subsidiaries—the Federal Cartridge Company and the Hoffman Engineering Company.

Our optimism at the time of the Federal Hoffman acquisition was bolstered by Pentair's financial position. The sale of $50 million in preferred stock in 1987, the sale of Port Huron, the conversion of convertible debentures to common stock, and strong earnings in 1988 had resulted in a 26-percent debt-to-total-capital ratio. The Federal Hoffman acquisition increased the ratio to about

50 percent, however, forcing tighter controls on capital expenditures and tempering any plans to expand our paper businesses.

Pentair was now predominantly an industrial-products company with only 30 percent of its sales in paper. Our changing corporate emphasis raised concerns as to the adequacy of our management structure and staffing. This concern was heightened with the departure of Tony Johnson as Pentair's president and chief operating officer in January 1989. Tony's departure followed a determination that his management style and long-term objectives would not be compatible with those of Pentair.

Early in 1989 the company was reorganized to meet the changing needs and to develop internal management succession. Jack Grunewald would serve as executive vice president, chief financial officer and secretary. The industrial-products business was split into two groups. Specialty products, headed by vice president Ron Kelly, accounted for about $400 million in annual sales and included 3,200 employees. General industrial equipment, under the direction of vice president Gerry Kitch, also reported sales of about $400 million, with a work force of roughly 3,800 employees. The paper group, with sales of $360 million and 1,600 employees, would be led by vice president Winslow (Windy) Buxton, who was also responsible for Pentair's interest in the LSPI joint venture (sales of $160 million and 340 employees). Gene retained the responsibility of president and chief operating officer in addition to his ongoing duties as chairman and CEO.

The reorganization did not identify Gene's successor, who planned to retire in 1992; whoever eventually took over would either be one of the above vice presidents or come from outside the company. Nonetheless, experienced and highly competent people were in our top management positions, and the outlook for the year (and years) ahead was bright.

———

The year 1989 proved more difficult than any of us expected. Pentair broke the billion-dollar mark, with sales for the year of $1.2 billion, and operating income was higher than in 1988. But net income per share was less than projected. While the industrial business performed pretty much according to plan (with a particularly strong showing by Hoffman Engineering), the paper group came in well below plan, due in part to soft markets. The biggest disappointment was the once-dependable Niagara mill, whose earnings were off by 50 percent from the year before. A diminished demand and lower margins for coated groundwood paper was aggravated by low morale among the plant's work force and by the delay in capital investment to upgrade machinery and facilities.

LSPI continued to perform well, yet we were coming to the conclusion that supercalendered paper did not enjoy the unique market position we thought it would when we launched the project. Supercalendered paper was becoming but another commodity, with profit margins dependent on production efficiency and cyclical, competitive market conditions. Our revised and less optimistic projections for the operation were further affected by estimates that the second paper machine we had been considering would cost more than $500 million. We could not justify such an amount by the cash flow we projected from it. For us, that meant going back to the drawing board to find ways to reach a lower construction cost for a second machine while increasing the profitability of the entire operation.

A new study by the First Boston Corporation, authorized at the July 1989 board meeting, pronounced our corporate defenses against an unfriendly takeover attempt to be sound and recommended no substantive changes. The portion of the study dealing with shareholder value, however, suggested that the company was not realizing an acceptable return on its paper operations. First Boston said the assets of the paper group could be sold for significantly more than our book value and for more than was represented by their earnings. It added that the investment community was not clear about Pentair's identity. Were we a paper company or an industrial-products company? Paper companies had stock price-to-earnings ratios of between eight and 10, while industrial-products companies had P/E ratios of 15. Pentair had the lower P/E ratio of a paper company but not a typical paper company's earnings per share. Thus, our stock price suffered despite our substantial growth and return on equity. Our vulnerability to unfriendly takeover attempts was higher in spite of our strong defenses.

The First Boston report supported the conclusions suggested by our experience. We must more effectively utilize our paper-manufacturing assets if we were to properly serve the best interests of our stakeholders. At our October board meeting, management targeted resolution of the matter within two years.

My personal discomfort had increased as the year wore on. Among the causes of my distress were the continuing problems at Niagara and the growing uncertainty as to what we should do with our paper business as a whole. While I once looked forward to trips to the Wisconsin mill, visits were now awkward and unpleasant. The quality of work life and morale at the facility deteriorated. The respect, trust, and confidence once afforded Pentair's corporate leadership by the local management and work force were now in question. Upcoming labor negotiations threatened to be difficult—early management proposals were hardening positions and open dialogue was being closed off. The situation seemed unnecessary to me and was all the more distressing because Niagara had played such an important role in Pentair's development and because Niagara's employees had made such significant concessions and worked so hard to assure the plant's success in years past. Niagara continued to be the corporation's primary profit contributor, but the outlook was not bright.

At the same time, Pentair was steadily evolving into an industrial-products company with a lessening emphasis on paper. To my mind, the trend was positive, but it was leading to conditions that would be contrary to the best interests of our paper businesses and their employees as well as to our stakeholders, and with the risk of undermining the morale of the entire organization. Progress seemed entirely too slow in developing a program for better utilization of our excellent assets in the paper business. I could only feel anxiety and frustration wishing for early corrective action.

———

Despite my fears and frustrations, I was not blind to the progress Pentair was making on several fronts.

Overall performance was good. We were becoming increasingly established in the industrial-products business, and recent changes in our paper business such as the Cross Pointe merger were showing positive results. We were continuing to make significant investments in our various businesses and had reorganized ourselves for future leadership succession and development. Plans for 1990 had forecast a 10-percent gain in both sales and earnings after the relatively disappointing results of 1989.

In late January 1990 we were surprised to receive notification, by way of a Form 13D filing with the SEC, that a group called Acadia Partners had acquired 5.6 percent of our outstanding shares. The filing raised immediate concerns that we had again been targeted for a hostile takeover. Other institutions each owned more than five percent of our stock, but those other large shareholders had accumulated their positions over a longer period of time and were regarded as long-term investors. Acadia was a surprise entrant, and some of the group's partners were known for unfriendly takeover proclivities. Despite our initial fears the stock market did not react much to the SEC filing. Apparently, the collapse of the junk-bond market a few months earlier had cooled the ardor of arbitrageurs, speculators, and opportunists. Had the Acadia announcement come a year earlier, we probably would have seen a feeding frenzy in the market, with the price of Pentair stock climbing in anticipation of a takeover.

Still, in spite of our strong defenses and the protection of Minnesota law, we decided to play the Acadia filing with caution. We alerted our legal and investment-banking counsel and informed Acadia of our determination to remain an independent public company. We were somewhat comforted by Acadia's insistence that its Pentair investment was for the long term. Our comfort was increased by the fact that nobody else was jumping into the water and gobbling up our shares.

Our policy was well established and unequivocal. We had made our decisions, fortified our defense, and would (as we always had) concentrate on maintaining good performance for the long-term benefit of all our stakeholders. The Acadia filing served, however, to focus our attention on an employee stock ownership plan. The plan would provide for establishing an ESOP trust that would borrow funds with which to acquire about 12 percent of the company's outstanding common shares. Those shares would then be issued annually to employees, beginning immediately and continuing for 10 or more years until all the shares had been issued. In shareholder voting, employees would individually vote the shares they had been issued. The ESOP trustee would vote the shares held in trust in the same ratio as the total vote of all ESOP shares held by employees. Assuming that the employees supported management, the arrangement would give management much greater voting power to wield against hostile takeover attempts.

The idea for an ESOP was not new to Pentair. In earlier years, I had been opposed to such a plan. I favored the principle of employees having ownership in the company, but only if that ownership was meaningful to them and if they knowingly accepted the risks that were always part of equities. In fact, back in 1972 we started an Employee Stock Purchase and Bonus Plan through which employees could acquire Pentair shares through payroll deductions and the company would provide 20 percent (later increased to 25 percent) in matching funds. Participation was excellent, with shares being purchased for participating employees on the open market and the company paying the transaction fees.

The earlier ESOP plans provided for very limited equity for each participating employee and represented a gift in which the employee had only minimal vested interest. Such plans, largely targeted for tax advantages for the company, tended to be short lived, and their administrative costs were high.

The newly proposed ESOP was different in that its design was not predicated on the limited tax advantages that still existed. Management instead promoted the new program with several nontax-related arguments: The plan would only negligibly dilute shareholder equity; employees would help buy their shares through a one-percent reduction in base pay and the application of the company's contribution to the employee savings plan; all employees would take part; employee communication and participation would be encouraged; the program could enhance the company's antitakeover defenses.

This ESOP, as it was soon established, has the real potential of further linking shareholder and employee interests. Management is committed to assuring that employees not only own company shares, but have a meaningful sense of ownership through programs of communication and participative management. Such an enlightened, essential, and ongoing human-resources effort will assure every participant a good understanding of corporate objectives and a satisfying role in decisions involving their work and their work place and their contribution to company success. The result can be a more productive organization, a higher quality of work life, and an appreciation in equity values benefiting shareholders and employees alike.

We continued to face operational difficulties at Niagara in 1990. Contract negotiations with the union dragged on beyond the February expiration date as both sides refused to give ground. Production slow-downs and minor acts of sabotage hurt quality, production, and profitability. When a new contract was finally agreed on in mid-April, the Pentair demands that had polarized the organization had been largely withdrawn and the work force responded with improved productivity.

Damage had been done, however. The on-site management had been demoralized and alienated by a dispute beyond their control, and several key members left. The result was a general lack of effective local leadership necessary to bring productivity and quality back up to fully competitive levels. The Niagara subsidiary suffered a net operating loss for the first six months of the year, and its slow recovery was further obstructed by a weak market for its product.

The program for optimizing our paper businesses had been confirmed at the January board meeting. The difficulties at Niagara, however, delayed real progress there until at least mid-year. In the meantime, capital investments, product development, and aggressive management attention were directed to strengthening all of the paper operations. Early definition of a program was becoming increasingly important to give direction to the larger capital investments, particularly at LSPI, that could be critical to the long-term performance of the businesses.

There was also the need to identify Gene Nugent's successor. Twice in the previous seven years we had recruited company presidents, expecting each in turn to gain the necessary experience and acceptance to be next in line for the top job, but neither individual had proved to be the right fit. We had, however, been developing a strong staff of corporate executives and were in the enviable position of having four vice presidents in the line of succession. All four were experienced and well qualified. The difficulty would be choosing the best one for the post.

The succession issue was of more concern to me than perhaps to others. I believed that a smooth transition of top management was one of the keys to a company's uninterrupted success. Such a transition required that the successor be identified early enough to be accepted within and outside the company as the logical new leader, so that the transition itself would be a nonevent. Now, though we had been preparing for succession for the past seven years, there was less than three years to identify and qualify the candidate for the top job. The plan was, first, to promote one of the vice presidents to the president-and-COO's post, then, a year to 18 months prior to Gene's retirement, name that person CEO. When Gene stepped down, the CEO would additionally become chairman.

The success of any such succession plan would rest with the CEO. The board of directors and its Compensation and Personnel Committee would play an important advisory role, but the CEO would identify the candidate and provide the guidance and support to prepare the new person for the forthcoming responsibility. We were fortunate to have four solid candidates from which to choose, and Windy Buxton was chosen to be Pentair's new president and chief operating officer, effective August 1, 1990.

If there was surprise about Buxton's selection, it was because that as vice president of our paper group he was experienced almost solely in the paper industry. The company now had nearly 70 percent of its sales volume in industrial products. However, Pentair had a track record of success in managing businesses outside the field of direct managerial experience. Windy had the personality, experience, and intellect necessary for the job. He would have the initial burden of being chosen from among four competitively qualified contenders and having to demonstrate corporate leadership skills and become knowledgeable in the industrial products business while earning the team support of the three vice presidents not chosen. Gene would have the key role in guiding this management transition to a smooth functioning new team.

We had long hoped that, with corporate help, our subsidiaries could augment their growth by making acquisitions of closely related businesses. Until June 29, 1990, that hope had gone unfulfilled. Then, on that date, F.E. Myers acquired Expert Pumps, Inc., of Chicago. It was a relatively small transaction of $1.4 million for $6 million in annual sales. Nonetheless, it promised to complement Myers' line of pumps, open new markets, and significantly expand both product lines. The Expert operation was quickly moved from

Chicago to the Myers plant in Ashland, Ohio, and early results bore out the promising value of the acquisition.

Overall Pentair had performed well during 1990 despite a weak national economy and great difficulty at Niagara. Cross Pointe came in at double its 1989 earnings. Sales reached a record of $1.2 billion; net income of $33 million was the third-best year in company history. The following year, 1991, promised to show even stronger performance notwithstanding an economic and political climate still clouded by the threat of war in the Persian Gulf.

Henry Conor and I were retiring as corporate directors effective April 23, 1991. In October of 1991 I would reach our mandatory retirement age of 70 years, making an additional term as corporate director impossible. Henry, our sage and senior outside director since 1970, was retiring to pursue other interests.

At our January 1991 board meeting, our directors approved an increase in the company's cash dividend, marking the 15th consecutive year we had paid quarterly cash dividends on common stock. That dividend had been increased every year.

The board's approval of new credit facility agreements was further evidence of the company's solid financial condition. Our revolving bank lending now stood at $315 million. New agreements had been negotiated at a time when the banking system was under extreme financial and regulatory pressure to maximize loan quality and reduce exposure to loss.

Reduced exposure to the unfriendly takeover threats that had plagued Pentair for years was manifested by Acadia Partners selling its stock holdings in February. We had remained firm in our defense, and Acadia was forced to liquidate its holdings to cover financial losses in other leveraged buyout activities; in my opinion, further evidence that well-managed companies faced little risk from opportunistic corporate raiders using high-yield financing.

On April 23, 1991, at our annual meeting of shareholders, two very qualified persons were elected to Pentair's board of directors: Harold Haverty, the CEO of Deluxe Corporation, and Kristine Johnson, a vice president at Medtronic, Inc., and the first woman to join our board. Henry Conor and I could feel honored to be replaced by such highly qualified individuals. We could also feel touched and honored as our shareholders and directors gave us resounding recognition for our years of service to Pentair.

My 25-year commitment to Pentair had come to a close. I felt a deep sense of personal satisfaction in knowing I had done my job as well as I could do it. The little company I had helped found was now a major corporation. *Fortune* magazine ranked Pentair, on the basis of 1990 sales, 310 in size among U.S. industrial companies. On the basis of 10-year total return to shareholders, Pentair ranked 120. Our 1990 sales of $1.2 billion, earnings of $33 million, and nearly 9,000 employees worldwide were a far cry from the numbers originally posted by our tiny start-up partnership. On the day of our annual meeting of shareholders, the market price for Pentair common shares was $35.25 per share, a gain of 500 times for those first public investors at $1 per share in 1966. I could feel secure knowing that in the first 25 years we had developed a respected company that had served our employees and all other stakeholders well.

Following the meeting there was a luncheon for corporate and subsidiary executives, directors, corporate office employees, founders, close associates of the company, and spouses. Henry Conor and I and our wives were recognized for our service. Henry and I each received a commemorative plaque from the directors and a gift as tokens of appreciation. The respect given me by employees, co-workers, directors, and friends was particularly meaningful. Without that respect, the entire quarter-century would have been a hollow success.

The honor accorded me by my business associates was overshadowed only by a surprise letter from my daughter, which Gene read to the assembled group.

Dear Mom and Dad,

As you retire and end your formal relationship with Pentair, I want to share with you what I have learned from watching you start and build this company. Your contributions to Pentair have made a significant impact on the organization, the business community, and the lives of many employees. But there have been other significant impacts made in a personal, more subtle way, that others would not know about, on the lives of your children.

My brothers and sister and I have grown up with Pentair in our lives and have acquired the strong values and beliefs that you and Mom live and work by. The values of having a strong work ethic, integrity, humility, a good education, and compassion for others are all things that I have learned from you and Mom and believe in for myself.

You are both truly examples of living day to day what you believe in and value most. I have watched you display these values in both your personal and professional lives.

Dad, as you are recognized and honored for your many contributions to Pentair, I want you and Mom to know that I thank you very much for the contributions you have made to my life. My goal is to each day display these values you have instilled in me and to be able to pass them on to my children. I am very proud of you and thank you both for your unending love and support. As the title to a popular song reads, "You are the wind beneath my wings."

Love, Jan

My dream had been fulfilled. With the loyal support of many, I had accomplished my goals. Without compromising personal standards or family relationships, I had participated in the development of a successful and respected corporation. Its momentum and direction had continued for five years beyond my tenure in management.

Success in an unpredictable future should come from maintaining our standards of fairness, commitment, integrity, and perseverance. These proven principles should enable Pentair to make the most of the economic, political, and social change that will occur. The organization, under the very capable direction of Gene Nugent and Windy Buxton, is positioned to meet the challenge. I view Pentair's future with the expectation that 25 years from now the company will remain an independent public company respected for its conduct of business and benefitting all of its stakeholders.

On October 18, 1982, the $23-million power plant at Flambeau was dedicated the Murray J. Harpole Power Plant. This was Pentair's largest single project to that date. Wood waste was used as its primary fuel.

Groundbreaking for Lake Superior Paper Industries (LSPI) took place April 26, 1986 (left to right): Pentair founder Murray Harpole; Duluth Mayor John Fedo; Minnesota Governor Rudy Perpich; LSPI President Ron Kelly; Minnesota Power Chief Executive Jack Rowe; Minnesota Power President Sandy Sandbulte; and Pentair Chief Executive Gene Nugent were on hand to turnover the first shovelsful.

Eighteen months after the LSPI groundbreaking, ahead of schedule and under budget, the first reel of paper merited thumbs-up from plant employees.

Pentair was committed to maintaining competitive facilities as illustrated by the installation of a $1 million dryer and calender stack on Port Huron's number 8 paper machine.

Pentair agrees to buy Anoka holding firm

Pentair Inc., Roseville, said it has reached a definitive agreement to buy FC Holdings Inc., the holding company for Federal-Hoffman Inc., for $93 million. Pentair said it will assume all of Federal-Hoffman's long-term debt for a total price of about $175 million.

Federal-Hoffman, Anoka, operates two businesses: Federal Cartridge Co., a manufacturer of sporting ammunition, and Hoffman Engineering Co., which makes electrical and electronic enclosures and wireways. The combined businesses, with 2,600 employees, had sales of $246 million in 1987, and $230 million for the first nine months of 1988. Federal-Hoffman was taken private in a 1985 leveraged buyout by members of management, Kelso & Co. and Banc-Boston Capital Inc.

"The friendly transaction fits long-term strategies of both Pentair and Federal-Hoffman," said D. Eugene Nugent, Pentair chairman and chief executive officer, in a prepared statement. "The businesses manufacture high-quality products with well-known names, and they are leaders in their respective markets."

David Lentz, chairman and chief executive officer of Federal-Hoffman, said the deal "provides us with access to capital. They will allow us to operate autonomously, which is very appealing."

The agreement, subject to acceptance by FC Holdings shareholders, is expected to be closed in December.

Pentair produces paper, electric tools and machinery, water pumps and systems and lubricating products and systems. Its 1987 sales were $789.2 million and net income was $21.9 million.

In 1988, Pentair tackled its largest acquisition, F-C Holdings, Inc., comprised of Federal Cartridge and Hoffman Engineering, two unrelated businesses, and established the businesses as separate entities. Now Pentair's business mix was about two-thirds industrial product businesses and one-third paper businesses. Annual sales approached the billion-dollar milestone.

The 1990 board of directors included (left to right):

Quentin J. Hietpas, senior vice president of external affairs at the University of St. Thomas

George N. Butzow, chairman of MTS Systems Corporation

H. William Lurton, chairman and CEO of Jostens, Inc.

Henry M. Conor, management consultant

Murray J. Harpole (seated), chairman emeritus of Pentair, Inc. and a founder of the company

Winslow H. Buxton, Pentair president and COO

D. Eugene Nugent, Pentair chairman and CEO

John H. Grunewald, Pentair executive vice president, CFO and secretary

James A. Thwaits, former director and retired president of International Operations and Corporate Staff Services of 3M Company.

In 1990, Pentair officers included:

1. Allan J. Kolles, vice president, human resources
2. John H. Grunewald, executive vice president, CFO, and secretary
3. Gerald C. Kitch, vice president, general industrial equipment
4. Richard W. Ingman, vice president, corporate development
5. Mark T. Schroepfer, vice president, controller
6. Richard F. Jost, vice president, industrial relations
7. Ronald V. Kelly, vice president, specialty products
8. Roy T. Rueb, vice president, treasurer

Subsidiary presidents included:

9. Fred C. Lavender, F.E. Myers Co.
10. James H. Frank, Hoffman Engineering Company
11. Barry J. Wetzel, Lincoln Automotive
12. Gunter Ostermeyer, Lincoln Industrial
13. Ritter H. Humphrey, Lake Superior Paper Industries
14. Robert V. Touchette, Cross Pointe Paper Corporation
15. Elmer C. Beale, Niagara of Wisconsin Paper Corporation
16. Thomas J. Ryan, Porter-Cable Corporation
17. Joseph R. Collins, Delta International Machinery Corporation
18. Ronald V. Mason, Federal Cartridge Company

Pentair enters its second quarter century under the helm of D. Eugene Nugent, Chairman and CEO (left), and Winslow H. Buxton, president and COO, International Distribution Center, Cross Pointe Paper Corporation.

Murray J. Harpole, chairman emeritus

Chapter Eleven

Lessons and Observations 1966-1991

For a quarter of a century, I focused my attention and energy on Pentair. Today, 25 years after our unremarkable beginnings, I feel a great sense of pride and satisfaction about what the company has achieved. I feel fortunate to have had the opportunity, health, luck, and assistance of many dedicated people to fulfill my dream.

Looking back, I wonder if I could do it all over again. My feelings are ambivalent, but speaking realistically I would have to say no. Although I still feel strong and energetic, I fear that I no longer have what it takes to succeed in a new venture. In fact, my experience might make the job more difficult. I have lost some of the mental agility and freshness born of naivete to respond to the the unpredictable challenges that inevitably arise from a fledgling operation.

That loss notwithstanding, my experience during the preceding 25 years has given me some basic beliefs about starting and running a business in contemporary America. These beliefs may not ring true to every entrepreneur and business person; however, I present them with the hope that they will benefit or at least be of interest to other entrepreneurs and to those who follow me.

Reasons for Pentair's Success

Why did Pentair succeed? That is not as simple a question as it sounds. If, as I believe, a company's long-term performance depends largely on the performance of its CEO, then I have to engage in some uncomfortable self-evaluation. On the other hand, the CEO is never a solo performer. A company's success depends on many people both within and outside of the organization. Other factors, not the least of which are luck and timing, also play important, difficult-to-quantify roles over the years.

I no longer recall whether starting the company back in July 1966 was Vern Stone's idea or mine, or whether the idea appeared unbidden during a series of discussions. In any event, getting Pentair off the ground depended on the willingness of five men to leave their comfortable jobs and to commit their time, resources, and energy to the cause.

The events that immediately followed the company's launching could not have been predicted; our response gives credence to my belief that new ventures also depend heavily on dumb luck, half of which is bad. I have come to believe success depends to a significant extent on surviving the bad luck while capitalizing on the good.

Perseverance is critical. At the time of the company's founding Ruth and I agreed that no matter how difficult conditions became, we would dedicate a minimum of five years to the project barring bankruptcy or debilitating illness. I did not agonize over quitting or forging ahead during those difficult early years; the decision had already been made. The company also benefitted from the perseverance and commitment of our early investors, most of whom took a long view of the future.

My partners and I also benefitted mightily from the savvy, good judgment, and dedicated support of earnest advisors and helpers such as accountant Stan Schweitzer, attorney Stan Efron, insurance expert Jim Partington, and office manager Irene Roettger. Ben Westby's contributions stand out as particularly important to both my business education and the company's early success.

Our string of early acquisitions enabled Pentair to survive and proved essential to developing the operating policies and philosophies documented in our Code of Business Conduct which appears on page 225. Driven initially by poverty and later by experience, we learned to acquire and to develop underperforming businesses that offered opportunity for long-term financial gain with minimal financial risk. The company's long-term success soon depended upon a total team effort.

Our first acquisition, which briefly put us in the plastic-thermoforming business, helped us raise desperately needed capital in our first public stock offering. The second, our purchase of the Peavey paper mill, provided a solid financial base for more than three years. The paper-mill venture on the island of Trinidad raised our corporate profile and helped generate increased support in the investment community. The purchase of the Niagara mill assured our success for more than a decade. Indeed, from a financial perspective, the Niagara acquisition was Pentair's springboard to major corporation status and success. Although capital-investment requirements became increasingly heavy, Niagara provided a substantial and consistent cash flow that underwrote much of the company's ongoing development.

Those early acquisitions proved also that we could grow effectively and efficiently with minimal corporate staff and highly autonomous subsidiaries, that we could manage businesses outside our existing area of experience and expertise, and that we could, through hard work, wise investment, and participative working relationships with the acquired staffs, transform underperforming businesses into profitable ones. Unquestionably, developing the support, trust, and confidence of the employees and the constituents of the acquired businesses was critical to our success. Those lessons define the company's modus operandi to this day.

Our eventual diversification was surely facilitated by the fact that our initial foray into the industrial-products business was the acquisition of Porter-Cable. Right from the start, Porter-Cable was an excellent performer, giving us both consistent growth in sales and earnings and industry recognition. Its performance not only helped dispel investor anxiety about our diversification, but gave us the confidence to pursue diversification aggressively. Jack Grunewald's creative direction to conservative financing provided for the necessary funding.

Fundamental to everything we accomplished was the fostering of a positive corporate culture. We were committed to building a successful corporation that would be respected for its business conduct and long-term achievements on behalf of its stakeholders. Personal gain, self-aggrandizement, and short-term profits were simply not allowed to obscure these objectives.

The Pentair Code of Business Conduct codified our basic principles, which had a very real effect on the company's development. The respect we were accorded as an upstanding, committed, and ethical corporation drew competent and high-minded managers and employees; it also enhanced our ability to acquire new businesses and obtain fresh financing. Internally, we were compelled by the code to treat people fairly and with respect, and to set aggressive performance goals for return on investment, annual growth in earnings per share, and return on sales with appropriate incentive compensation.

Motivated people require tools to work with, and underperforming businesses need investments in facilities and products to stay in business and to compete. These needs drove us to retain earnings and invest heavily in new machinery and facilities and to develop products and approaches to business suited to both the market and our capabilities. Soon giving a committed organization the tools with which to compete and succeed in productivity, service, quality, and product innovation became our operating practice.

The reasons for Pentair's success are many, obvious, and unending. To the extent that future managements maintain their integrity, compassion, and commitment, and control their egos, the company will continue to prosper. The outlook is bright as the organization under the dedicated leadership of Gene Nugent exemplifies these principles.

The Qualities of a Successful CEO

Truth be told, I never gave much thought to the position of chief executive officer prior to Pentair's founding. Literally, the company had no CEO during its first decade in business. I suppose I was its chief executive from the beginning, only without the formal title.

Sometime during our formative years I realized that I would determine what kind of company Pentair would be. There was simply no one else with the responsibility, authority, and incentive to do it. Over time my conduct, my work ethic, my treatment of others, and my goals and objectives would shape the corporate culture. I never felt my ideas and management style were the only ones that could be effective and appropriate to a growing company. I did believe, though, that it was up to me to set the tone. Moreover, if I did the job right, my influence would be strongly and positively felt for many years after my retirement.

I have strong feelings about what it takes to be a successful CEO. I truly believe that while a chief executive's intellect, training, and experience are important, that person's strength of character, moral and ethical standards, compassion for others, level of commitment, control of ego, and inherent leadership qualities are even more essential.

The range of a CEO's responsibilities requires long hours, extensive travel, and constant wrestling with complex problems. Often, the CEO's determination to deal with large, strategic concerns causes that person to overlook or neglect many smaller matters that are just as critical to the organization. Ironically, there is always help in dealing with the big items; only the CEO can handle many of the smaller points that are so important, perhaps critical, to the company's culture and long-term performance.

Many distractions and temptations face even the most conscientious and tightly focused CEO. As CEO, you are constantly expected to set direction and make decisions, making it very easy to believe you are someone special. Power, perquisites, publicity, and a dizzying variety of privileges all work to reinforce a sense of self-importance. That can obscure the fact that a CEO is a fiduciary for the employees, shareholders, and other stakeholders who are counting on commitment, integrity, and hard work to protect and enhance their interests.

I have encountered other distractions and temptations for CEOs over the years:

- Too many memberships on corporate, civic, and charitable boards can unduly interfere with corporate responsibilities.
- Too much time spent with other CEOs in trade associations, special-interest groups, and other organizations.
- Too much effort expended trying to emulate other CEOs' success instead of tailoring strategies and tactics to specific organizational realities.
- Too much time and effort given to outside speaking engagements, club memberships, and other diversionary public appearances.
- Too many executive privileges in expense accounts, travel, personal services, and other areas, which undermine the company's perceptions of fairness, cost-control, and commitment, and degrade the corporate culture.

Other pitfalls include the tendency to maintain tight control over major corporate decisions and public contacts while delegating vital internal personal relationships and constituent contact to subordinates, and procrastinating in both developing a management structure and identifying a successor.

CEO compensation is a large and potentially troublesome issue that demands special consideration. The temptation is great for a CEO to ask for and receive outsized financial rewards. In addition to a large salary, generous bonuses, and hefty options, they can usually command first-class travel, accommodations, and entertainment, high-priced luxury cars, expensive club memberships, and the like—thwarting the short-term control of the board and independent of the financial situation of the company. Sooner or later the example set by the CEO will be reflected throughout the organization, with the risk of long-term damage to costs, morale, and culture. I strongly believe that the culture of the organization is determined almost entirely by the CEO's example.

Sometimes, in truth, it is lonely at the top. The hours are long, the work demanding, and the pressure often intense. On the other hand, satisfaction and emotional reward derive from playing the single most important role in leading the company along a successful track. Although many tough decisions must be made by the CEO alone, there is ample opportunity to exchange information and discuss alternatives in a participatory management structure. The CEO's designated successor, the executive staff, and the company's board of directors should be trusted confidants, providing essential advice, counsel, and dialogue.

The CEO above all others determines the long-lasting quality and character of the corporation. The CEO should be held to a much higher level of accountability than anyone else in the organization. As I have said, the CEO's overall performance must be fairly measured over a term extending at least five years beyond the person's tenure. If the job has been done right and a successor has been carefully chosen, that CEO will have the satisfaction of knowing that his or her influence for the corporate good will extend much farther.

Years ago I read a poem attributed to the sixth-century B.C. Chinese philosopher Lao-tzu and committed its words to memory. To this day I believe the words of that poem sum up the essence of a leader, especially a corporate CEO.

A leader is best
When people barely know he exists,
Not so good when people obey and acclaim him,
Worse when they despise him.
But of a good leader,
Who talks little,
When his work is done,
His aim fulfilled,
They will say:
We did it ourselves.

The Board of Directors

The role of a publicly held corporation's board of directors has sometimes puzzled me. I was entirely comfortable with the job performed by Pentair's board over the years. Its members provided us with a valuable service. However, in recent years society has looked on directors as having more power and influence than I think is possible. I cannot help but wonder how so many corporations with so many brilliant and prestigious board members could have gotten into so much trouble.

My experience is that the real power and authority for directing a corporation's course are concentrated in the hands of the CEO. It is exceedingly easy for a CEO to keep a board in the dark on important matters until after-the-fact financial reports or a crisis illuminates a problem. The board's most important responsibility is hiring and sometimes firing the CEO. Beyond that it is constrained to advising, counseling, critiquing, and supporting the CEO. Thorough understanding of and trust in the CEO's commitment and integrity is essential for a board to be effective. If board members lose their confidence or trust in the CEO, they should act swiftly to replace that individual. If they are unable to persuade the majority of the directors to do that, then the minority should resign their seats at the table.

Pentair has had 28 different directors in the course of its first 25 years. The company's charter and bylaws provide for no more than nine directors at a time but no fewer than three. Initially, there were seven members of the board; at times during the ensuing decades there were only three, and not until our 25th year did we seat a full nine.

In our experience, the flexibility afforded by a small board was essential to growth. As the business grew in both size and complexity, a larger board became necessary. All in all, though, I believe that a company's board should comprise as small a number as reasonably possible. Outside board members should make up the majority and be sufficient in number to staff committees as specified by law. Contrary to current popular thinking, I have concluded that good corporate governance is enhanced by having several employee members as directors, too. These management directors can provide better insights and a diversity of information regarding current affairs and the effects board decisions can have on operations.

Our board membership reflected the general need and condition of the organization. The original group consisted of the company's five founders, plus legal counsel and a major investor. During our first few years, board membership decreased because of deaths, terminations, and business uncertainty. Our early attempts to recruit outside directors were frustrated by an understandable reluctance among candidates to commit time and energy to an unknown company with uncertain prospects. In fact, it was 1970 before two outsiders joined the Pentair board and 1980 before outside members outnumbered the insiders. After 1975, I never had a director candidate decline consideration for fear of Pentair's stability or legal liabilities.

As CEO, I recruited all of our new directors until a nominating committee was established in 1985. From the beginning, no potential director was nominated without first being interviewed by the entire sitting board. I insisted that a candidate for the board have no prior significant social or business relationship with me or any of the other directors. I also excluded from possible membership lawyers, bankers, brokers, and public accountants because of the potential for real or perceived conflict of interest. I looked for candidates whose own experience would be of value and who would be both objective and candid in their observations and opinions. To be effective, directors had to have the time, interest, integrity, and compatibility to mesh effectively with the rest of the board. It did not matter if the candidates held any Pentair stock. What mattered was whether they could objectively represent and serve the best interests of the corporation and its stakeholders.

I have always believed that directors should feel part of the corporate team and that open and candid communication supported by mutual respect and confidence is vital to the board's effectiveness. Our board meetings tended to be informal, with frank and thorough discussion of all pertinent issues. When I was chairman and CEO, I made it a point to meet occasionally with our outside directors to review operations, discuss options, ask for advice, and develop a consensus on potentially controversial items. All of our directors were supplied financial data and management analyses on a regular basis, not only before board meetings. Such ongoing information-sharing helped eliminate surprises, enhanced the efficiency of our meetings, and made the board an effective force. A complete list of Pentair's directors and their terms of service appears on pages 229-230 of the Appendix.

Executive Recruitment and Compensation

Over the years, while we occasionally made mistakes in recruiting and promoting executives, there is no question that we succeeded in developing a competent group of top-level managers.

Our management staff is remarkably small; today it numbers only 43 persons for a company of nearly 9,000 employees. By necessity that staff has found ways to establish priorities, delegate responsibilities, and efficiently use time and energy.

At a certain point, the size and complexity of the operation required that entrepreneurs give way to a larger executive staff with decidedly different characteristics. In place of the free-wheeling, seat-of-the-pants mentality of our entrepreneurial phase, we placed more emphasis on professional management and administration, more formal organizational structure, and greater long-range planning.

Experienced persons recruited for executive positions often were from larger, established companies. Along with their managerial credentials, many new applicants arrived with expectations that Pentair could not or would not meet: large support staffs, fancy cars, and other perks foreign to our company culture. I was more than once disappointed to find a competent person whose satisfaction in a job well done was overshadowed by an oversized ego.

Filling an executive position at Pentair was and still is expensive and time consuming. Finding persons with technical skills and solid experience has not been difficult. It is far tougher to also find persons with inherent management skills, controlled egos, commitment, integrity, and compatible personalities who will retain these qualities in an executive position. Even after careful screening and selection, six months to a year was necessary for a new manager to become a truly effective corporate team member. In a few instances, it became apparent that an individual was not right for Pentair or vice versa. In those cases, we believed it was in the best interest of both parties to quickly come to grips with the problem and end the relationship. Then favorable termination benefits were in order as primary responsibility rested with the company for making a poor hiring decision. Performance failures and personality flaws that developed over a longer period were usually less the fault of the company.

Pertinent to the recruiting of topnotch executive talent was the need to provide opportunity for promotions. There would be little incentive for an outstanding candidate to accept an executive position with Pentair if that candidate did not have assurance there would be openings in the top positions that he or she could aspire to. Thus, the policy that no executive officer would remain in office after age 65 not only encourages succession planning but assures younger persons of executive position openings at specific times in the future.

Initially, promotions of subsidiary personnel to corporate executive positions were very few. This was largely due to our having acquired manufacturing units with limited opportunity for the staff to gain the necessary broad experience in sales, finance, engineering, human resources, etc. As persons gained more experience with Pentair in managing our autonomous subsidiaries, we were able to make more promotions from within the company. However, a promotion to the corporate office is a difficult adjustment in almost every instance. The transition from an operating position to an executive staff job was difficult. The job satisfaction and rewards in operations came from having direct control, getting quick response to decisions, seeing results, and being recognized for work done. A corporate executive had to sell his or her ideas to subsidiary management for their implementation. More time was spent on the very important but less recognized areas of planning, guidance, and selling. As a result, most operations people when moving to corporate had difficulty finding job satisfaction. Broad training and exposure to a variety of work experiences became important to giving candidates the capabilities and personal insights necessary to succeed in the promotion.

There was also a tendency for corporate executives to want to build a staff. This seemingly came from a traditional belief that an executive's stature and importance are measured by the size of the organization. There are always arguments for increasing staff to handle complex matters, provide more service to the subsidiaries, and save money by handling common services at corporate. However, Pentair's success had been built upon autonomous subsidiaries and a small corporate staff. The autonomous operations made for a pride of ownership, a sense of responsibility, and rapidity of response benefitting performance to a degree that overshadowed any duplication of effort. A small corporate staff minimizes the time available for corporate executives to interfere in subsidiary operations.

Executive compensation changed significantly as the company developed. At the beginning, money was scarce and survival was the goal; salaries were low and benefits nonexistent or scanty. Equity grants and options were used in lieu of cash. Later, with sales approaching and then soaring past the $100 million mark, the company was expected to match if not exceed the salaries and benefits of established, prospering businesses. By the late 1970s, Pentair was hiring consultants to help prepare and update the company's executive compensation programs. Together, we set up a conservative salary and incentive-pay program that represented an increase over past levels which was sound enough to provide a foundation for future programs. Equity participation in the form of options, incentives, and rewards have been an important component in tying compensation to shareholder interests. Simple and effective, the incentive program was enthusiastically embraced within the company and has contributed to stronger corporate performance.

However, fixing executive compensation was never truly pleasant or satisfying for either the board members or the CEO. Common sense suggested that above-average performance goals required above-average executives and compensation levels. Average compensation was determined by outside compensation specialists who had databases on the salaries and compensation programs for all industry including our competitors. But an uneasy feeling persisted that these specialists might be enhancing the sale of their services by escalating salaries to satisfy the egos of demanding clients. The results seemed to be compensation inflation without any meaningful tie to performance, fairness, or equity. Even our executives were occasionally uneasy with pay greater than they may have anticipated. Increasing criticism from shareholders and unions and derision of foreign competitors only added to our uncertainty. A sense of frustration existed as the board of directors and the CEO worked to develop pay programs that would attract, retain, and motivate competent people while maintaining equity and fairness tied to performance and long-term shareholder interests.

While CEO, I sensed a need and a desire by the organization that the CEO control, by example and by enforced policy, the hidden costs that can creep into executive expense. Those hidden costs tend to develop as executives may secure personal services for themselves and their family members; receive entertainment and meals; cover personal expenses; take extended leave; obtain special perquisites, etc. If not controlled, a modest excess will develop into a spirit of one-upmanship. Left unchecked, these practices become viruses that debase management, spread thoughout the organization, and undermine morale and performance. Positive example and evenhanded control by the CEO not only contain cost, but more importantly, strengthen the spirit of the entire organization.

The key to success is a staff of corporate executives working as a compatible team. A spirit of open and candid communication, fair play, mutual respect, and commitment to succeed will stimulate the entire company. Not only will there be rewards through better business performance but in the satisfaction of a higher quality of work life as well. Sound recruitment and promotion, fair compensation, and strong but sensitive leadership will secure these results.

Using Consultants

When we founded Pentair, our knowledge of business was more limited than we realized. Fortunately, our counsel in legal and accounting matters were willing to provide technical advice and service without trying to make business decisions. This forced us to research, study, and think through issues so that we could establish direction and manage the business. We struggled and made mistakes, but we also learned fast and we were guided around legal or accounting disasters.

Certainly there were times when we wished for help from some consultant or specialist who could cut through the jungle of details and show us the way to success. Fortunately, there was no money to hire such a person. We were forced to do our homework, handle our own problems, and gain an understanding of when and how to make the best use of specialized help.

An important lesson for us was just how much free help is available to the entrepreneur. Employees, suppliers, customers, bankers, and peers can be important sources of specialized information and are often glad to give it. More important, some of those sources are in tune with the needs of your business and have a vested interest in its success.

We did find it necessary to purchase expert legal and accounting advice and assistance. Other areas included labor law, hostile-takeover defense, compensation and benefits, financial deal-structuring, insurance, investor relations, proxy solicitations, and computer systems. The outside experts had the benefit of broad and ongoing experience in the industry and with governmental regulatory agencies.

Working effectively with outside advisors was not always easy. We frequently felt the urge to turn the entire matter over to the specialists and be free of the problem once and for all. The problem was usually new and complex and often exhausted our best efforts to get our arms around it. In some cases, there was a tendency for the outsider, motivated by a desire to be thorough, to increase the consulting fee, or to take part in our business decision making, to want to take over and increase the scope of the task.

We never turned business decisions or responsibilities over to outside experts or advisors. After all, it was our responsibility to know more about our business, employees, and markets than anyone on the outside. When we did use outside help, we learned to work closely with the experts and guide their work to make sure it met our needs. It was important to know enough about the area in question so that when the experts left, we could carry on effectively without them.

We selected competent, reputable individuals or organizations. We tried to make certain that there was a feeling of mutual respect and compatibility of personalities. If long-term or repeat assignments were contemplated, particularly in accounting, legal, or insurance, a long-term relationship with that person or organization was desirable. Through such a relationship, outsiders became well acquainted with our organization, culture, thought processes, and modes of operation. In turn, their work could be more effective and efficient.

On some occasions, advisors and consultants have had to work with our employees, customers, and financiers. Of course, in those cases they were representing us. Thus, their ethical standards and personal habits were a reflection on us individually and as a company. We had a few experiences in which a consultant reflected poorly on Pentair, which emphasized the need to carefully select and closely work with all consultants to help prevent unpleasant surprises and to keep the company's reputation unsullied.

Consultants, special counsel, and outside specialists are expensive. While it is wise to use them sparingly and only when needed, do not skimp on quality. Selecting competent firms and individuals, making efficient and effective use of their time, supporting them fully, and learning as much from them as possible will help control costs. In the meantime, never underestimate how much a CEO and the organization can do alone.

Responsibilities to Shareholders

With the sale of Pentair shares in a public stock offering in 1968, the company's five founders suddenly became its minority owners, an odd and unsettling sensation. While we collectively owned less than 20 percent of the company at that point, I felt the company was still ours to operate. We were like the farmer who sold his land and then stayed on to tend it for its new owner.

In any case, I felt a strong and personal obligation to those early shareholders who had made it possible for me to continue to develop the company I had helped found. While a few were speculators looking for a quick return, most were friends and relatives and sincere investors who were interested in the company's long-term success. I vividly recall an elderly gentleman greeting me at one of our annual meetings. "I'm counting on you, Sonny," the man said. "I've invested my savings in your company and hope to have a comfortable retirement." Whether that Pentair investor enjoyed his retirement, I do not know. I do know that many have done very well. On my own retirement, I received a letter from the wife of a local machinist, who had converted a $2,000 loan to us into Pentair stock then valued at $1 per share. The letter read in part: "My husband...bought the original stock years ago when Pentair was just starting out. With great faith in the company (the only time we cashed in stock was the purchase of our home) we have accumulated eight thousand shares. This will assure us the money for the education of our two sons." At the time she wrote that letter, those 8,000 shares were worth $250,000 and were earning $5,300 annually in cash dividends.

Our original public offering comprised the sale of 200,000 shares at $1 a share and attracted individual investors like the elderly gentleman and the savvy machinist. In 1979, the next time we offered equity in the company we sold, at $25 per share, 365,000 shares of preferred stock convertible into common stock and drew many institutional investors. Our closely knit family of individual shareholders now included sizable numbers of pension funds, mutual funds, banks, and other institutions. In the decade between offerings, the company had grown large and successful enough to meet their requirements.

The change in the nature of our stockholders has since been dramatic. Indeed, between 1979 and 1990, institutional holdings of outstanding shares increased from about five percent to about 70 percent. That change resulted in changes in how we viewed our company and its obligations. Our concern about the threat of unfriendly takeovers increased as many of the institutional holders of Pentair stock displayed an interest in short-term profits.

During the same period, my colleagues and I grew increasingly obligated to other groups and individuals who held a stake in the company such as employees, customers, suppliers, and the communities in which we operated. Most of these had made sacrifices or some extra effort to help the business succeed. While those stakeholders did not necessarily own a share of Pentair stock, they did have a moral claim on the company. In fact, I came to believe that the long-term interests of stockholders and other stakeholders were essentially the same. As a result, management was obliged to take into account and balance all of their interests when making key corporate decisions.

In the meantime, the transformation of public company ownership from small individual investors to large impersonal institutions has made a lasting impact felt by most public corporations in contemporary America. The long-term interest of investors and employees must be continually evaluated and defended against the short-term interests of fiduciaries, with compromise often being an unsatisfactory result. Unfortunately for society as a whole, the role of the small investor has probably been diminished forever. In the wake of that loss, I only hope that institutional shareholders can be persuaded to place greater emphasis on long-term investing for the long-term benefit of all. I believe both business and society depend on it.

Unions

I had little contact with labor unions prior to founding Pentair. In 1957, I scuffled through a picket line while working for General Mills, Inc. to get to my office and laboratory, but that was the extent of it. My feeling about unions was that they were necessary in the face of abusive working conditions in the past, but they had since evolved into a negative influence on business. Struggling to get my own company on its feet, I wanted the chance to establish a positive working environment without a union's interference and then let our employees decide whether they wanted organized representation.

Pentair's initial experience with unions followed the Peavey paper mill acquisition. Though Peavey had a history of fractious labor relations, we found the local union leadership dedicated, competent, and free of constraints from its international office. At the outset, the mill's business was in such bad shape that there was little choice but for everybody to pull together. But even as business conditions improved, our relationship with the union there continued in the main upbeat and productive.

At the Niagara facility, we also found strong local union leadership, a cooperative international, and a willingness to work together to preserve a troubled business. In the years following our initial contact, working relationships remained good, the plant's productivity was high, and negotiations were tough but fair.

However, back at corporate headquarters, we never satisfactorily answered the question of why we needed a third party to deal effectively with our employees. We were dedicated to treating our workers fairly, openly, and respectfully. As we acquired more businesses, the question evolved into a nagging dissatisfaction. As managers, we were not particularly objective; the company was our baby, and we had an emotional reaction to anyone or anything that interfered with our running it. At times, the dissatisfaction was exacerbated by having to work with what we considered inexperienced and marginally qualified union officials. Frequently, their agendas had little to do with the legitimate aims of the company and its work force. Further complicating the picture were external factors such as rapid technological changes, pressing environmental concerns, and heightened foreign and domestic competition. New forms of organization and work practices also were transforming the nation's industry.

We eventually faced very serious labor problems that degenerated into prolonged strikes, picket-line violence, and destruction of property. There was even an attempt to blow up one of our facilities. The costs in terms of lost business, jobs, and friendships were at times enormous.

At our Miami subsidiary, the combination of a failing business and an acrimonious labor situation finally resulted in a significant replacement of the organized labor force and finally decertification of the union. Although that change hurt many individual workers and their families, it resulted in a much improved workplace and turned Miami into a successful business with dramatic gains in productivity, product quality, and employee satisfaction. A short time later, our experience of establishing a nonunion mill at Lake Superior Paper Industries was equally gratifying. There, the labor force was organized in a team structure that facilitated a high level of employee participation. Production and morale remain strong at the Duluth plant.

However, I do not argue for a nonunion shop as a necessity of doing business. As strongly as I craved the chance to create my own relationship with employees, I also believe in the right of workers to organize into a union if they so desire. Employees must have complete freedom to choose between union and nonunion.

Management-union relations should be conducted fairly and even-handedly. Both management and unions have the responsibility to work openly for the long-term interests of both the company and its employees, keeping in mind that the workers are real people with real families and have a genuine desire to be productive members of a successful organization.

Takeover Attempts

The goal of corporate raiders is to influence control over a corporation for the primary purpose of assuring themselves a large, short-term profit paid at the expense of the corporation and the long-term welfare of its stakeholders.

Pentair has been the target of three serious takeover attempts involving the two most prevalent forms of corporate raid: a leveraged buyout and a tender offer. In either form, the raids, had they been successful, would have paid the raider handsomely and placed a heavy debt burden on the company. The effect would have been to pay the finance costs of the takeover at great risk to the company's future. The raids, at least during our earlier years, were unexpected. Pentair acquired its subsidiaries through friendly, negotiated transactions; a takeover was as unthinkable to us as piracy or hostage-taking. The notion of our management participating in the takeover, behaving like a fox in the chicken coop, was also unacceptable.

The three attempts to take over Pentair were not directed against an incompetent management, as raiders like to suggest. Within three years of each of the three attempts (1974, 1976, and 1981), Pentair's share prices rose to more than double the takeover offer. Today those share prices are from three to sixteen times the premium price offered during the takeover attempts; the premium was in each case about 50 percent above the market price at the time. Additionally, the company has continued to grow and to provide benefits to many more employees, communities, and shareholders.

Pentair was nonetheless an excellent target for corporate raiders. We boasted solid assets and a strong cash flow. Our stock was valued at less than the break-up value of the company, which together with our strong cash flow, could provide handsome profits to a raider. A purchase price of a 50-percent premium over market price for 51 percent of our stock was considered a bargain. The debt of any such deal could be easily serviced by the company's cash flow. If operations faltered, the company's assets, in particular our autonomous subsidiaries, could be sold piece by piece.

The attempts to take over Pentair would have been legal and hugely profitable for the few who would gain by the transaction. But by our standards such a takeover would have been unfair, unethical, and diametrically opposed to our objective of developing a strong and respected public company that would benefit many. We in management could never have recommended that our shareholders sell out under the circumstances. We would have been betraying the entire company and all of its stakeholders. Trust in a company's management is essential not only to the survival of publicly held corporations but to the health of our private enterprise system. We were not about to give our stakeholders reason to doubt either our responsibility or our resolve.

I took such takeover attempts as a personal affront. I had worked hard and taken considerable personal risk to get Pentair up and running. I looked on our stakeholders as part of the corporate family and felt that I was better qualified than any outsider to operate the company on their behalf. It outraged me to think that some opportunist could come in, wrest control of the company from its current management, and in exchange for short-term profit, place the entire enterprise in grave danger. I was insulted by the pious pronouncements of the raiders, who insisted that they targeted only underperforming companies with incompetent management in order to make sure that corporate assets were put to the best possible use. That was sheer, unadulterated nonsense.

We managed to fight off all unfriendly attempts with an arsenal of defensive weapons that are frequently reviewed and updated. I have personally been active in antitakeover organizations whose aim has been to inform the public about takeover abuses and to work for preventive legislation. In Minnesota, the efforts of many hard-working persons in both private and public sectors have resulted in state laws that, together with our own defensive measures, have greatly reduced Pentair's vulnerability. This is not to say the threat no longer exists. Pentair still receives proposals from persons or groups seeking some sort of change in corporate control. Fortunately, management is equipped to handle the proposals with much less concern than had been possible a few years ago.

Sadly, corporate raiders have already done their damage to American business. The hostile takeover activity in concert with increased multinational ownership during the past 20 years has forever altered our private enterprise system and its public ownership of independent corporations. The role of the small individual investor has been reduced while the role of the large institutional investor has been enhanced. Emphasis has shifted from long-term objectives to short-term performance.

In today's environment it would be virtually impossible to finance a start-up company like Pentair with the public sale of shares the way we did almost 25 years ago. That alone should give us cause to reflect.

Entrepreneurship

Bud Ruvelson was right when, in 1966, he cautioned me that entrepreneurs risk not only their financial well-being, but their physical and mental health and the well-being of their families. My experience and observations of others confirm the wisdom of Bud's words, and my own experience suggests that success may be an even greater hazard than failure. Bruised egos tend to heal; inflated egos tend to explode.

On Day One at Pentair I was enthusiastic, almost in a mild state of euphoria. I made the break and joined the world of entrepreneurs heading my own company. My friends applauded my courage and wished me success.

Such days can be pretty heady. You are convinced you are on the way to developing a successful company. Of course, it is essential to be optimistic and confident in yourself and your concept, or you will never make the commitment, pledge your assets, and cut the ties with a secure position. Sooner or later, the clarity of your original vision becomes cloudy. Things go wrong. The intended market falls to technological change, product development takes longer and is more expensive than planned. Your capital is insufficient, a serious personality conflict disrupts operations, a cloudburst literally floods the laboratory. My experience confirmed that several such things can and probably will happen in a struggling start-up operation.

Suddenly your landlord, bankers, suppliers, and customers are not impressed with your title and company. It is the balance sheet, cash flow, product quality, delivery schedule, payment of invoices, and personal guarantee that really count.

Long gone are the eight-to-five workdays you enjoyed as somebody else's employee. Now it is six to six (more likely 10 or midnight), seven days a week. Furthermore, you can never forget the business. Problems, plans, alternatives, and administrative details are constantly on your mind. Sleep becomes difficult. While at home, out to dinner, or trying to enjoy a brief vacation, your mind is back at the office mulling over one problem or another. That preoccupation is not restricted to just the first few years in business, either. Even after you have achieved success and mastered most of the start-up problems, the business requires round-the-clock attention. At some point you realize that your business is your life. In those early days you test your resilience and adaptability. Your ability to handle the needs of the business while still maintaining your health and your family is sorely challenged. If you fail, you could lose everything.

Compounding your problems can be the attitude of society if the enterprise is successful. As a struggling entrepreneur, you found your efforts applauded and supported. Later, you realize that a little favorable publicity and evidence of a growing company tend to transform the perception of you from one of a heroic entrepreneur to one of a greedy businessperson. Attitudes of society, the church, and even some acquaintances suggest that you have joined the ranks of grasping industrialists who exploit their workers and jeopardize the environment. You are surprised, hurt, perhaps even alienated by the change in perception. There may even be an inclination to abandon your previous lifestyle and associates and become the person you are perceived to be.

Given the high failure rate of new ventures, I was somewhat conditioned to accepting an unsuccessful end to my efforts in starting Pentair. That would have been a bitter pill to swallow. On the other hand, I certainly hoped and expected Pentair to be successful. I was not prepared for the societal pressures and temptations that accompany success. I can see how some entrepreneurs, having achieved a measure of success, lose perspective and end up destroying not only the enterprise but also their families and their own good reputation.

The seeds of failure are sometimes sown with an entrepreneur's successful sale of a large initial stock offering. The newfound money is spent on lavish offices, fancy automobiles, and extensive perquisites. Organizational development, better products, and a more effective corporate culture are neglected. Inflated egos enjoy a brief run in the sun before the clouds of failure appear.

In other enterprises, success comes after several years of hard work and disappointment. By the time it arrives, a substantial company has been created, with cash flow and equity exceeding previously imagined levels. Favorable publicity, the praise of peers, and the expectations of society induce a person to believe he or she is a genius who deserves to luxuriate in the company's success. Previous lifestyles, friends and associates, and even families no longer seem appropriate to the newfound acclaim.

Even when surviving such pressures and temptations, the entrepreneur will notice changes in him- or herself. Surviving in business and building a strong organization requires dealing with many competent people, most of whom have strong egos of their own. To prevail and to succeed, you find yourself taking firm positions and matching their egos with your own. A quiet and mild-mannered entrepreneur can become an egocentric autocrat in the eyes of family and friends.

Another danger derives from the virtue of trust. Coming from an engineering background, I was accustomed to working in an environment with a high degree of integrity, openness, and trust. I believed then, and I believe today, that business can only be successfully conducted when there is trust and confidence between and among the participants. I soon learned that in business, where money is involved, there are a few people with an entirely different set of ethics and code of conduct. Greed, ego, and self-interest can overwhelm their sense of fairness, honesty, and compassion. A person's trust can sometimes be lost on such people.

Our survival required accepting some risk, learning to recognize danger signs, and taking quick action when problems developed. Failure comes from becoming either paranoid about the risk or oblivious to potential dangers. Success lay in understanding my dependence on the support of many people—always expecting the best from them, but being alert to the worst. I also learned the value of setting the best possible example for others to follow.

Pentair Guidelines

I want to share a few guidelines I have found especially helpful over the past several years. Some of them were passed on to me by acquaintances, some were developed jointly with colleagues, and some evolved out of my own observations. Together, these guidelines, Lao-tzu's poem, and our Code of Business Conduct lie at the core of the Pentair experience.

- If you work hard and smart, try new ideas, and take some risks, more good things will happen than bad.
- Never believe your own advertising.
- It is not a good business deal unless all parties gain something.
- Never let consultants and advisors run your business. Your responsibility is to manage. Engage consultants sparingly for expert advice and opinion.
- A timely decision, even though flawed, is always better than a decision rendered too late.
- A good leader makes his or her job appear easy. A poor leader becomes experienced in handling crises.
- Strong egos are good but become a great liability when they are out of control.
- A company tends to be autocratic. It cannot be democratic. However, it must have positive elements of egalitarian participation in decisions and rewards for long-term success.
- Never abandon a successful practice unless you have overwhelming evidence that there is a better way.
- Never try to sell an idea to others if you are not first sold on it yourself.
- Management is a talent, like music or art, that people are blessed with in varying degrees. Training and experience may sharpen that talent, but there is no practical amount of training that will make a good manager out of a person who does not have inherent management skills.
- Few actions destroy credibility faster than lies, idle threats, and unkept promises.
- A reputation for trust and confidence is developed over years. It can be destroyed in hours.

- Business dealings are with individuals and not with institutions.
- Open and candid conversation resolves most differences, accommodates most concerns, and dispels most rumors.
- Underpromise and overdeliver.
- Success is measured less by what you accomplish than by what you should have accomplished with available assets and opportunities.

APPENDIX

Pentair Code of Business Conduct

Pentair, Inc. chooses to be an independent, publicly owned company, and this statement is to guide the development of its organization and the conduct of its business affairs.

Our businesses are to be managed in keeping with the highest business, ethical, moral and patriotic standards applicable to a publicly owned corporation.

Our businesses are to be operated so that we are respected for our actions by shareholders, employees, plant communities, customers, suppliers, investors and all other stakeholders.

Our approach to business is intended to make Pentair, Inc. a top performing company managed and operated to provide long-term benefits to all constituents.

Operating Guidelines

Balanced consideration will be given to the interests of shareholders and employees in managing the corporation.

The corporate staff will be kept to minimum size, and subsidiary operations will be as autonomous as practicable.

A strong work ethic is expected of all constituents.
Good performance will be freely recognized.
Poor performance will not be condoned.

The dignity and self-worth of all persons involved with the Company will be respected.

Safety in the workplace and in work practices shall be maximized.

We will encourage, aid and promote the physical and mental health, and wellness of employees and their families.

Qualified employees will be given priority for internal employment opportunities.

Standards of ethics, integrity and work practices shall apply equally to all employees.

We will honor agreements, meet obligations timely, maintain the spirit and intent of our commitments, and will value good relationships.

Hiring emphasis will recognize ability, compatibility and integrity, and will not discriminate on the basis of sex, religion, race or age.

We will promote open and candid communications with emphasis on informality and on conversational exchanges.

Corporate Officers
1966-1991

Buxton, Winslow H.
Vice President Paper Group,
1988-1989; President and Chief
Operating Officer, 1990-present.

Conor, Henry M.
Treasurer, 1972-1973.

Conway, Martin E.
Secretary, 1967-1968.

Follmer, Vincent J.
Treasurer, 1966-1968.

Frank, James H.
Vice President Corporate
Development, 1987-1988.

Grunewald, John H.
Vice President Finance, 1977;
Vice President Finance and
Treasurer, 1977-1978; Vice
President Finance, Treasurer
and Secretary, 1979-1980; Vice
President Finance, Chief
Financial Officer, Treasurer and
Secretary, 1981-1985; Vice
President Finance, Chief
Financial Officer and Secretary,
1986-1987; Executive Vice
President, Chief Financial
Officer and Secretary,
1988-present.

Harpole, Murray J.
President and Chief Executive
Officer, Chairman, 1966-1981;
Chairman, 1982-1986.

Ingman, Richard W.
Vice President Corporate
Development, 1989-present.

Johnson, Sankey A.
Executive Vice President and
Chief Operating Officer, 1985;
President and Chief Operating
Officer, 1988-1989.

Jost, Richard F.
Vice President Industrial
Relations, 1978-present.

Kaufenberg, James H.
Vice President Corporate
Development, 1977-1978.

Kelly, Ronald V.
Vice President Corporate
Development, 1980-1984; Vice
President Industrial Group,
1988-1989; Vice President
Specialty Products,
1990-present.

Kitch, Gerald C.
Vice President Industrial Group,
1988-1989; Vice President
General Industrial Equipment,
1990-present.

Kolles, Allan J.
Vice President Human
Resources, 1985-present.

Lentz, David J.
Senior Vice President,
1988-1989.

Miller, Daniel J.
Secretary-Treasurer, 1969-1971.

Neilson, Dennis C.
Vice President Corporate
Development, 1988-1989.

Corporate Officers

Nugent, D. Eugene
Vice President Operations, 1975-1976; President, Chief Operating Officer and Treasurer, 1976; President and Chief Operating Officer, 1977-1981; President and Chief Executive Officer, 1982-1986; Chairman and Chief Executive Officer, 1987; Chairman, Chief Executive Officer and President, 1988-1989; Chairman and Chief Executive Officer, 1990-present.

Olson, Tharlie E.
Senior Vice President Paper Group, 1981-1985; Senior Vice President, 1986.

Pieri, Aldo D.
Secretary, 1966-1967.

Poe, Lawrence J.
Executive Vice President Operations, 1982-1983; Senior Vice President Industrial Products Group, 1984.

Roettger, Irene M.
Secretary, 1972-1979.

Rueb, Roy T.
Vice President and Treasurer, 1987-present.

Schroepfer, Mark T.
Vice President and Controller, 1989-present.

Stone, Vernon H.
Vice President, 1966-1968.

Thomsen, Thomas J.
Vice President Corporate Development, 1979; Vice President, 1980.

Touchette, Robert V.
Vice President Specialty Papers Group, 1986-1987.

Wells, Wallace S.
Vice President, 1969-1970.

Westby, Benjamin F.
Executive Vice President, 1970-1973.

Whiting, Fred N.
Vice President, 1968-1969.

Winn, James W.
Vice President Uncoated Paper Group, 1980; Vice President Paper Group Operations, 1981-1983.

Zolchonock, William M.
Vice President and Treasurer, 1974-1975.

Corporate Directors*
1966-1991

Baird, John
Vice President Research,
Control Data Corporation;
5/22/74-8/28/81 (death).

Butzow, George N.
Chairman, CEO, MTS Systems
Corporation; 10/17/79-present.

Buxton, Winslow H.
President, COO, Pentair, Inc.;
7/2/90-present.

Conor, Henry M.
Founder, Secretary-Treasurer,
Data 100 Corporation;
2/16/70-4/23/91 (retired).

Conway, Martin E.
Legal Counsel, Pentair, Inc.;
9/7/67-12/6/68 (resigned).

Follmer, Vincent J.
Founder, Treasurer, Pentair,
Inc.; 8/31/66-1/31/69 (resigned).

Grunewald, John H.
Executive Vice President, CFO,
Pentair, Inc.; 1/13/89-present.

Harpole, Murray J.
Founder, CEO, Chairman,
Pentair, Inc.; 8/31/66-4/23/91
(retired).

Haverty, Harold V.
President and CEO, Deluxe
Corporation; 4/23/91-present.

Hietpas, Quentin J.
Vice President
Communications, Data 100
Corporation; 5/18/76-present.

Hoaglund, James B.
Chairman and CEO, McQuay,
Inc.; 12/15/83-2/9/85 (death).

Johnson, Kristine
Vice President, Medtronic, Inc.;
4/23/91-present.

Johnson, Sankey A.
President, COO, Pentair, Inc.;
7/17/87-1/12/89 (resigned).

Lurton, H. William
Chairman and CEO, Jostens,
Inc.; 2/9/82-present.

Miller, Daniel J.
President, Peavey Paper Mills,
Inc.; 12/6/68-5/31/72 (resigned).

Nelson, Leroy E.
Founder, Pentair, Inc.;
8/31/66-2/5/68 (resigned).

Nugent, D. Eugene
Vice President, COO, Pentair,
Inc.; 9/29/75-present.

Ostrand, Gary G.
Founder, Pentair, Inc.;
8/31/66-10/26/68 (resigned).

Pieri, Aldo D.
Legal Counsel, Secretary,
Pentair, Inc.; 8/31/66-6/11/67
(death).

Roberg, Donovan L.
President, Conserve Industries,
Inc.; 5/31/72-5/1/78 (resigned).

Siegel, Marshall J.
Vice President, Secretary, Alpha
Distributing Company;
4/12/73-1/31/74 (resigned).

Stone, Vernon H.
Founder, Vice President,
Pentair, Inc.; 8/31/66-6/13/68
(death).

Corporate Directors

Thayer, William, H.
Vice President,
Woodard-Elwood & Company;
2/16/70-5/16/73 (resigned).

Thwaits, James A.
President International
Operations, 3M Company;
10/19/85-present.

Wallace, Kenneth L.
President, Niagara Paper
Corporation; 5/22/74-4/24/84
(retired).

Wells, Wallace S.
Engineering Manager, Control
Data Corporation;
8/31/66-4/12/71 (resigned).

Westby, Benjamin F.
President, Peavey Paper Mills,
Inc.; 7/1/68-12/6/68;
1/31/69-12/12/69;
12/16/70-10/31/74 (resigned).

Whiting, Fred N.
Vice President Sales Manager,
Peavey Paper Mills, Inc.;
7/1/68-11/3/69 (resigned).

In alphabetical order, listing occupation at time of election, term of service and reason for leaving the board.

Acquisitions

Company	Acquisition Date	Description	Acquisition Cost	Annual Sales
American Thermo-Vac Company Arden Hills, Minnesota	January 26, 1967	Tooling for vacuum-forming large plastic items, including a canoe.	$14,500 cash	$0.00
Peavey Paper Mills, Inc. Ladysmith, Wisconsin	June 3, 1968	Manufacturer, absorbent tissue paper.	$10,000 down, $20,000 in one year, and 5% of after-tax profits for five years	$4 million
Caribbean Paper Industries, Ltd. Trinidad and Tobago	November 27, 1968	Toilet paper mill.	$150,000 capital infusion plus 2% of profits for 10 years	$0.00
Universal Systems, Inc. Rockville, Maryland	February 27, 1970	Computer software system for trucking industry. (Investment and management agreement with option to buy)	$196,000	$0.00
Federated Industries, Inc. Spooner, Wisconsin	March 31, 1970	Leather moccasins and fashion wear.	$9,980 cash (acquired 61% of a corporate shell, Plastineers, Inc.; changed name to Federated Industries, Inc., and caused it to acquire Namekagon Leather Company and What's New, Inc.)	$100,000
Conserve Industries, Inc. Arden Hills, Minnesota	October 19, 1971	Rendering meat by-products and grinding high-protein livestock feed in Minneapolis Hide and Tallow and Kem Milling Companies.	$700,000 in cash and notes	$1.3 million
Niagara of Wisconsin Paper Corporation Niagara, Wisconsin	April 3, 1972	Coated groundwood paper.	$9.8 million in cash and notes	$30 million
Miami Paper Corporation West Carrollton, Ohio	July 29, 1974	Book grade papers.	$6 million cash	$20 million
Flambeau Paper Corporation Park Falls, Wisconsin	July 31, 1978	Business and commercial printing papers.	$16 million cash	$40 million
Porter-Cable Corporation Jackson, Tennessee	October 19, 1981	Portable electric tools.	$16 million cash	$45 million
Port Huron Paper Corporation Port Huron, Michigan Detroit, Michigan Leitchfield, Kentucky	October 17, 1983	Light-weight printing paper. Specialty tissue paper. Office paper products converting.	$15.6 million cash and Pentair stock plus $15.7 million assumed debt	$120 million
Delta International Machinery Corporation Pittsburgh, Pennsylvania; Tupelo, Mississippi; Memphis, Tennessee; Limeira, Brazil; Guelph, Ontario, Canada	April 1, 1984	Woodworking machinery.	$39 million cash	$100 million

Acquisitions (continued)

Company	Date	Description	Acquisition Cost	Annual Sales
McNeil Corporation Ashland, Ohio; St. Louis, Missouri; Jonesboro, Arkansas; Waldorf, Germany	August 15, 1986	Lubrication and material dispensing systems. Automotive lifting equipment. Water pumps.	$83 million cash	$180 million
Federal-Hoffman Corporation Anoka, Minnesota; Milwaukee, Wisconsin; Richmond, Indiana; Cwmbran, South Wales, United Kingdom	December 15, 1988	Electrical equipment enclosures and sporting ammunition.	$93 million cash plus $18 million preferred stock and $78 million assumed debt	$300 million
Expert Pumps, Inc. Chicago, Illinois	June 29, 1990	Water sump pumps.	$1.4 million cash	$6 million

Divestitures

Company	Date of Divestiture	Sale Price
Vacuum Forming and Canoe Business	July 29, 1968	$25,000 cash
Balloon and Inflatables Business	September 30, 1968	$5,000 cash
Universal Systems, Inc.	June 30, 1970	Write off $200,000
Federated Industries, Inc.	February 15, 1971	$9,000 in notes for stock interest
Caribbean Paper Industries, Ltd.	February 15, 1974	$12,500 cash for stock interest and write off $172,000
Peavey Paper Mills, Inc.	August 13, 1976	$3.2 million cash and note
Conserve Industries, Inc.	October 18, 1983	$930,000 cash
Huron Office Products	April 9, 1985	$13 million cash
Port Huron Paper Mill	September 10, 1987	$42 million cash
Detroit Paper Mill	March 31, 1988	$13 million cash and note

Subsidiary Profiles

Corporation	Products	Markets	Locations/No. of Employees
Porter-Cable Corporation	Porter-Cable electric tools including circular saws, reciprocating saws, band saws, sanders, drills, and routers.	Woodworking, residential and industrial construction; industrial fabrication and maintenance; and home craftspeople.	Jackson, Tennessee; 840
Delta International Machinery Corporation	General purpose woodworking machinery, including table saws, band saws, planers, jointers, grinders, drill presses, shapers, lathes, other tools, and accessories.	Industrial plants, particularly cabinet manufacturers, case goods, and furniture makers; commercial, residential and industrial construction; and do-it-yourself/homeshop craftspeople.	Pittsburgh, Pennsylvania; Tupelo, Mississippi; Memphis, Tennessee; Guelph, Ontario, Canada; Limeira, Brazil; and Taichung, Taiwan; 1,172
Federal Cartridge Company	Shotshell, centerfire and rimfire cartridges, ammunition components, and clay targets.	Federal products serve over 16 million licensed hunters, trap, skeet, sporting clay and target shooters; U. S. government; and law enforcement agencies.	Anoka, Minnesota and Richmond, Indiana; 775
Hoffman Engineering Company	Metal and composite enclosures for electrical and electronic controls, instruments, and components.	Original equipment manufacturers; plant maintenance and repair markets; and construction markets.	Anoka, Minnesota; Brooklyn Center, Minnesota; Oak Creek, Wisconsin; and Cwmbran, South Wales, United Kingdom; 1,962
F. E. Myers Co.	Pumps for water well systems, pumps and grinders for environmental engineering applications, industrial pumps, and pumps for do-it-yourself markets.	Residential users, municipal environmental organizations, and industrial manufacturing companies.	Ashland, Ohio and Kitchener, Ontario, Canada; 643
Lincoln Industrial	Lubrications systems and equipment, and material dispensing systems.	Products are distributed to manufacturers and general industrial markets.	St. Louis, Missouri and Waldorf, Germany; 1,029
Lincoln Automotive	Vehicle service equipment, including lubricating equipment, hydraulic jacks and specialty products for the repair and service of automobiles, trucks, buses and construction and agricultural equipment.	Products are marketed through a distributor network to professional mechanics and vehicle maintenance facilities.	St. Louis, Missouri; Jonesboro, Arkansas; and Mississauga, Ontario, Canada; 510
Cross Pointe Paper Corporation	Premium uncoated text and cover papers, and commercial printing and writing papers, including products made from recycled fiber.	Paper merchants, commercial printers, graphic design houses, business copy centers, educational institutions and converters.	St. Paul, Minnesota; West Carrollton, Ohio; Park Falls, Wisconsin; and West Chicago, Illinois; 1,002
Niagara of Wisconsin Paper Corporation	Coated publication papers, including recycled-fiber grades.	Magazines, catalogs, periodicals, advertising literature, trade books, and general commercial printing.	Niagara, Wisconsin; 667
Lake Superior Paper Industries (joint venture)	Supercalendered publication and printing grade papers.	Catalogs, newspaper supplements, magazines, advertising inserts, and other commercial printing.	Duluth, Minnesota; 327

233

Growth Record

Year Ending	Net Sales (millions)	Net Earnings (millions)	Common Shares ** (millions)	Total Equity *** (millions)	Common Equity x (millions)	Number of Employees xx	Corporate Staff xxx
* 1966	--	--	--	$0.03	$0.03	5	5
1967	$0.03	$(0.11)	--	0.15	0.15	15	6
1968	0.16	(0.13)	0.28	0.02	0.02	175	3
1969	5.55	0.54	1.13	0.90	0.90	100	3
1970	5.23	0.43	1.13	1.32	1.32	94	5
1971	5.46	0.38	1.14	1.70	1.70	152	6
1972	25.38	0.64	1.22	2.42	2.42	765	5
1973	44.26	3.39	1.36	5.87	5.87	734	6
1974	69.68	3.62	1.51	9.52	9.52	1,100	6
1975	76.93	1.91	1.65	11.43	11.43	1,169	10
1976	90.65	4.35	1.70	15.38	15.38	1,115	10
1977	100.24	5.74	1.70	20.41	20.41	1,121	11
1978	135.43	8.46	2.66	27.77	27.77	1,738	12
1979	192.77	11.84	2.76	48.05	38.05	1,850	14
1980	210.85	12.30	2.76	57.39	47.39	1,800	14
1981	223.98	8.15	2.60	58.47	48.47	2,400	16
1982	271.09	10.51	3.28	66.20	56.20	2,400	21
1983	319.29	11.92	5.58	101.53	92.16	3,200	21
1984	545.44	21.25	6.21	119.33	119.33	4,800	24
1985	534.20	20.06	7.82	134.56	134.56	4,800	31
1986	623.88	15.23	8.64	145.39	145.39	7,000	28
1987	789.25	21.86	8.69	208.58	158.58	6,200	33
1988	823.28	39.84	10.70	281.75	214.17	8,740	37
1989	1,163.63	36.41	10.82	306.90	241.00	8,750	47
1990	1,175.93	33.01	10.37	316.20	247.84	8,650	43

* At date of inception 7/6/66
** Common shares outstanding
*** Total shareholder equity, includes preferred
x Total equity of common shareholders
xx Total employees worldwide excluding LSPI
xxx Total employees in corporate office
( ) Indicates negative value

Performance Record

Year Ending	Reported EPS *	Adjusted EPS **	ROE Common ***	Debt to Equity x	Book Value xx	ROS xxx
1966	--	--	--	--	--	--
1967	$(0.53)	$(0.04)	(73)%	0%	$0.04	(367)%
1968	(0.46)	(0.03)	(650)	0	0.00	(81)
1969	0.45	0.10	60	27	0.17	9.7
1970	0.35	0.07	33	16	0.25	8.2
1971	0.32	0.07	22	28	0.32	7.0
1972	0.53	0.11	26	337	0.42	2.5
1973	2.38	0.55	58	153	1.00	7.7
1974	2.40	0.62	38	144	1.62	5.2
1975	1.16	0.33	17	93	1.95	2.5
1976	2.44	0.69	28	73	2.55	4.8
1977	3.18	0.90	28	54	3.38	5.7
1978	3.12	1.32	30	61	4.42	6.2
1979	4.00	1.69	31	25	5.85	6.1
1980	3.90	1.65	26	49	7.26	5.8
1981	2.71	1.15	17	63	7.88	3.6
1982	2.79	1.47	19	23	9.07	3.9
1983	2.28	1.52	13	28	10.93	3.7
1984	3.40	2.25	18	56	12.69	3.9
1985	2.46	2.03	15	56	14.23	3.8
1986	1.70	1.55	10	98	15.29	2.4
1987	2.15	1.95	14	43	16.59	2.8
1988	3.35	3.35	19	89	20.02	4.8
1989	2.85	2.85	15	82	22.28	3.1
1990	2.43	2.43	13	71	23.91	2.8

*   Reported earnings per common share – diluted

**   Earnings per common share – restated for stock dividends

*** Earnings as percent of common equity

x   Long-term debt as percent of total equity

xx   Book value per common share – restated for stock dividends

xxx ROS – Earnings as percent of sales

( ) Indicates negative value

Share Value

| Year | Appreciation of Initial Shares* | | | Per Share Values | |
	Number of Shares**	Market Value***	Dividends+	Cash Dividends++	Market Price+++
1966	100	$100	$ --	$ --	$1.00
1967	100	150	--	--	1.50
1968	100	200	--	--	2.00
1969	300	2,250	--	--	7.50
1970	300	1,800	--	--	6.00
1971	300	1,050	--	--	3.50
1972	300	2,400	--	--	8.00
1973	330	4,745	--	--	14.38
1974	363	3,721	--	--	10.25
1975	399	2,195	--	--	5.50
1976	399	4,090	120	0.30	10.25
1977	399	5,738	200	0.50	14.38
1978	599	13,705	282	0.47	22.88
1979	599	12,807	383	0.64	21.38
1980	599	11,609	479	0.80	19.38
1981	599	14,304	575	0.96	23.88
1982	749	17,227	599	0.80	23.00
1983	936	27,144	636	0.68	29.00
1984	936	27,256	711	0.76	29.12
1985	1,170	38,903	796	0.68	33.25
1986	1,287	41,828	849	0.66	32.50
1987	1,287	41,506	888	0.69	32.25
1988	1,416	50,622	949	0.67	35.75
1989	1,416	48,498	1,133	0.80	34.25
1990	1,416	46,374	1,246	0.88	32.75

*   Based on 100 shares purchased 12/31/66 for $100.00
**   Increase from stock dividends
*** Based on highest market price during year
+   Annual cash dividend on total shares
++   Annual cash dividend paid per share
+++ Highest market price during year

Stock Dividends:

200%	5/23/69	25%	2/12/82
10%	10/15/73	25%	11/1/83
10%	10/25/74	25%	3/15/85
10%	10/15/75	10%	3/21/86
50%	7/28/78	10%	6/4/88

Net Earnings

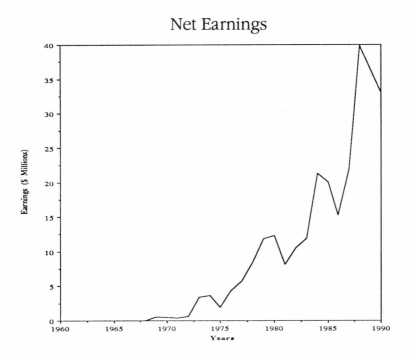

Net Sales

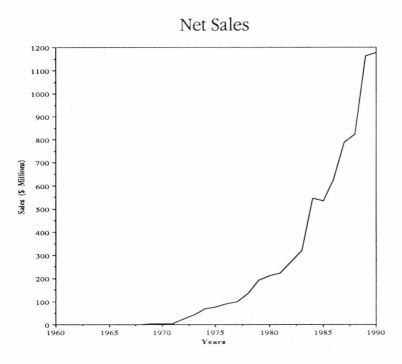

Market Value of Shares*

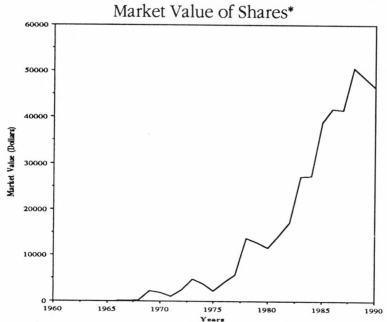

*Based on highest market price during year.

Book Value of Shares*

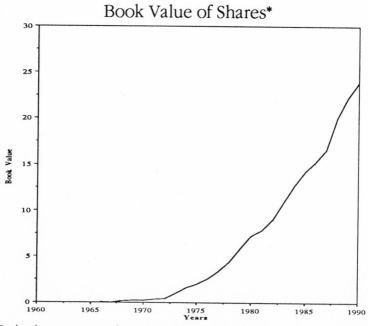

*Book value per common share, restated for stock dividends.

238

Capital Investments

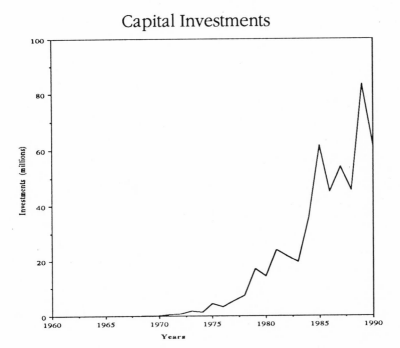

Significant Events in Pentair History

1966

July 6	Pentair Industries founded as partnership
August 31	Pentair Industries, Inc. became a Minnesota corporation
December 6	Effective date for offering 200,000 shares at $1.15 per share
December 16	Committed to enter vacuum-forming business

1967

January 10	Completed public sale of shares
January 26	Agreed to acquire American Thermo-Vac
June 1	First significant delivery of balloons and inflatable systems
July 2	Founder Vernon Stone ill with cancer
September 6	Delivery of canoe mold
October 17	Produced first vacuum-formed products
October 30	Held first annual meeting of shareholders
November 21	Delivered first 17-foot canoe

1968

February 6	Founder Leroy Nelson resigns
February 21	Initial bank borrowing to finance canoe receivables
April 1	First visit to Peavey Paper Mill
April 16	Terminated canoe production, defective raw material and shortage of cash
May 24	Ben Westby joined Pentair
June 3	Acquired Peavey Paper Mills
June 7	Founder Gary Ostrand resigns
June 13	Death of founder Vernon Stone
July 29	Sold canoe and vacuum-forming business
September 30	Sold balloon and inflatable business
November 27	Preliminary agreement to acquire Trinidad paper mill

Significant Events in Pentair History

December	Trial production of absorbent wadding for Pampers-brand disposable diapers

1969

January 31	Founder Vincent Follmer resigns
March 6	Closed on acquisition of Trinidad paper mill
March 10	Contracted Peavey production to Procter & Gamble
May 16	Common stock split 3 for 1
August 15	Produced first paper in Trinidad
September 1	Political unrest halted operations in Trinidad

1970

February 2	Elected Henry Conor first outside director
February 27	Investment and management agreement with Universal Systems, Inc. (USI)
March 10	Tests of USI system fail
March 31	Acquired 61% of shares in Federated Industries, Inc. (corporate shell which acquired Namekagon Leather, Inc. and What's New, Inc.)
June 30	Terminated agreement with USI

1971

February 15	Sold controlling interest in Federated Industries, Inc.
October 19	Acquired Conserve Industries, Inc.
October 27	First visit to Niagara paper mill

1972

January 27	Signed conditional purchase agreement for Niagara paper mill
March 30	Niagara labor union accepted proposed contract
March 31	Venture capitalists withdrew funding for Niagara purchase

Significant Events in Pentair History

April 3	Acquired Niagara paper mill from Kimberly-Clark Corporation
August	Peavey completed deliveries under Procter & Gamble contract
September 20	Village of Niagara officially welcomed Pentair
December	Niagara's production enters a seller's market

1973

August 22	Conserve Industries, Inc. agreement to process packing house material
October 1	Sold $3.3 million pollution control bonds for Niagara

1974

February 15	Sold Caribbean Paper Industries, Inc.
July 29	Acquired Miami Paper Corporation
August 28	Moved corporate offices to present location
October	Pentair subjected to serious takeover attempt
December 18	First annual long-range business planning meeting

1975

January	Established Pentair pension plan
February	Paper market collapsed causing periodic paper machine shutdowns over next six months
August 1	Hired Gene Nugent as vice president for operations

1976

January 22	Pentair takeover attempt and proxy fight initiated then abandoned in April
April 19	Declared first cash dividend on common stock
August 13	Sold Peavey Paper Mills, Inc.
September 1	Gene Nugent became president and COO

Significant Events in Pentair History

1977

April 1	Hired Jack Grunewald as vice president for finance
April 12	Initiated investor relations program with New York City presentation
December 31	Net annual sales reached $100 million

1978

July 31	Acquired Flambeau Paper Corporation
October 17	Decided to diversify outside of paper manufacturing

1979

January 16	Established policy guidelines for directors, including retirement at age 70
May 2	Sold 400,000 preferred shares at $25 (first equity sold since initial offering in 1966)

1980

March	Published corporate policy statement in annual report
August 31	Authorized construction of new power plant at Flambeau
November 17	Peter Wray initiated Pentair takeover discussion
December 22	Takeover action started with 13-D filing

1981

February 9	Terminated takeover attempt by paying $4.5 million in greenmail
April 12	Shareholders approved takeover defense measures
October 19	Acquired Porter-Cable
December 15	Gene Nugent promoted to CEO and Murray Harpole continued as chairman

Significant Events in Pentair History

1982

October 18	Dedicated Flambeau Power Plant

1983

July 15	Sold 600,000 common shares at $24
October 17	Acquired Port Huron Paper Corporation
October 18	Sold Conserve Industries, Inc.

1984

January 13	Set mandatory retirement age of 65 for corporate officers
April 12	Acquired Delta International Machinery Corporation
July 20	Board adopted "Pentair Code of Business Conduct"
December 31	Ranked by *Fortune* magazine among the 500 largest industrial companies in the United States

1985

March 29	Sold $25 million in convertible debentures
April 9	Sold Huron Office Products Company
June 27	Initiated joint venture feasibility study with Minnesota Power for paper mill in Duluth
August 29	Labor strike began at Miami Paper Corporation
November 15	Hired permanent replacements for Miami employees on strike
November 21	Signed joint venture agreement with Minnesota Power for building paper mill in Duluth, Lake Superior Paper Industries, Inc. (LSPI)

1986

April 26	Ground breaking for LSPI paper mill
July 6	Murray Harpole retired as Pentair Board Chairman; Gene Nugent became Chairman and CEO
August 15	Acquired McNeil Corporation

Significant Events in Pentair History

October 31   Murray Harpole retired from Pentair

1987

March 18   Sold two million convertible preferred shares at $25
September 10   Sold Port Huron Paper mill
November 4   LSPI produced first roll of paper at Duluth mill

1988

March 31   Sold Detroit paper mill
June 16   Established Cross Pointe Paper Corporation (a merger of Miami and Flambeau)
December 15   Acquired Federal-Hoffman, Inc.

1989

January 12   Tony Johnson resigned as president and COO
December 31   Annual sales exceeded $1 billion

1990

March 6   Authorized Employee Stock Ownership Plan (ESOP)
June 29   Acquired Expert Pump, Inc.
August 1   Appointed Winslow (Windy) Buxton president and COO

1991

April 23   Henry Conor and Murray Harpole retired from board of directors

Note: Record ends as of April 23, 1991

INDEX

A

Abdo, John 32
Acadia Partners 184
Alexy, Jim 93
American Can Company 143
American Hoist & Derrick Company 77
American Paper Institute 146
American Thermo-vac Tooling
    acquisition 18 - 22, 24
Ampad Corporation 160
Anderson, Harvey 18
Anderson, Robert 18, 23
Apache Office Park 37
Arden Hills, Minnesota 8
austerity program 9

B

bagasse 40
Baird, John 79, 144
Banks, Odos 163
Bartolac, Karen 70
Beaver Delta Machinery Corporation 150
Beerman, Bill 73, 102
Blandin Paper Company 104
Bloomington, Minnesota 32
Blythe, Eastman 120
Breitman, Orenstein & Schweitzer 6, 106
Brown Company of Eau Claire,
Wisconsin 93
Buffalo, New York 6
Burwell, Gary 102
Butzow, George 114
Buxton, Winslow 181, 187

C

Canadian Pacific Investments of
Montreal 104
canoes
    cease production 29
    manufacturing 26
    molds 22
    Penta Craft 27
    shipping 28
    vacuum-forming 24
Capital Cities Communications 107
Caribbean Paper Industries, Ltd. 47
    acquisition 41
Caterpillar 115
Cellu-Products, Inc. 75

Clary Corporation 49
College of St. Thomas 165
Collins, Joe 150
Commercial Trading Company 35
Community Investment 52, 54
Conde Nast Publications 50
Conor, Henry 42, 55, 77, 79, 117, 188
    retirement 188
Conserve Industries, Inc. 68, 109
    acquisition 50
    divestiture 147
    expansion 103
    Kem Milling, Inc. 50
    Minneapolis Hide and Tallow 50
Control Data Corporation 10, 21, 144
Cross Pointe Paper Corporation
    consolidation of Flambeau and
    Miami Paper 178
Cummins Engine Corporation 158

D

Dain, Bosworth 120
Dain, Kalman & Quail 111
Delta International Machinery Corpora-
tion 150
Delta Manufacturing Company 150
Deluxe Corporation 188
Donenfeld, Ken 92
Doubleday 79
Drexel Burnham 89
Duluth, Minnesota
    See Lake Superior Paper Industries, Inc.

E

Efron, Stanley 11 - 12, 49, 83, 120
    corporate legal counsel 50
Encyclopedia Britannica 79
entrepreneurship 218 - 220
Ernest, Robert 51
Ethyl Corporation 78
executive recruitment and
compensation 207 - 210
Expert Pumps, Inc. 187

F

Federal Cartridge Company 180
Federal Hoffman Corporation
    acquisition 179 - 180
Federated Industries, Inc.

Namekagon Leather 45
    sale of 46
    What's New 45
Fedo, John 151, 168
Fidelity Bank & Trust 7, 13
First Boston Corporation 182
First Midwest Capital Corporation 14
First National Bank of St. Paul 28, 52, 54, 81, 90
Flambeau Paper Corporation 111, 118
    acquisition 107 - 108
    consolidation with Miami Paper Corporation 178
Flambeau River 48
Foley and Lardner 120
Follmer, Vincent 2, 12, 35, 46
Fortune magazine 165, 189
Frame, Clarence 28
Frank, James 169, 179

G

Garmer, Ben 120
General Electric 115
General Electric Credit Corporation 143
General Mills, Inc. 1
Georgeson and Company 91 - 92
Grove, Jim 85, 95, 126, 179
Grunewald, Jack 102, 111, 113, 181, 201
Guiliano, Francis 160

H

Harpole, Murray J. 1 - 2, 12, 79, 157, 166, 171, 188
Harpole, Ruth 5, 200
Haskins & Sells 106
Haverty, Harold 188
Hawes, Donald 44
Hietpas, Quentin 92, 180
Hoaglund, James 158
Hoffman Engineering Company 180
Hyduke, David 28

I

inflatable products 1, 21
    aerodynamic-shaped balloons 1
    high-altitude balloons 1
    roughened spheres 1
    tethered balloons 1
Internal Revenue Service 22, 77
International Harvester Company 115
Invicta-Delta 150

Iowa State University 143
ITT Industrial Credit Company 87

J

Jacobs, Irwin 165
Johnson, Kristine 188
Johnson, Lyndon 5
Johnson, S.A. "Tony" 158, 181
Jost, Dick 87, 113
Jostens, Inc. 144

K

Kamp, Charles 108
Kansas City Star 107
Kapaco Group, Inc. 176
Kaufenberg, James 87, 102, 113, 117
Kelly, Ronald 117, 125, 151, 160, 169, 181
Kem Milling, Inc. 49
Kidder Peabody 165, 167, 177
Kimberly-Clark Corporation 50, 69, 94
King, Peter 77, 87
Kitch, Gerald 181
Klein, Melvyn 122
Kolles, Allan 158

L

Ladysmith, Wisconsin 29, 31
    municipal waste-water facility 48
Lake Superior Paper Industries, Inc. 167, 176
    beginnings 159 - 160
    first meeting to discuss joint venture 151
Lapp, William 40
Life magazine 50
Litton Industries, Inc.
    Applied Science Division 1
Look magazine 50
Lucey, Patrick 70
Lurton, H. William 144
Lynchburg Foundry Company 145

M

Macmillan 79
Marathon pulp mill 143
Master-Matte grade paper 109
McNeil Corporation 169, 175
Mead Corporation 145
Meadows, Glenn 170
Medtronic, Inc. 188
Menominee River 51
Miami Paper Corporation 79

break-up of union 160 - 163
consolidation with Flambeau Paper
  Corporation 178
Midland Hills Country Club 127
Miller & Schroeder 89
Miller, Daniel 39, 42, 46
Minneapolis Hide and Tallow 49
Minnesota Business Hall of Fame 166
Minnesota Power Company 159
  See Lake Superior Paper Industries, Inc.
moccasin manufacturing 43
Montgomery Ward 20
Morseth, Gordon 145
MTS Systems Corporation 114
Murray J. Harpole Power Plant 143
Myers, F.E. 170, 176, 187

N

Namekagon Leather, Inc. 43
NASA 21, 24, 35
National Labor Relations Board 162
Nelson, Leroy 2, 27
New York Stock Exchange 105
The New Yorker magazine 50
Niagara of Wisconsin Paper
Corporation 68, 143, 177
  acquisition 52 - 53, 55
Niagara welcomes Pentair 70
Niagara, Wisconsin 50
Nicollet, Joseph 171
Northwest Growth Fund 52
Nugent, D. Eugene 88, 113, 129, 142,
148, 151, 155, 157, 171, 181, 187, 202

O

Oliver, Tom 78
Olson, Tharlie 74, 151
Onan Corporation 158
Orenstein, Harvey 6
Ostrand, Gary 3, 33

P

Paine Webber 90, 111, 120, 122
Pampers brand disposable diaper 40
Park Falls, Wisconsin 107
Parke-Davis, Inc. 80
Parker, Bobby 127
Partington, James 36
Patrician Paper Company 31, 39
Paulucci, Jeno 168

Peavey Paper Mill 29
  acquisition 31 - 32, 34, 36 - 38
  divestiture 94
Peavey, Pete 32
Pentair Industries, Incorporated 5
  articles of incorporation 12
  beginnings 7
  corporate charter 39
  first annual meeting 25
  first board of directors 12
  name change to Pentair, Inc. 106
  stock offering 11, 19
  subscription agreements 13, 20
Pentair, Inc.
  adding industrial-products
    subsidiary 115
  approach to business statement 128
  Code of Business Conduct 128, 156,
    170, 201
  equity offering 111
  establishment of ESOP trust 184
  fifteenth anniversary 127
  guidelines 221
  long-term executive performance
    plan 105
  management incentive plan 105
  mandatory retirement policy 148
  reasons for success 199 - 201
  Shareholder Rights Plan 167
  stock offering 175
Perpich, Rudy 168
Peterson, Leland 38, 73
Peterson, P.R. 10, 18
Peterson, P.R. Company 10
Pieri, Aldo 4, 12, 23
The Pillsbury Company 119
Plastineers, Inc. 43
  acquisition 45
Plus brand toilet tissue 49
Poe, Larry 144, 155
Politte, Robert 72, 92, 106
Ponzio, Martin V. 53
Port Huron Paper Company 107
  acquisition 145, 147
  divestiture 176
  Huron Office Products Division 160
Porter-Cable subsidiary 126, 141, 201
Prince Albert Pulp Company 152
Pritzkers 120
Procter & Gamble 40

Q

qualities of a successful CEO   202 - 204

R

Resource Management Corporation of
Bethesda   44
responsibilities to shareholders   212, 214
Robel, Inc.   73
Roberg, Donovan   68, 79, 114
Roberg, Ernie   68, 147
Rockwell International Corporation   150
    acquisition of power tool division   126
Roettger, Irene   43, 68, 77, 83, 114
role of board of directors   205 - 207
Romitti, Blossom   166
Roseville, Minnesota   81
Rotary International   142
Rueb, Roy   113
Rust Engineering Company   159
Ruvelson, Alan   14
Ryan, Tom   127

S

Sail brand toilet tissue   48
Schultz, Allen   32
Schweitzer, Stanley   6, 9 - 10, 12, 83
Seaman, Ken   86
Sears Roebuck   50
Securities and Exchange Commission
(SEC)   7, 10
    Regulation A offering   11
Semenchuk, Steve   108
Shearson Hayden Stone   99, 111
Soukup, Don   54
Southern Living magazine   50
Spooner, Wisconsin   43
St. Anthony's Catholic church   70
St. Joseph, Missouri   73
St. Regis Paper Corporation   107
Stakeholders of America   167, 175
Steak and Ale   119
Steiger Tractor, Inc.   115
Stephens, John R.   12, 19
Stone, Vernon   1 - 2, 9, 12, 23, 27, 33

T

takeover attempts   216 - 218
Technical Products, Inc.   36
Thayer, William   42

thermo-forming business
    sale of   36
Third Northwestern Bank of
Minneapolis   32, 40
Thomsen, Tom   69
Thunder Aircraft and Marine
Company   18
Thwaits, James   158
Touchette, Robert   179
Trinidad   42
    tissue-paper mill   39

U

Ulmer, John   127
Unidynamics Corporation   17
unions   214 - 215
United States Navy   17, 24
Universal Systems, Inc.
    acquisition   43
    divestiture   45

V

The Victorio Company (TVC)   119
Vietnam   5

W

The Wall Street Journal   41, 87, 120
Wallace, Kenneth   74, 79, 102
Wells, Wallace   4, 12, 46 - 47
West Carrollton, Ohio   78
Westby, Ben   25, 29 - 30, 34, 40, 76, 79,
83, 86, 103
Whiting, Fred   32, 34, 39 - 40, 42
Wilkins, Paul   97
Winn, Jim   95, 147, 179
Wisconsin Department of Natural
Resources   48, 52, 108, 118
Wisconsin Investor   50
working with consultants   211 - 212
Wray, Peter
    takeover attempt   119 - 123

Y

YMCA   142

Z

Zolchonock, Bill   68, 77, 83